Interest-Rate Rules in a New Keynesian Framework with Investment

Schriften zur Wirtschaftstheorie und Wirtschaftspolitik

Herausgegeben von
Klaus Beckmann, Michael Berlemann, Rolf Hasse,
Jörn Kruse, Franco Reither, Wolf Schäfer,
Thomas Straubhaar und Klaus W. Zimmermann

Band 44

PETER LANG
Frankfurt am Main · Berlin · Bern · Bruxelles · New York · Oxford · Wien

Elena Pavlova

Interest-Rate Rules in a New Keynesian Framework with Investment

PETER LANG
Internationaler Verlag der Wissenschaften

Bibliographic Information published by the Deutsche Nationalbibliothek
The Deutsche Nationalbibliothek lists this publication in the Deutsche Nationalbibliografie; detailed bibliographic data is available in the internet at http://dnb.d-nb.de.

Zugl.: Hamburg, Univ. der Bundeswehr, Diss., 2010

Gratefully acknowledging financial support
by Helmut Schmidt University/University of the
Federal Armed Forces Hamburg.

D 705
ISSN 1433-1519
ISBN 978-3-631-61128-9

www.peterlang.de

Acknowledgements

This book is based on research carried out during my activity as Teaching and Research Assistant at the Institute for Theoretical Economics at the Helmut Schmidt University. It has been accepted as PhD thesis by the Helmut Schmidt University. I am exclusively responsible for any errors and omissions.

Preparing and successfully completing a PhD thesis has been an intensive learning experience for me, which required intellectual curiosity, innovative thinking, hard work and persistence. My efforts have been supported by a number of colleagues and friends. In the first place, I would like to express my deep gratitude to my academic advisor Prof. Dr. Franco Reither, who has offered continuous and most valuable guidance and support during all stages of the process in the form of in-depth thematic exchanges, targeted insights and excellent cooperation. In addition, I would like to thank my second advisor, Prof. Dr. Barbara Dluhosch and Prof. Dr. Klaus Zimmermann for their open attitude and the interesting discussions. I would also like to acknowledge the moral support and assistance of all my colleagues at the Helmut Schmidt University, in particular Lars Bennöhr and Sabine Michels.

Finally, I would like to thank my family for their motivating influence and their understanding. Their appreciation and firm belief in my dreams have been the basis for any professional success so far. This is why I would like to dedicate this book to my parents and to my partner Peter.

Brussels, February 2011

Elena Pavlova

Table of Contents

List of Figures and Tables 11

List of Symbols 13

I. Introduction 17

II. Monetary policy design and criteria for assessing monetary policy rules 21

1. Monetary policy issues 21
   - 1.1. The case for rules rather than discretion 23
     - 1.1.1. Analytical distinction between rules and discretion 23
     - 1.1.2. The problem of dynamic inconsistency 24
     - 1.1.3. Advantages of central bank commitment to a monetary policy rule 25
   - 1.2. Design of monetary policy rules 26
     - 1.2.1. Rules, instruments and targets 28
     - 1.2.2. Choice of instruments 30
     - 1.2.3. Choice of target variables 31
2. Criteria for assessing monetary policy rules 37
   - 2.1. Operationality/Simplicity 38
   - 2.2. Local determinacy of rational-expectations equilibrium and monetary policy analysis 41
     - 2.2.1. An overview 41
     - 2.2.2. Presenting the criterion 42
     - 2.2.3. Determinacy and reactions to shocks 43
   - 2.3. The Taylor principle 45
3. Preliminary summary 49

III. A New Keynesian model with endogenous capital with adjustment costs 51

1. New Keynesian framework: an overview 52
2. Modelling capital and investment 55
3. The model with endogenous capital and adjustment costs 60

3.1. Household utility function and optimality conditions 60
3.2. The “IS sector” 63
3.3. Capital accumulation adjustment costs 64
3.4. Inflation and real wage equations under sticky prices and wages 66
3.5. Interest-rate rule specifications 67
4. Determinacy analysis 68
4.1. Calibration 69
4.2. Determinacy and the Taylor principle: some numerical examples 72
4.2.1. Active rule 74
4.2.2. Passive rule 75
4.2.3. Interest-rate rule response coefficient values and determinacy: a global perspective 77
5. Preliminary summary of results 79
IV. Shock impulse responses 81
1. Some preliminary remarks on the adjustment mechanisms in the system 81
1.1. Monetary policy unit shock 82
1.2. Technology unit shock 84
1.3. Consumption preference unit shock 86
2. Active rule 87
2.1. The case of inflation-targeting only 87
2.1.1. Monetary policy unit shock 88
2.1.2. Technology unit shock 92
2.1.3. Consumption preference unit shock 95
2.2. The case of inflation- and output-targeting 98
2.2.1. Monetary policy unit shock 98
2.2.2. Technology unit shock 101
2.2.3. Consumption preference unit shock 104

2.3. The case of inflation- and output-targeting with interest-rate smoothing 107
2.3.1. Monetary policy unit shock 107
2.3.2. Technology unit shock 110
2.3.3. Consumption preference unit shock 113
3. Passive rule 116
3.1. The case of inflation-targeting only 116
3.2. The case of inflation- and output-targeting 116
3.2.1. Monetary policy unit shock 117
3.2.2. Technology unit shock 120
3.2.3. Consumption preference unit shock 123
3.3. The case of inflation- and output-targeting with interest-rate smoothing 126
3.3.1. Monetary policy unit shock 126
3.3.2. Technology unit shock 129
3.3.3. Consumption preference unit shock 132
4. Preliminary summary of results 135
V. Discussion and conclusion 137
Appendix: Optimising IS-LM model with endogenous investment and capital adjustment costs 139
References 145

List of Figures and Tables

Figure 2.1. The monetary policy framework 30
Figure 2.2. Stable and unstable monetary policy rules 46
Table 3.1. Parameter values 69
Figure 3.1. Determinacy regions (3D) 78
Figure 3.2. Determinacy regions (2D) 78
Figure 4.1. Responses to a monetary policy unit shock under an active rule with inflation-targeting only 90
Figure 4.2. Responses to a technology unit shock under an active rule with inflation-targeting only 94
Figure 4.3. Responses to a consumption preference unit shock under an active rule with inflation-targeting only 97
Figure 4.4. Responses to a monetary policy unit shock under an active rule with inflation- and output-targeting 100
Figure 4.5. Responses to a technology unit shock under an active rule with inflation- and output-targeting 103
Figure 4.6. Responses to a consumption preference unit shock under an active rule with inflation- and output-targeting 106
Figure 4.7. Responses to a monetary policy unit shock under an active rule with inflation- and output-targeting and interest-rate smoothing 109
Figure 4.8. Responses to a technology unit shock under an active rule with inflation- and output-targeting and interest-rate smoothing 112
Figure 4.9. Responses to a consumption preference unit shock under an active rule with inflation- and output-targeting and interest-rate smoothing 115
Figure 4.10. Responses to a monetary policy unit shock under a passive rule with inflation- and output-targeting 118
Figure 4.11. Responses to a technology unit shock under a passive rule with inflation- and output-targeting 121
Figure 4.12. Responses to a consumption preference unit shock under a passive rule with inflation- and output-targeting 124
Figure 4.13. Responses to a monetary policy unit shock under a passive rule with inflation- and output-targeting and interest-rate smoothing 128
Figure 4.14. Responses to a technology unit shock under a passive rule with inflation- and output-targeting and interest-rate smoothing 130
Figure 4.15. Responses to a consumption preference unit shock under a passive rule with inflation- and output-targeting and interest-rate smoothing 134

List of Symbols

Chapter III

Latin symbols

A	coefficient matrix
B	column vector of constant parameters
E	expectation operator
g	stochastic shock (IS relation)
I	identity matrix
i	nominal interest rate
m	number of non-predetermined variables
$\overline{m}$	number of eigenvalues of the coefficient matrix outside the unit circle
$\overline{r}$	equilibrium (steady-state) real interest rate
t	arbitrary point in time
u	stochastic shock (AS relation)
X	vector of predetermined variables
Y	vector of non-predetermined variables
y	actual output
$\overline{y}$	potential/steady-state output
$\hat{y}$	output gap
Z	vector of exogenous variables

Greek symbols

α	price stickiness parameter
γ	coefficient matrix
θ	eigenvalue
λ_π^*	effective inflation response coefficient (monetary policy rule)
λ_y	output gap response coefficient (monetary policy rule)
π	inflation rate
π^*	inflation target
φ	interest-rate elasticity of the output gap
Ω	information set

Other symbols

$\Re$	set of real numbers
$\Re^n$	n-dimensional Euclidian space

Chapter IV

Latin symbols

A	(labour-augmenting) technology shock
a	matrix coefficient
b	one-period government bonds
C	capital adjustment costs
$\overline{C}$	steady-state unit adjustment cost
$\overline{C}_1$	steady-state marginal adjustment cost
c	consumption
$\hat{c}$	deviation of consumption from its steady-state level
E	expectation operator
F	coefficient matrix
G	coefficient matrix
g	government consumption of goods and services
H	coefficient matrix
i	nominal interest rate
$\bar{i}$	steady-state nominal interest rate
inv	investment
$\overline{inv}$	steady-state investment
$\widehat{inv}$	deviation of investment from its steady-state level
J	coefficient matrix
k	capital
$\bar{k}$	steady-state capital
$\hat{k}$	deviation of capital from its steady-state level
l	leisure
m	real money balances
mpk	marginal product of capital
$\overline{mpk}$	steady-state marginal product of capital
mpl	marginal product of labour
n	labour input in the production function
n^A	aggregate labour
n^d	labour demand
P	price of the household's product
P^A	aggregate price level
r	real interest rate
$\bar{r}$	steady-state real interest rate
rmc	real marginal cost
$\overline{rmc}$	steady-state real marginal cost
$\widehat{rmc}$	deviation of real marginal cost from its steady-state level
W	household's nominal wage
W^A	aggregate nominal wage

y	actual output
$\overline{y}$	potential/steady-state output
$\hat{y}$	output gap
Y^A	aggregate demand
y^n	natural rate of output

Greek symbols

α_{PF}	elasticity of substitution between capital and labour
β	discount factor
ε_i	monetary policy unit shock
δ	capital depreciation rate
η	elasticity of total adjustment costs with respect to investment
η_P	probability that households cannot adjust their price
η_W	probability that households cannot adjust their nominal wage
Θ_1, Θ_2	adjustment-cost function parameters
θ	elasticity of substitution between differentiated goods
θ_W	elasticity of substitution between differentiated labour units
ϑ	Lagrange multiplier
λ	Lagrange multiplier
λ_i	interest-rate smoothing coefficient (interest-rate rule)
λ_π	inflation response coefficient (interest-rate rule)
λ_π^*	effective inflation response coefficient (interest-rate rule)
λ_y	output gap response coefficient (interest-rate rule)
λ_y^*	effective output gap response coefficient (monetary policy rule)
Ξ	semi-elasticity of investment with respect to the real asset's premium
ξ	scale parameter (investment adjustment costs)
π	inflation rate
$\overline{\pi}$	steady-state inflation rate
ρ_A	autocorrelation coefficient (technology shock)
ρ_υ	autocorrelation coefficient (consumption preference shock)
σ^{-1}	intertemporal elasticity of substitution in consumption
ς	consumption preference shock
τ	leisure relative risk aversion coefficient
υ	consumption preference shock
ω	real wage rate
ϖ	Lagrange multiplier
ω_c	steady-state share in output of consumption
ω_g	steady-state share in output of government expenditure
ω_{inv}	steady-state share in output of investment

I. Introduction

At the beginning of the 21st century, after the wide-scale collapse of centrally planned economies, the consensus perception prevails that prosperity and economic growth are generated by private enterprise and free markets. Nevertheless, government policy has maintained its role as a major factor, responsible for creating the necessary conditions for promoting enterprise and growth. In this context, monetary policy has emerged as an important means for achieving these goals[1]. The arguments for this statement are twofold, concerning both how quickly and how accurately the intervention takes effect on the market. In the first place, unlike fiscal policy, which often serves multiple (sometimes conflicting) goals and may be subject to political influences and lengthy legislative decision-making and approval procedures, monetary policy conducted by an independent central bank can be adjusted relatively quickly to respond to the latest macroeconomic developments. Furthermore, the impact of monetary impulses especially on the financial markets under a sufficient degree of central bank credibility takes place immediately. Sometimes the financial market response even precedes the actual central bank intervention, as market participants anticipate the envisaged measures and act accordingly in advance.

The last decades have witnessed major transformations pertaining to both monetary policy theory and practice. Since the Bretton Woods collapse central banks exposed not only to a higher degree of freedom, but also to the need to define clear monetary policy goals and communicate them to the public. In the last two decades, a growing number of central banks (such as the Bank of England, Bank of Canada, the Reserve Bank of New Zealand and the Swedish Riksbank) have opted for systematic policy behaviour by means of introducing inflation-targeting. On the theoretical side, major advances have been made in the last two decades. One facet of the new consensus on monetary policy is that low, stable inflation is crucial for market-driven growth and that the monetary policy stance in the medium to long run is the major determinant of inflation. After a long period of focusing on the impact of non-monetary factors on the business cycle, empirical studies since the late 1980s have argued that monetary policy significantly influences the short-term course of the economy. Another facet is the strengthened focus on monetary policy design and the interest for optimal rule-based monetary policy in particular. Recent macroeconomic research features nominal rigidities and output fluctuations and focuses on the stabilization role of monetary policy, by allowing the monetary authorities to choose from a

---

1 Or, as Bernanke *et al.* (1999) argue: "… of all the government's tools for influencing the economy, monetary policy has proven to be the most flexible instrument for achieving medium-term stabilization objectives."

variety of monetary policy rule specifications[2] in terms of policy instruments, target variables and size of the response coefficients assigned to the target variables. Since the results obtained in the literature when assessing the different monetary policy rule specifications are to a large extent model-dependent, the choice of a macroeconomic framework based on sufficiently realistic assumptions is crucial for the analysis of the implications of different rule specifications.

Building on the arguments of the New Classical Critique[3] in the 1970s, New Keynesian models that incorporate rational expectations, as well as microeconomic foundations, have been developed. The optimizing behaviour on the part of households and firms, as well as the intertemporal methodology of New Keynesian models with nominal rigidities enable detailed study of the monetary transmission mechanism and optimal monetary policy design. However, with respect to investment and capital, most of these models (e.g. Woodford (1995), Rotemberg and Woodford (1999) and McCallum and Nelson (1999b)) abstract from investment (constant-capital specification). One reason is that introducing endogenous capital and investment to a model with sticky prices may lead to multiple rational-expectations equilibria under certain monetary policy rule specifications[4]. Moreover, the exclusion of capital is often justified on the grounds that capital does not exhibit substantial volatility at business cycle frequencies (e.g. McCallum and Nelson, 1997). However, such an approach is clearly unsatisfactory, as it leaves out an important monetary transmission channel and shock propagation mechanism.

In the following chapters, the analysis is carried out within a New Keynesian framework with endogenous capital, sticky prices and wages and capital adjustment costs. The purpose of this study is to assess different interest rate rule specifications with respect to the degree of activeness (measured by the inflation response coefficient) and the target variables included, based on two criteria: (i) the existence of a determinate rational expectations equilibrium and (ii) the characteristics of the convergence path towards steady state after a shock occurs. In particular, policy rule specifications that yield determinacy of rational expectations equilibrium and in addition involve quantitatively smaller deviations and fast, monotonic convergence after a shock occurs would be preferred. The results obtained confirm that the introduction of endogenous capital and investment has important implications for the monetary policy outcomes. A stronger than one-on-one nominal interest rate response to inflation in the policy rule (i.e.

---

2 The most famous example in recent years being the Taylor rule as in Taylor (1993).

3 The New Classical Critique focused on the use of conventional methods of econometric policy evaluation (Lucas (1976)) and of optimal control (Kydland and Prescott (1977)). In general, according to the real-business cycle theory, monetary policy has no relevance for economic welfare when rational expectations of economic agents are assumed.

4 E.g. forward-looking rules (see Huang and Meng (2007)).

adherence to the Taylor principle) does not *per se* guarantee the best outcomes in terms of equilibrium uniqueness and responses to shocks. Under endogenous capital and investment, the inclusion of an output target in the policy rule is crucial under both criteria.

The study is organised as follows. In Chapter II, I summarise the main issues in monetary policy theory and practice, including the possible rule specifications (Section 1). In Section 2, I give an overview of the criteria for assessing the performance of monetary policy rules. The focus is on determinacy of rational expectations equilibrium and the response to shocks, explicitly used for the analysis in Chapters III and IV. In the last subsection I present formally the Taylor principle, which since 1999 has been a benchmark for formulating rule-based policy and forms the basis for the distinction between "active" and "passive" policy rules made in the subsequent chapters. Section 3 provides a preliminary summary.

In Chapter III I derive the New Keynesian framework with sticky prices and wages, endogenous capital and investment and capital adjustment costs and study the system's determinacy properties under different values assigned to the inflation and output gap response coefficients in the interest-rate rule. In particular, Section 1 provides an overview to the New Keynesian framework, while Section 2 presents the main approaches to modelling capital and investment in the literature. Then in Section 3, I concentrate the model with endogenous capital and adjustment costs, by examining the household optimisation problem and the resulting first-order conditions, deriving the "IS block" equations, the aggregate supply and real-wage relation and adding an interest rate rule to the system. As a next step, in Section 4 I complete the calibration of the model, so as to permit quantitative analysis of its properties. In addition, I provide some numerical analysis of the systems' determinacy properties under different rule specifications.

The findings from Section 4 in Chapter III are then considered when assessing the shock impulse responses under different monetary policy specifications in Chapter IV. Active and passive rules in three possible specifications for each class are tested in this chapter: (i) rules with a sole inflation target; (ii) rules with an inflation and output target and (iii) rules with inflation and output gap target and interest-rate smoothing. Results are obtained for three types of shocks: (i) a monetary policy unit shock; (ii) a technology unit shock and (iii) a consumption preference shock. The results are summarised in Section 4. Chapter V summarises the main findings and concludes.

II. Monetary policy design and criteria for assessing monetary policy rules

In this chapter, I provide a more general perspective to the main theoretical and practical issues in monetary policy design, which are relevant for the assessment of the several interest rate rule specifications in the subsequent parts. The issues covered in Section 1 include the advantages and implications of systematic policy behaviour (as opposed to discretionary measures) and choice of instruments/target variables that enter the rule specification. In addition, Section 2 presents the main criteria that will be used in the subsequent determinacy and impulse response analysis in Chapters III and IV. The Taylor principle, which forms the basis for the classification of monetary policy rules in terms of the degree of their "activeness" (measured by the size of the inflation response coefficient), is presented formally in the last subsection. Later on, in Section 4 in the subsequent chapter the main findings will be centred on the question whether adherence to the Taylor principle guarantees a determinate rational-expectations equilibrium when endogenous capital with adjustment costs is introduced to a New Keynesian model with staggered price-and wage-setting.

1. Monetary policy issues

In the 1960s and 1970s "activist" monetary policies, aimed at achieving "full employment" have been widely discussed and implemented[5]. The rise of such policies has been motivated by the conviction that there exists a stable long-run trade-off between inflation and unemployment, captured by the Phillips curve[6]. According to this view, in the long run the monetary authority can attain a permanent reduction in the unemployment rate by allowing for a higher rate of inflation. At the same time, estimates of these (allegedly) stable relations between inflation and unemployment have been computed by using large econometric models that assigned precise quantitative dimensions to the policy trade-off. The actual experience with the activist pursuit of full employment by monetary policy means has contradicted the policy-makers' anticipated outcome. Not only did the business cycle fluctuations not disappear in the 1970s, but the worldwide recessions of 1973-74 and 1981-82 were among the most severe in the second half of the twentieth century, characterised by high unemployment and inflation ("stagflation"). Thus, in spite of not attaining the aspired policy objective, the "sacrifice" in terms of higher inflation rate has still been realised: the late 1960s and most of the 1970s were characterised by rising and variable rates of inflation in many countries.

5 For a more detailed discussion of monetary policy strategies in the 1960s and 1970s, see Mishkin (2006).

6 See Phillips (1958) and Samuelson and Solow (1960).

Parallel to the practical experience with activist policies, there has also been an academic critique of using monetary policy as a tool to obtain full employment at the expense of a higher inflation rate. Among the most influential arguments are Milton Friedman's monetary critique concerning the uncertain outcomes of monetary policy interventions[7], the Lucas critique of the optimal control paradigm for monetary policy[8], the conclusion reached by Friedman (1968) and Phelps (1968) that there is no long-run trade-off between inflation and unemployment, as well as the warning against the perils of time inconsistency under discretionary policy delivered by Kydland and Prescott (1977), Calvo (1978) and Barro and Gordon (1983).

Without denying the significant impact of monetary policy on the economy, Friedman argued that monetary policy is a tool that cannot be used with precision for stabilisation purposes. In "The Role of Monetary Policy" he explicitly warns against "the belief that the state of employment itself should be the proximate criterion of policy", adding that

> ...I fear that... the pendulum may well have swung too far, that... we are in danger of assigning to monetary policy a larger role than it can perform, in danger of asking it to accomplish tasks that it cannot achieve, and, as a result, in danger of preventing it from making the contribution that it is capable of making (Friedman, 1968, p. 5).

Friedman emphasised that, due to long and variable lags of monetary policy, a too strong policy response might have a destabilising effect on the economy. This forms the basis for the subsequent discussion on the appropriate degree of activism of monetary policy. As argued by Blanchard and Fischer (1993), under long and variable lags very strong policy responses to shocks could create instrument instability. Instrument instability arises when the current effects of changes in the monetary policy instrument are small and the lagged effects large, so that large changes in the policy instrument are required to offset the effects of a recent shock, creating the need for even larger changes later on. An even more powerful argument for more moderate policy responses has to do with uncertainty about the structural coefficients in the model, i.e. to what extent the variability of the instrument increases the variability of the target variables.

Although Friedman's criticism emphasises the technical difficulties in controlling the policy outcomes, it does not fundamentally rule out activist central bank behaviour. If the pitfalls of the active pursuit of short-run output stabilisation had been predominately of instrumental nature, implementing more elaborate methods such as the (at that time increasingly popular) techniques of optimal control would have been sufficient to compensate for lags between policy measures and their effects. Thus, for policy activism to be ruled out as an appropriate central bank strategy, a formal methodological critique of the proposed

---

7 See Friedman and Schwartz (1963).

8 See Lucas (1976).

techniques of optimal control or a substantial re-evaluation of the implied stable relation between inflation and unemployment were needed.

The formal methodological critique of optimal control has been put forward by Lucas (1976) who argues that macroeconomic models that are not based on consistent microeconomic underpinning are non-structural and cannot be useful for policy evaluation. The underlying reason for that finding is that the estimated coefficients of such models' equations include both structural and policy parameters and are therefore not invariant to the choice of monetary policy regime.

1.1. The case for rules rather than discretion

The general equilibrium framework adopted in recent research permits explicit utility-based welfare analysis by introducing a quadratic central bank loss function that involves stabilizing inflation around an inflation target and stabilizing the real economy, represented by the output gap. Some examples of research incorporating such a loss function include Clarida *et al.* (1999), McCallum *et al.* (1999, 2000), Svensson *et al.* (2000), Woodford (2001).

One of the main issues in monetary policy research in recent years has been whether central banks should commit themselves to a systematic approach to monetary policy that involves an explicit framework for decision-making and is communicated to the public.

1.1.1. Analytical distinction between rules and discretion

For the subsequent analysis, it is necessary to introduce an analytical distinction between the two main strategies of monetary policy conduct - discretionary and rule-based monetary policy. In an argument on rule—based monetary policy Friedman (1962) notes that under a policy rule decisions are made by following a procedure applicable to many distinct cases and not on a case-by case basis, which has favourable effects on expectations. He notes that, under discretionary policy, wrong decisions are likely to be made in a large fraction of cases because the decision-makers are not taking into account the cumulative consequences of the policy as a whole. By contrast, adopting a general rule is adopted for a group of cases as a bundle would have favourable effects on people's attitudes and expectations that would not follow even from the discretionary adoption of precisely the same actions on a series of separate occasions.

Taylor (1993) emphasises that under pure discretion, "the settings for the instruments of policy are determined from scratch each period with no attempt to follow a reasonably well-defined contingency plan for the future." Alternatively, rule-based behaviour is systematic, or in other words "methodical, according to a plan, and not casual or random." McCallum (1993) argues that although this condition is necessary, it is not sufficient for a rule-based policy. Under rational expectations, in order for rule-like behaviour to be at place, the central bank should not only be systematic in the sense of applying the same type of response each period, but should also design the systematic response pattern taking into account the private sector's expectational behaviour. Under a theoretical point of view the distinction is between: (i) responding to existing conditions as prescribed by a prearranged formula specifying instrument settings. The formula could be derived as a result of optimisation analysis, but is not influenced by current conditions in each period; and (ii) period-by-period optimisation based on current conditions while treating past experiences and policies as irrelevant bygones.

Last but not least, a rule-based monetary policy procedure should rule out the temptation to exploit existing expectations for temporary output gains by creating an inflationary bias as in the baseline framework on dynamic inconsistency developed by Kydland and Prescott (1977).

1.1.2. The problem of dynamic inconsistency

According to the definition of Blanchard and Fischer (1993) "a policy is dynamically inconsistent when a future policy decision that forms part of an optimal plan formulated at an initial date is no longer optimal from the viewpoint of a later date, even if no relevant new information has appeared in the meantime". Extensive theoretical research has been devoted to this subject since Kydland and Prescott (1977) first argued that optimal macroeconomic policies could be dynamically inconsistent. The basic question refers to the costs of a government not being able to commit itself to implementing announced policy actions or, equivalently, of the benefits of policy rules over discretion. Under rational expectations, a policy commitment (such as following a rule) means carrying out the policy that is optimal and expected. By contrast, under discretionary policy the private sector in each period may anticipate that the government will opt for the short-run optimal decision and react accordingly.

Barro and Gordon (1983) reveal the motivation behind inconsistent behaveiour in monetary policy conduct. They point to two main sources of temporary benefits from inducing surprise inflation. One source of benefits can be derived from the dependence of the output gap on inflation expectations, whereby unanticipated monetary expansions lead to increases in real economic activity, lowering the unemployment rate below the natural rate[9]. The other source of potential benefits from surprise inflation involves the reductions in real value of the government's liabilities that are fixed in nominal terms. However, since under rational expectations the private sector is able to understand the central bank's incentives and adjust its inflationary expectations accordingly, surprise inflation

9 The natural rate is defined by Barro and Gordon (1983) as "the value that would be ground out by the private sector in the absence of monetary disturbances". The natural rate can shift over time because of supply shocks, demographic changes, shifts in governmental tax and transfer programs, etc. As the authors point out, the natural rate need not be optimal.

and the benefits arising from it cannot be induced systematically in equilibrium. If the private sector anticipates the potential for introducing inflationary shocks, in equilibrium the average rate of inflation and its corresponding costs will be higher than under maintained credible monetary policy commitment. Thus, under rational expectations, nothing is gained from opportunism and the outcome is in general worse compared to the commitment scenario.

1.1.3. Advantages of central bank commitment to a monetary policy rule

Based on the time-inconsistency literature findings presented in the previous subsection, two main advantages of central bank commitment to an explicit policy rule can be derived[10].

The first benefit of such an approach includes increased predictability of central bank actions, which is essential for improving policy effectiveness that depends not only on the actual measures taken, but also on the public's expectations about future policy. This provides central banks with an important tool of stabilisation policy, as market expectations about the future path of short-run interest rates influence other financial-market prices (such as long-term interest rates, equity prices and exchange rates) that ultimately affect spending decisions. In order for this mechanism to function, the public needs to have a clear enough understanding of the rule that the central bank follows in deciding on policy actions. To this end, it could be enough that the central bank commits itself to a systematic way of determining an appropriate response to future developments, without having to explicitly specify actions under every circumstance possible.

The second main benefit from a systematic approach has to do with the optimal outcomes of a behaviour bound by past commitments. As first postulated by Kydland and Prescott (1977), even if the central bank has a correct quantitative model of the economy and of its policy trade-offs in each period and the private sector forms correct expectations about future policy, the outcome under discretion may be substantially worse than under commitment. In this line of argument, Woodford (2003) argues that the main gains from commitment in this respect are in terms of eliminating the inflation bias[11] characterising sequential (discretionary) optimisation and an optimal reaction to shocks/real disturbances[12].

---

10 It should be noted that the benefits that are elaborated in this subsection are model-specific.

11 For further elaboration on inflation bias under discretion, see Kydland and Prescott (1977) und Barro and Gordon (1983).

12 Rule-based (forward-looking) decision making allows for a more persistent reaction to real disturbances over time and thus implies reducing the volatility in short-run interest rates.

An interesting new topic in the rules vs. discretion debate concerns the role of credibility. The main finding is that in the presence of a trade-off between the two policy objectives (price stability and actual output), a credible central bank commitment to a state-contingent policy results in a greater welfare gain as compared to discretionary policy. An example for this approach can be found in Woodford (1999), where the inefficiency that arises from discretionary policy-making equals the discounted present value of current and future period losses (squared deviations of inflation and output from their target levels).

1.2. Design of monetary policy rules

The issue of how a monetary policy rule should be designed has been subject to much theoretical debate in the last several decades. The discussion could be traced back to Friedman's arguments in the 50s and 60s for a rule of constant money growth[13]. Apart from that particular instrument setting, in more general terms Friedman argued that monetary policy should be fixed by a rule, thus ruling out discretionary policy.

Before discussing the theoretical and practical developments concerning monetary policy design, it would be useful to identify the transmission channels of monetary impulses to the economy. Among others, Arestis and Sawyer (2002, 2003) identify six channels of monetary policy transmission: (i) the interest rate channel; (ii) the wealth effect channel; (iii) the exchange rate channel (under an open-economy perspective); (iv) the monetarist channel; (v) the narrow credit channel and (vi) the broad credit channel.

Both the narrow and the broad credit channel refer to how changes in the financial positions of borrowers and lenders affect aggregate demand in an economy with credit market frictions. The narrow credit channel emphasised by Hall (2001)[14] and Bernanke and Blinder (1988) concerns the role of the banking sector as lender. When monetary policy induces changes of banking sector's total reserves, the supply of loans to the private sector will be affected. Given the fact that normally a significant number of producers and consumers depend on bank lending to finance their investment and consumption spending, ultimately monetary policy interventions are bound to affect aggregate demand and inflation in the economy. In addition, the broad credit channel described by Hall (2001)[15], Bernanke and Gertler (1999) and Bernanke *et al.* (1998) takes into consideration the effect of the monetary policy stance on the financial position of borrowers. If imperfect information in terms of the supply of external finance to the private

13 See Friedman (1960, 1962).

14 Hall (2001) originally refers to the narrow credit channel as "bank lending channel".

15 The broad credit channel is called "balance sheet channel" in the Hall (2001) classification.

sector is assumed, lenders charge a (risk) premium[16] on loans dependent on the borrower's financial position. Generally, low gearing[17] implies small external finance premium and vice versa. In this setting, the monetary policy stance affects aggregate demand through corporate cash flows and asset price developments. As to the former mechanism, a policy-induced increase in the interest rate raises the individual firm's gearing ratio, thereby boosting the required premium on external finance. The second effect of policy-induced interest rate hikes pertains to asset prices that determine the value of loan collateral. According to this "financial accelerator" effect, higher interest rates may lead to falling asset prices and consequently a decline in the value of the collateral, thus leading to an increase in the borrower premium. On a broader scale, monetary impulses channelled through the financial sector by means of the narrow or broad credit channel affect investment and consumption decisions and consequently aggregate demand in the economy.

Apart from the importance for gaining access to external finance, asset prices affect aggregate demand through the wealth effect channel. If the consumption function is constructed to depend on consumer wealth, consumption expenditure is affected by the value of real consumer wealth (i.e. by asset prices).

Next, the distinction between the interest rate and the monetarist channels is explained by the choice of a monetary aggregate or the interest rate as a monetary policy instrument. If the nominal interest rate is the policy instrument, the money supply is endogenous and vice versa. The choice between both instruments determines the particular type of the initial monetary impulse; still, if the degree of substitutability between money and financial (especially short-term liquid) assets is very high, changes in money supply have a significant impact on interest rates. Under a sufficient degree of price stickiness, the real interest rate and the return on capital will also be affected. As a result, as long as consumption and investment decisions are interest-rate sensitive, the interest rate changes influence aggregate demand. Of course, the transmission of the monetary policy impulse to the economy is to a great extent dependent on the functioning of the financial sector. Instead of symmetrically adjusting their interest rates in response to the policy-induced interest rate changes, financial institutions may choose to perform some type of credit rationing[18]. In the context of the interest and the monetary transmission channels, a broader perspective to the implications of money supply as a policy instrument beyond the effect on interest rates may also be relevant. In case a high degree of substitutability between money

16 In this context, Arestis and Sawyer (2003) mention a "premium to cover monitoring costs" charged by lenders.

17 I.e. a low debt-to-equity ratio.

18 For a thorough study of the determinants and forms of credit rationing, see Jaffee and Modigliani (1969), Stiglitz and Weiss (1981) and Blinder and Stiglitz (1983).

and real assets is assumed, the impact of money supply changes would also depend on relative price changes. In this case, apart from interest rates, asset prices also affect aggregate demand and should be considered by the monetary authority.

The last monetary policy transmission channel, the exchange rate channel, concerns the open economy and links monetary policy to inflation through several effects. One of them pertains to aggregate demand and functions through the uncovered interest rate parity condition, matching interest rate differentials to expected exchange rate changes. Another type of effect works through import prices.

The six transmission channels identified by Arestis and Sawyer (2002, 2003) all describe variations of aggregate demand channel. Thus, from a broader perspective, monetary policy transmission can be classified as giving an initial impulse either to aggregate demand or to aggregate supply[19]. In this context, Taylor (2000) speaks of "aggregate demand" and "staggered price adjustment" component of the monetary transmission mechanism. As far as monetary policy transmission from the aggregate demand perspective is concerned, Taylor (2000) identifies the "financial market price view" and the "credit view". The former emphasizes the impact of monetary policy on the prices and rates of return on financial assets (e.g. bonds prices, interest and exchange rates) and consequently on firm and household spending decisions. The credit view stresses the impact of monetary policy on lending by banks or other financial institutions as alternative to internal finance. The "staggered price adjustment" channel (denoted "expectations channel" in Svensson (1999b)) allows monetary policy to affect inflation expectations which, in turn, affect inflation with a lag via the wage- and price-setting decisions of economic agents.

Last but not least, incorporating an aggregate supply transmission channel of monetary policy allows for a more thorough analysis of monetary policy outcomes. The framework with endogenous capital presented in the next chapter enables tracking the supply-side response to shocks induced under several rule specifications, thus offering a broader insight into medium- to long-run adjustments in the economy.

1.2.1. Rules, instruments and targets

In the recent decades interest-rate rules have attracted much theoretical attention. Despite the fact that central banks have been reluctant to publicly commit to an interest-rate rule of a specific form, there is some evidence that past behav-

19 For a closed-economy setting, building blocks, micro-foundations and different specifications of these two general transmission mechanism channels are modeled by King and Wolman (1996), Woodford (1996), Yun (1996), Goodfriend and King (1997), Rotemberg and Woodford (1998), McCallum and Nelson (1999) and Clarida et al. (1999).

iour of some monetary authorities can be described by an explicit rule[20], the central banks of some major economies nowadays apply explicit inflation targets (*inter alia*, the ECB, the Bank of England and Bank of Canada).

In the subsequent exposition, I will concentrate on interest-rate rules for conducing monetary policy. Although other definitions of a monetary policy rule could be possible, for the purpose of this work I adopt the definition of Taylor (1998):

> "...a monetary policy rule is defined as a description—expressed algebraically, numerically or graphically-of how the *instruments* of policy, such as the monetary base or the federal funds rate, change in response to economic variables" (Taylor, 1998, p.3).

Furthermore, for the subsequent analysis it is necessary to provide a definition of instruments, targets, goals/objectives and indicators of monetary policy. From a practical perspective, Borio (1997) and Ho (2008) distinguish between the strategic and tactical level of the monetary authorities' pursuit of policy goals (see Figure 2.1). At the strategic level, certain macroeconomic goals or final objectives are pursued, such as price stability, long-term growth or employment. By contrast, the tactical (operating) level covers the choice of instruments and operating objectives/targets. The latter are variables which can be influenced quite fast and closely by the central bank[21]. Examples of monetary policy instruments include the official interest rates (e.g. on standing facilities), market operations (e.g. repo tenders, FX operations), reserve requirements and, in the past, direct controls (e.g. ceilings on loans or on bank depositor loan rates).

According to McCallum (2001b), instruments are variables that the central bank can control quickly and directly or at least accurately, the usual contenders being short-term interest rates, the monetary base or a measure of bank reserves. Goals/Objectives are variables that enter the central bank objective function. In case the ultimate goals are not promptly observable, the central bank employs a two-step procedure, attempting to hit target variables that are treated as surrogates for the ultimate objectives. Examples for target variables are the monetary aggregates M1, M2 and nominal GDP. Indicators are information variables, for which the central bank does not try to hit specified paths.

20 For example, the Taylor rule (Taylor (1993)) seems to have described the actions of the Fed remarkably accurately during most of the 80s and 90s of the past century.

21 For example, short-term financial market interest rates, exchange rates, etc.

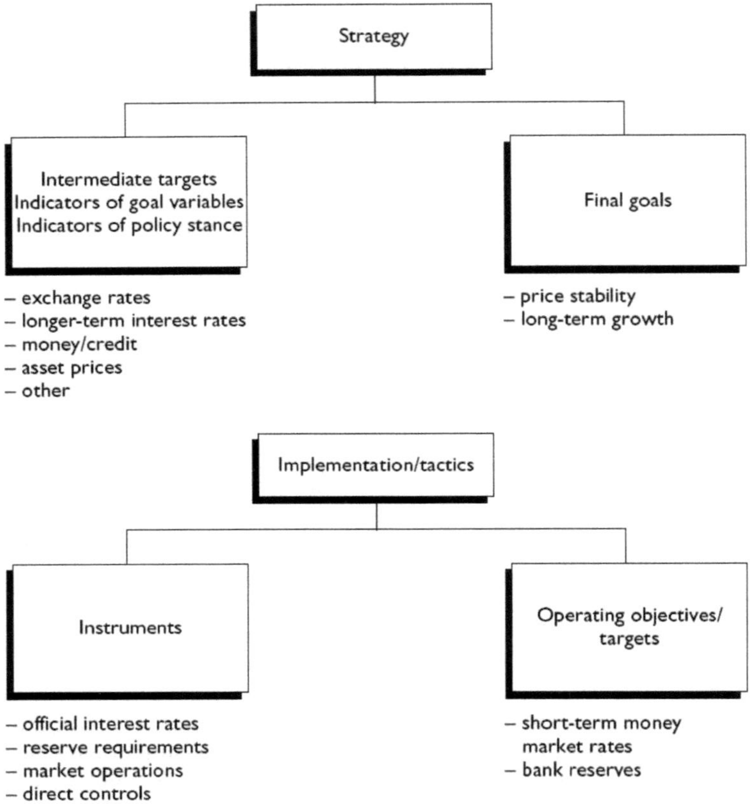

Figure 2.1: The monetary policy framework (Borio (1997)

1.2.2. Choice of instruments

A long-standing discussion in monetary policy research has concentrated on the issue whether the monetary authority should use money[22] or the interest rate to target inflation and/or output. Money supply as a policy instrument gained increasing popularity in the 1960s and 1970s. In fact, in his policy proposals Friedman went even further and argued for a rule involving money supply not only as an instrument, but as a policy target as well. Actually, Friedman (1960) acknowledged that a constant money growth rule does not correspond to optimal policy. Still, arguments such as imperfect knowledge about the "true" objectives inflation and output, the possibly inaccurate estimation of the unobserved natu-

22 In the form of a monetary aggregate.

ral rates of interest, output or employment and their dynamics, as well as the difficulties with obtaining real-time measures of policy objectives seemed to support choosing a rule expressed in terms of money supply only.

Of course, the above arguments to a greater extent address the question whether the central bank should target an intermediate variable or its final objectives directly and provides less insight to the choice of instruments. A further contribution by Poole (1970) analyses the conditions under which pegging money or interest rates are appropriate. For a static IS-LM framework, Poole suggested that if disturbances originate primarily in the money demand, fixing the level of the interest rates is appropriate. For the case of goods market shocks, the money stock should be pegged. Despite the simplicity of the framework and the lack of supply side in particular, the Poole model provides an essential insight to understanding the choice between money and interest rates as monetary policy instruments.

Taylor (1995, 1998) suggests that a constant money growth rule will generally induce an interest rate response to inflation and output similar in form as in the case of interest rate policy rules, but not necessarily similar in size. For example, for very high or negative inflation rate, the resulting variability of inflation expectations can render interest rate rules less efficient than controlling the money supply[23]. That is why, even when pursuing an interest rate rule, it is advisable for the central bank to still monitor money supply.

Recent models, such as Casares and McCallum (2006), McCallum and Nelson (1999b) and Rotemberg and Woodford (1998a) all include an interest rate instrument, whereby the money supply is endogenous since the central bank must vary it in order to sustain its desired interest rate level. In these models the path for money growth followed by the monetary authority in the long run under an interest rate instrument exactly coincides with the one that would be followed under a money supply instrument. In line with the choice of instrument in these studies and the recent central bank practice, the monetary policy rules that I introduce in the next chapter include the nominal interest rate as a policy instrument.

1.2.3. Choice of target variables

A second issue in policy design (apart from the choice of the instrument) concerns the choice of target variables. In this subsection, the variables entering the rule specifications in Chapter III (inflation, the output gap and the lagged interest rate) will be briefly discussed from a theoretical point of view.

---

23 As Taylor (1995) shows, in such circumstances interest rate rules can break down completely.

Inflation-targeting

There has been consensus in the literature on the fact that in the recent years a growing number of countries has opted for some form of inflation targeting[24] combined with central bank independence[25]. Inflation-targeting is subject to differing definitions in the literature. For example, according to Svensson (2002) inflation targeting involves stabilizing inflation around an inflation target[26]. With respect to the target variables selected, it could be distinguished between inflation targeting in a narrower sense[27] (involving a central bank reaction to inflation deviations from a target level only) and a broader definition where inflation and a measure of real economic activity are both considered. Adhering to the former perspective, Bernanke *et al.* (1999) define inflation-targeting as a framework, rather than a rule for monetary policy[28]. According to them, inflation-targeting is characterised by public announcement of official quantitative targets (or target ranges) for the inflation rate over one or more time horizons, and by explicit acknowledgement that low, stable inflation is monetary policy's primary long-run goal.

Arestis and Sawyer (2003)[29] offer a definition of inflation targeting complemented by certain institutional requirements. Thus, inflation targeting involves more than just targeting the rate of inflation as an objective of economic policy and implies: (i) setting a numerical target range for the inflation objecttive; (ii) using monetary policy as an instrument to achieve the target by adjusting the nominal interest rate; (iii) central bank independence; and (iv) monetary policy only targeting the inflation rate with the possible effects of monetary policy on other objectives ignored, with the exception of short-term effects.

---

24 Snowdon and Vane (2005) distinguish between four types of monetary regimes that have been implemented since the middle of the 20th century: exchange rate targeting (e.g. in the UK, 1990-1992), monetary targeting (e.g. in the UK, 1976-1987), explicit inflation targeting (UK, 1992-to date) and implicit inflation targeting (USA).The difference between explicit and implicit inflation targeting pertains to whether the central bank announces an exact inflation target. In this sense, the ECB policy would qualify as "explicit inflation targeting".

25 For more detailed contributions on modern central bank practice issues, see Alesina and Summers (1993), Fischer (1995a, 1995b, 1996), Bernanke and Mishkin (1992, 1997), Bernanke and Woodford (1997), Bernanke *et al.* (1999), King (1997), Svensson (1997a 1999b, 2000), Mishkin (1999, 2000), Bernanke and Woodford (2006).

26 P. 6.

27 The inflation-targeting rules referred to in Chapter IV abide by this narrower definition of the term.

28 In the terms of Bernanke et al. (1999) inflation-targeting as a framework for monetary policy implies that the inherent discipline of a rule is extended by maintaining some degree of flexibility.

29 See p. 2.

The broader definition of inflation targeting with reference to the target variables entering the central bank's loss function (or monetary policy rule) is denoted as "flexible" inflation targeting[30]. Svensson (1997b, 2002) argues that in the central bank practice inflation targeting is flexible[31], as it also involves some concern about the stability of the real economy. The latter means that monetary policy should contribute to the welfare of the representative citizen. However, as this objective is not operational, stabilising output around potential output is in-cluded in the central bank reaction function[32].

There exists a general consensus in the recent empirical literature that maintaining a low and stable rate of inflation is an appropriate monetary policy objective[33]. Yet the justification of such a policy emphasis from a theoretical point of view may not be straightforward. According to the real-business-cycle models of the 1980s relative prices rather than the absolute level of prices are relevant for the allocation of resources in the economy[34]. Traditional Keynesian models, by contrast, postulate that variations in the growth rates of prices and wages induce variations in output and employment[35]. However, this inflation-output relation has typically been considered as an argument in favour of achieving output and employment goals rather than a justification for establishing price stability as a primary objective of monetary policy.

With the introduction of rational expectations to a framework with nominal rigidities, keeping inflation low and less volatile "locks in" expectations about future inflation and helps to contain the possible inflationary impact of macroeconomic shocks. Furthermore, in the short run and with sluggish price adjustment inflationary impulses can have a destabilising impact on output and employment. In this line, Woodford (2003) argues that, since instability of the general level of prices causes substantial real distortions – leading to inefficient variation both in aggregate employment and output and in the sectoral composition of economic activity –price stability is important and should therefore be the primary aim of monetary policy.

In addition, the theoretical literature so far suggests a distinction between the costs of anticipated and unanticipated inflation. Anticipated inflation causes loss of social welfare because it promotes economising on real money balances, generates costs for frequent price adjustments and increases relative price uncer-

30 As opposed to "strict" inflation targeting, with low and stable inflation being the only goal of monetary policy (i.e. when the reaction coefficient to inflation solely is different from zero).

31 See pp. 6-7.

32 For further analysis of the output target, see Subsection 3.2.3.2.

33 See, for example, Fischer (1996) and Mishkin (2000).

34 Real business cycle authors support „real" as opposed to "monetary" theories of fluctuations. For example, Kydland and Prescott (1982) and Prescott (1986) construct models that include real variables only.

35 For a thorough discussion, see Leeson (1994, 1997a, 1997b).

tainty. Unanticipated inflation, on the other hand, increases relative price variability and costs of information gathering and leads to income redistribution. Finally, as Blanchard and Fischer (1993)[36] put it: "Its presence as the only macroeconomic variable in addition to output in the loss function reflects in part the fact that, right or wrong, inflation is perceived as costly by people and is costly for policymakers to ignore."

An essential practical issue in policy design concerns the specification of the inflation target. Commonly under inflation-targeting the rule followed by the monetary authority includes a weighted measure of the deviation of the inflation rate from its target value. Concerning the choice of an appropriate target, Taylor (1986) emphasises that the policy objective is to minimize fluctuations around the target, regardless of what the actual value of the target is.

Output-targeting

Svensson (1997a) and Rudebusch and Svensson (1998) show that it is advisable that the monetary policy instrument responds to the determinants of the target variables rather than the target variables themselves. Thus, even under a primary price stability goal, it is generally appropriate to respond to both current inflation and the output gap, since both are determinants of future inflation. The relevance of simple policy rules that, as proposed by Taylor (1993), include both an inflation and an output target for recent central bank practice can be substantiated by the following statement by Federal Reserve Board Governor Yellen, made in January 1995:

> "Now, if you take the case of the FOMC, it seems to me that a reaction function in which the real funds rate changes by roughly equal amounts in response to deviations of inflation from a target of 2 percent and to deviations of actual from potential output describes tolerably well what this Committee has done since 1986. This policy, which fits the behavior of this Committee, is an example of the type of hybrid rule that would be preferable in my view, if we wanted a rule. I think the Greenspan Fed has done very well by following such a rule, and I think that is what sensible central banks do." (Federal Reserve Board, 1995, pp. 43-44)

Different definitions of the output gap with respect to the reference term are common in the literature. According to Galí (2002) the output gap is defined as "the deviation of output from its equilibrium level in the absence of nominal rigidities". Woodford (1999) on the other hand, distinguishes in his proposed model between "potential output" and "natural rate of output" as reference values for the deviation of actual output. The former term represents steady state (or long-term equilibrium) output in the presence of nominal rigidities and market frictions, while the second term denotes the "equilibrium level of output under perfectly flexible prices". The natural rate of output can is relatively time-

36 Chapter 11, p.569.

invariant and, at least in the short run, cannot be influenced by economic policy actions.

Walsh (2003) provides an alternative definition of the output policy objective - a "speed-limit policy" that targets growth in demand relative to growth in potential, i.e. output gap changes. He finds that targeting the change in the output gap introduces inertia into monetary policy under central bank discretion, as the lagged output gap becomes an endogenous state variable. The final outcome is that targeting the output gap change is superior to inflation targeting unless inflation adjustment is prevailing backward-looking. In contrast, McCallum (2001a) argues that the output gap is unobservable and instead assesses the implications of using a trend-type measure. His results show that highly undesirable consequences in terms of higher inflation variability arise in case policy responds strongly to the measured gap. However, this result is obtained in a framework with constant capital. By contrast, the results obtained in Chapter IV in a model with endogenous capital and adjustment costs reveal that including the output gap in the monetary policy rule plays an important stabilising role in the occurrence of shocks.

The central bank's output objective is often included as a quadratic term on output deviations in the loss function, so that deviations of output from the target (natural or potential) level are symmetrically penalised. This feature is subject to critique by some authors[37] who argue that in sticky-prices Keynesian models in the presence of market frictions (e.g. monopoly power by firms), the equilibrium level of output is too low, in which case a negative output gap should be penalised more heavily by the central bank. Whereas this argument rests on the subtleties of defining target output[38], a more general critique point could be elaborated in terms of whether a positive and a negative gap actually impose the same welfare loss to the economy.

Another critique on interest rate rules including an output gap target (such as, for instance, the Taylor rule as in Taylor (1993)) arises from measurement difficulties. In the first place, no real-time data on the value of current output are available to policy-makers. Thus, the operational usefulness of the output gap target is limited by the availability of timely and reliable estimates[39]. This shortcoming can be alleviated to a certain extend by assuming that the current output gap is equal to the expectation in the previous period. Secondly, as McCallum and Nelson (1999b) point out[40], "...there is considerable uncertainty regarding

37 See Blanchard and Fischer (1993), Chapter 11.

38 In Blanchard and Fischer (1993) the full-employment level of output denotes potential level of output when certain distortions have been taken account of, instead of the level of output under flexible prices and perfect competition.

39 This argument has been used by Orphanides and van Norden (2004) to describe the difficulties when using the output gap to predict inflation within the Phillips curve relation.

40 P. 5.

the realised value of real GDP even at the end of the quarter in actual economies". The reason is that empirical estimates of the output gap are in general subject to significant and highly persistent revisions. The third source of practical difficulties when measuring the output gap target pertains to correctly estimating the value of potential output[41]. Kuttner (1994) and McCallum (1997) argue that monetary policy decisions are in practice complicated by the risk of output gap mismeasurement. Smets (1998) analyses the effect of measurement error in the output gap on efficient policy rules in a simple estimated model of the US economy. The conclusion is that output gap uncertainty can have a significant impact on the efficient response coefficients in instrument rules (such as the Taylor rule) by reducing the response to the current estimated output gap relative to current inflation. Orphanides (1998)[42] shows that output gap real-time measurement errors "lead to a significant deterioration of feasible policy outcomes and cause efficient policies to be less activist".

Interest-rate smoothing

A policy rule with the short-term interest rate as instrument can be designed to involve interest-rate smoothing. Here it should be differentiated between smoothing in the sense of lowering the variance of the level of interest rates, as opposed to lowering the variability of interest-rate changes. According to Woodford (1999) reducing short-term interest rate level variability can be justified under the assumption that the distortions associated with positive nominal interest rates are described by a convex function of the interest rate. In this case, for any average level of nominal interest rates, a lower variance in them will reduce the size of the distortions. The case for lowering interest rate level variability could easily be illustrated by analysing the implications of significant interest rate changes in the two extreme scenarios of a low and a high average level of nominal interest rates respectively. A policy consistent with a low average rate of inflation and nominal interest rates faces the zero nominal interest rate bound and therefore cannot apply large interest rate reductions to combat deflationary shocks. On the other hand, when the levels of inflation and nominal interest rates are already relative high, in order to avoid distortions (as private sector's resources are wasted on attempts to economise on cash balances), the monetary authority should avoid significant further increases in interest rates in response to inflationary shocks.

Interest-rate smoothing in the sense of seeking to minimise the variability of interest rate changes is a widely observed phenomenon in actual central bank

41 The difficulties associated with measurement of potential (and, by analogy, the natural rate of) output and resource utilization and their implications for monetary policy and macroeconomic stabilization have a long tradition in modern economic literature, beginning with Friedman (1947, 1953).

42 See also Orphanides *et al.* (2000).

practice. From a theoretical point of view, minimising the variability of interest-rate changes by adjusting official interest rates in a sequence of relatively small steps in the same direction means that central bank behaviour depends not only on current states and current forecasts of future conditions, but also on past conditions and commitments. Sack (1998)[43], for example, estimates the optimal federal funds rate policy given the structural form of the US economy and compares it to actual historical data. He finds that in the absence of parameter uncertainty, the calculated optimal policy responds more aggressively to changes in the economy than the observed policy, resulting in a substantially higher volatility of the funds rate than observed. He explains lower variability of interest rates in actual policy with the existence of parameter uncertainty, which limits the willingness of the Fed to deviate from the policy rule that has been previously implemented.

There are several possible explanations of interest-rate smoothing that have been discussed in the recent literature on central bank practice. First, as Lowe and Ellis (1997) point out, policy-makers are averse to frequent changes in the direction of interest rate movements as it may undermine confidence in the central bank and therefore its ability to influence private sector expectations and behaviour in a desirable manner. Second, it can be argued that the nature of the decision-making process on monetary policy leads to conservatism that is at the heart of interest-rate smoothing[44]. According to this line of argument, central banks are not able to gain broad political support for prospective interest rate changes until sufficient evidence has been gathered. Because the evidence needed accumulates slowly, interest rates tend to be changed gradually. A third motive for interest-rate smoothing, as discussed by Sellon and Roley (1995), concerns the fact that a predictable path for short-term interest rates confers the central bank greater influence over long-term bond yields, and consequently over future output and inflation. Similarly, Lowe and Ellis (1997) provide the explanation that central banks tend to modify interest rates gradually in order to be able to assess the policy impact on longer rates and adjust the direction and pace of changes accordingly.

2. Criteria for assessing monetary policy rules

After having presented some main theoretical insights concerning monetary policy design (which are taken into account when specifying the policy rules to be assessed in the next two chapters), I will discuss several criteria for assessing rule-based monetary policy performance, including operationality/simplicity, local determinacy of rational expectations equilibrium and its implications for response to shocks, as well as adherence to the Taylor principle. In the next

43 For further empirical evidence of interest-rate smoothing, see Clarida *et al.* (1998) and Rudebusch (1995).

44 Also in Lowe and Ellis (1997).

chapters, I will assess several interest-rate rule specifications in terms of whether they induce a locally determinate rational expectations equilibrium and desirable responses to a number of shocks[45]. By definition, the operationality/simplicity criterion is fulfilled for all the interest-rate rule specifications assessed in Chapters III and IV. In the next parts, adherence to the Taylor principle is discussed from a broader perspective in terms of critically examining whether within the model chosen fulfilling this criterion actually guarantees local determinacy of rational expectations equilibrium[46].

2.1. Operationality/Simplicity

In a series of studies on monetary policy rules, McCallum (1988, 1989, 1993, 1994) has emphasised operationality[47] as a crucial property when deciding on a policy strategy. The operationality criterion limits consideration to policy rules (i) that are expressed in terms of instrument variables that could be controlled on a high-frequency basis by the monetary authority and (ii) that require only information that could actually be possessed by this authority.

The use of simple instrument rules to specify rule-based monetary policy behaviour has a long tradition in the literature. Wicksell (1898) and Henderson and McKibbin (1993) suggested simple instrument rules with the interest rate as the instrument. Meltzer (1987) and McCallum (1988) proposed simple instrument rules with the monetary base as the instrument. The most prominent simple instrument rule is the Taylor rule (Taylor (1993)), incorporating an interest-rate instrument responding to the inflation and output gaps. Recent discussions of Taylor rules include Clarida *et al.* (1999), Hetzel (2000), Kozicki (1999), Woodford (2001b).

A certain degree of disaccord pertains to the definition of a simple rule in the existing literature. Earlier contributions, such as Blanchard and Fischer (1993) use the term "simple rules" to refer to non-activist rules[48]. Schmitt-Grohe and Uribe (2004) define simple rules in terms of restricting attention to rules whereby policy variables are set as a function of a small number of easily observable macroeconomic indicators. In compliance with this criterion they propose studying central bank interest-rate feedback rules that include measures of inflation and output.

Svensson (1997b, 1999a, 2002) offers a more detailed classification of monetary policy rules. According to him, a rule-based monetary policy procedure could take the form of either an instrument or a targeting rule. An instru-

45 „Desirable responses to shocks" here refers to quantitatively modest and short-lived model variable deviations from steady state as a result of a shock.

46 This means that solely the fact that a policy rule is active is not seen as a positive trait. The determinacy results in Section 4 in Chapter III support this critical perspective.

47 In the studies mentioned, McCallum treats simple rules as being operational as well.

48 See pp. 581-583.

ment rule expresses the central bank's instrument (e.g. the short-term nominal interest rate) as an explicit function of information available to the monetary authority. In particular, in the case of a simple instrument rule (such as the Taylor rule, for instance)[49] the monetary policy instrument is a function of a small subset of the information available and no optimal reaction function is derived. Apart from the simple type, instrument rules (at least in theory) can be designed to involve optimisation, whereby the monetary policy problem is solved once-and-for-all for the central bank's optimal reaction function. After the optimal explicit reaction function is determined, the central bank makes a commitment and follows it ever after[50].

However methodically appealing the optimal-control approach may seem, it is hardly practicable. Its complexity renders it unverifiable, i.e. it cannot be objectively and unambiguously determined whether monetary policy actions diverge from the prescriptions of the underlying reaction function. In addition, it cannot be expected that every possible circumstance be anticipated as required by the optimal reaction function. What is more, even if the perspective is limited to a certain number of realistic assumptions, the complexity of the optimal reaction function is still exuberant.

Targeting rules are designed by presenting a central bank loss function whose arguments are the monetary policy targets. The loss function is then minimised subject to aggregate demand and aggregate supply equations describing the model of the economy. Thus, the monetary policy rule is an implicit reaction function and can be written as the optimal response of the monetary policy instrument to current and/or expected values of state variables. A general targeting rule is a high-level specification of a monetary-policy rule that specifies operational objectives, the targets and the loss function to be minimised. A "specific targeting rule" is instead expressed directly as an operational condition for the target variables (or their forecasts)[51].

The use of simple monetary policy rules has both practical advantages and disadvantages. According to Rotemberg and Woodford (1998a), the simplicity of such rules makes them more easily understandable, so that the central bank should have less difficulties in explaining its course of action. Indeed, once the decision to adopt a simple rule is made and announced to the general public, the decision process of the monetary authority becomes exceedingly transparent and simple. Based on the data on the target variables available, the instrument-setting can be calculated. As a result, the public is to a greater extent able to monitor the monetary authority's compliance with the adopted rule. Taylor (1998a) summarises simulation results on simple policy rules and concludes that

49 Taylor-like specifications of the monetary policy rule enter the analysis in Chapter IV.

50 According to Svensson (2002) this can be called a commitment to an optimal instrument rule.

51 See Svensson (2002), p. 30.

they seem to be “a surprisingly good approximation to fully optimal policy.” He also states a further advantage of this type of rules, namely their greater robustness in comparison with complex rules across a variety of models. The idea has been recently restated by McCallum (1997) and supported by the results of Levin *et al.* (1999) who find that simple monetary policy rules may be robust across a set of models of the U.S. economy. In a later study, Levin and Williams (2003) offer a more sophisticated analysis of the robustness property of simple rules and conclude that a robust outcome is attainable only when the objective function places substantial weight on stabilising not only inflation, but output as well[52].

As far as the disadvantages of adopting a simple monetary policy rule are concerned, Svensson (1999a, 1999c) argues that a commitment to a simple instrument rule does not leave any possibility for judgmental adjustments and extra-model information. He concludes that for both of these reasons, a commitment to an instrument rule would be inefficient. An interesting example for practical difficulties with implementing the theoretically much appealing concept of a simple Taylor rule refers to the inclusion of the output gap as a target variable, to which nominal interest rates respond. As McCallum (2000b) points out, various measures of potential or natural-rate output levels differ widely and there is no professional consensus regarding the most appropriate measure or even concept to be used. Furthermore, McCallum and Nelson (1999b) argue that most detrending procedures in use inappropriately attribute the effects of technology shocks to the output gap, instead to the reference value of potential output itself. A more general critique refers to the real-time availability and reliability of output gap data. Orphanides (2001) provides real-time non-revised data series for 1987-1992 on macroeconomic indicators available for the Federal Open Market Committee’s decisions on the federal funds rate. In this respect, potential output estimates are particularly problematical. Data revisions had such a decisive magnitude that, as a result policy recommendations based on real-time data might differ widely from those obtained with the revised published data employed later on. Lastly, Svensson (1999a) emphasises the fact that, however appealing the idea of a simple monetary policy rule might seem, no central bank has yet actually committed to such a rule, as this would mean that “Monetary policy could be delegated to the staff, or even to a computer, and it would be completely static and mechanical… Such a degradation of the decision-making process would naturally be strongly resisted by any central bank and, I believe, arguments about its inefficiency would also easily convince legislators to reject it”.

52 For the case when the monetary policy objective is to stabilize inflation only, the authors are unable to find a robust simple rule.

2.2. Local determinacy of a rational-expectations equilibrium and monetary policy analysis

2.2.1. An overview

A central issue when evaluating alternative monetary policy rules is whether they can induce a determinate rational expectations equilibrium[53]. A vast literature starting with Sargent and Wallace (1975)[54] and McCallum (1981) has considered the fact that certain types of monetary policy rules may be associated with multiple rational expectations equilibria, some of which involving fluctuations of inflation and output as a result of self-fulfilling expectations. Such rules should clearly be avoided if the monetary authority aims at stabilising the variables previously mentioned. Giannoni and Woodford (2002) define determinacy of a rational-expectations equilibrium[55] as "A unique equilibrium with the property that bounded disturbance processes result in bounded fluctuations in the endogenous variables".

Blanchard and Fischer (1993) offer a classification of various types of multiplicity of equilibria, such as bubbles, "components that explode in expected value over time" and equilibria that exhibit sunspots. As McCallum (2004, 2003b) emphasizes, apart from finding a unique determinate equilibrium, a well-defined policy rule should lead to a bubble-free solution[56].

A related issue often consistent with the existence of a rational expectations equilibrium is what is called a "sunspot equilibrium", i.e. endogenous variables changing according to random states that are not associated with any changes in economic fundamentals. This is the case of changes in equilibrium resulting from self-fulfilling expectations. Such self-fulfilling arbitrary changes in expectations introduce endogenous instability. Therefore, the design of a set-up that

---

53 Here a steady-state equilibrium (also known as a stationary equilibrium, a rest point, an equilibrium point, or a fixed point) is referred to. According to Galor (2007), a steady-state equilibrium of a n-dimensional system is a value of the n-dimensional vector of the state variables that is invariant under further iterations to the dynamic system. Thus, once each of the state variables reaches its steady-state level, the system will not evolve in the absence of exogenous disturbances.

54 For more recent research on determinacy of rational expectations equilibria under different monetary policy rules see Bernanke and Woodford (1997), Bullard and Mitra (2000), Carlstrom and Fuerst (2000), Clarida, Gali and Gertler (2000), McCallum (2002b) and Rotemberg and Woodford (1998, 1999).

55 In the subsequent exposition only real determinacy is being considered.

56 In other words, a solution reflecting only "market fundamentals", as specified in the model. For a detailed definition of a bubble, see Burmeister, Flood and Garber (1983).

does not allow multiplicity of equilibria is of very important practical significance for the design of macroeconomic policies[57].

2.2.2. Presenting the criterion

In order to assess in terms of determinacy the implications of different model settings with forward-looking elements, it is important to specify how individuals form expectations. In the subsequent analysis I assume rational expectations consistent with the definition of Muth (1961), that is, expectations equal to the mathematical expectation of the variable in $t+1$ based on information at time t. For simplicity, I further assume that individuals know the underlying model and its parameters and all have the same information set at time t[58]. In the next chapter, the assessment of monetary policy alternatives regarding determinacy of rational-expectations equilibrium will be based on the formal setting provided by Blanchard and Kahn (1980). The structural model is described by:

$$\begin{bmatrix} X_{t+1} \\ E_t Y_{t+1} \end{bmatrix} = A \begin{bmatrix} X_t \\ Y_t \end{bmatrix} + \gamma Z_t \tag{2.1}$$

where X is an $(n \times 1)$ vector of variables predetermined at time *t*; Y is an $(m \times 1)$ vector of variables non-predetermined at time *t*; *Z* is a $(k \times 1)$ vector of exogenous variables; $E_t Y_{t+1}$ is the expectation of Y_{t+1} at time *t*; A and γ are $(n+m)\times(n+m)$ and $(n+m)\times k$ matrices, respectively. Rational expectations are formalised by

$$E_t Y_{t+1} = E\left[Y_{t+1} \mid \Omega_t\right] \tag{2.2}$$

where *E* is the expectation operator; Ω_t is the information set at *t*, such that

$$\Omega_t = \left\{X_{t-i}, Y_{t-i}, Z_{t-i}; i = 0, ..., \infty\right\}. \tag{2.3}$$

The above specification of the information set implies no loss of memory, as all the information known at time *t* is still known at time *t+1*. In order to rule out exponential growth of $E_t Z_{t+i}$, the following condition needs to be met:

$$-(1+i)^{\Theta_t} \bar{Z}_t \leq E\left[Z_{t+i} \mid \Omega_t\right] \leq (1+i)^{\Theta_t} \bar{Z}_t, \tag{2.4}$$

$$t \geq 0,\ \bar{Z}_t \in \Re^k,\ \Theta_t \in \Re.$$

57 An exception to this consensus opinion in the literature is expressed by McCallum (2003b), who argues that in the case of multiple equilibria only fundamental, minimal state variable solutions are likely to be observed in practice, and therefore the existence of a number of non-fundamental equilibria should be granted less attention in the literature.

58 As opposed to the alternative assumption that individuals are learning about the model as they are forming their expectations. The issues of learning and expectational stability have been studied by several key papers in the 1980s, including Bray (1982), Evans (1985), Lucas (1987), and Marcet and Sargent (1989).

Analogously to (2.4), for a unique determinate rational expectations solution it is required that the expectations of X_{t+i} and Y_{t+i} at time t do not explode. Thus, condition (2.4) can be applied as follows:

$$\begin{bmatrix} \overline{X}_t \\ \overline{Y}_t \end{bmatrix} \in \Re^{n+m}, \quad \tau_t \in \Re \text{ such that} \tag{2.5}$$

$$-(1+i)^{\tau_t} \begin{bmatrix} \overline{X}_t \\ \overline{Y}_t \end{bmatrix} \leq \begin{bmatrix} E(X_{t+i} \mid \Omega_t) \\ E(Y_{t+i} \mid \Omega_t) \end{bmatrix} \leq (1+i)^{\tau_t} \begin{bmatrix} \overline{X}_t \\ \overline{Y}_t \end{bmatrix}, \qquad \forall t \geq 0.$$

According to Blanchard and Kahn (1980), in order to obtain a unique solution, the number of eigenvalues of A outside the unit circle (denoted by $\overline{m}$) should be equal to the number of non-predetermined variables (m). The unique solution is "forward-looking" in the sense that the non-predetermined variables depend on the past only through its effect on current predetermined variables. The condition $\overline{m} = m$ actually states that a unique solution exists if and only if A has the strict saddle point property. If $\overline{m} > m$, there is no unique non-explosive solution satisfying all necessary conditions (2.1)-(2.5). For the opposite case, $\overline{m} < m$, i.e. when the number of eigenvalues outside the unit circle is less than the number of the predetermined variables, there is an infinity of solutions. In particular, it could be the case that the non-predetermined variables depend directly on the past or that a variable not belonging to Z directly affects X and Y. By contrast, these possibilities are ruled out when $\overline{m} = m$.

2.2.3. Determinacy and reactions to shocks

When assessing the impact of shocks, the issue of dynamic stability (convergence) plays a crucial role. Stability analysis facilitates the study of the local (and sometimes the global) behaviour of a dynamic system and of the implications of disturbances occurring once the system is in the vicinity of a steady-state equilibrium. According to Heijdra and van der Ploeg (2002) a stable system is defined as "one in which the unique equilibrium (also called steady state) is eventually restored following a shock to one or more of the exogenous variables". In case of multiple equilibria (or stationary points), there may exist stable (convergent) and unstable (divergent) equilibria. Still, even under multiple equilibria, if there is a unique stable equilibrium, the system can still be regarded as stable. The arguments in favour of using stable systems only can be traced back to the correspondence principle in Samuelson (1947)[59]. Indeed, unstable systems are not particularly useful for economic analysis. Even if one or more (unstable) equilibria exist, the system is not very likely to be at any of these at a particular point in time. Moreover, even if, by coincidence, the system is in an equilibrium, a minor shock will suffice to displace it permanently from that equilibrium. Sta-

59 Early applications of dynamic methods in macroeconomics can also be found in Baumol (1959) and Allen (1967).

ble systems, by contrast, converge along an adjustment path to a stable equilibrium. An additional convenient feature of stable systems is that it is often possible to derive steady-state multipliers for the impact of changes in government policy and other exogenous variables on the endogenous ones in the system. Heijdra and van der Ploeg (2002) distinguish between backward-looking and forward-looking stability. The former implies that, at a particular moment, the model determines the endogenous variables as a function of the exogenous and the predetermined state variables. Under forward-looking stability, lagged (historical) and expectational (future) values jointly determine the current situation.

A perhaps more important issue for stability analysis is the distinction between local and global stability of a dynamic system[60]. In the mathematical literature stability refers to situations in which trajectories that are initiated from an ε-neighbourhood of a fixed point remain sufficiently close to this fixed point subsequently. Galor (2007) defines a system as being locally (asymptotically) stable if for a sufficiently small perturbation the dynamic system converges asymptotically to the original equilibrium. In the case when, regardless of the magnitude of the perturbation, the system converges asymptotically to the original equilibrium, the system is globally (asymptotically) stable. In other words, a steady-state equilibrium is locally (asymptotically) stable if there exists an ε-neighborhood of the steady-state equilibrium such that for every initial condition within this neighborhood the system converges to this steady-state equilibrium, whereas a steady-state equilibrium is globally (asymptotically) stable if the system converges to the steady-state equilibrium regardless of the initial condition.

Local stability of a steady-state equilibrium requires the local uniqueness of the steady-state equilibrium[61]. Thus, if the system is characterized by a continuum of equilibria none of these steady-state equilibria is locally stable. Local stability necessitates therefore local uniqueness of the steady-state equilibrium. Global stability of a steady-state equilibrium requires global uniqueness of the steady-state equilibrium[62]. In the case of a linear system, local uniqueness implies global uniqueness and local stability necessarily implies global stability.

In Chapter IV (Sections 2 and 3), the model variables' responses to a number of shocks (monetary policy unit shock, technology shock and consumption preference shock) under a variety of interest-rate rule specifications are illustrated by impulse response analysis. Clearly, convergence to the steady state values is regarded as crucial when assessing the performance of different policy rule specifications. Beyond that, the existence of a monotonic convergence path

60 In the subsequent analysis in Chapter IV, local determinacy of rational-expectations equilibrium will be assessed.

61 I.e. the absence of any additional point in the steady-state neighbourhood from which there is no escape.

62 I.e. the absence of any additional point in the space from which there is no escape.

and relatively small and short-lived initial variable deviations from steady state values are also considered to be advantageous[63].

2.3. The Taylor principle

Taylor (1999) derives a relationship between the stability of inflation and the size of the interest rate coefficient on inflation in the policy rule. He shows that it is crucial to set the interest rate response coefficient on inflation above a critical "stability threshold" of one. The interest rate rule is given by[64]

$$i_t = \bar{r} + \pi_t + \lambda_\pi (\pi_t - \pi^*) + \lambda_y \hat{y}_t, \tag{2.6}$$

where i_t is the nominal interest rate in t, π_t denotes the inflation rate over the previous four quarters, π^* is the central bank's inflation target[65], $\hat{y}_t$ is the output gap[66], $\bar{r}$ is the equilibrium (steady-state) real interest rate[67], λ_π and λ_y are policy parameters, denoting the central bank's response to inflation and output gap deviations from target[68]. The total response to inflation in (2.6) is given by $\lambda_\pi^* = 1 + \lambda_\pi$. It is assumed that the monetary policy stance is counter-cyclical, i.e. $\lambda_\pi^*, \lambda_y > 0$. Taylor (1999) combines (2.6) with backward-looking IS- and AS-specifications given by

$$\hat{y}_t = -\varphi(i_t - \pi_t - \bar{r}) + g_t \tag{2.7}$$

and

$$\pi_t = \alpha \hat{y}_{t-1} + \pi_{t-1} + u_t, \tag{2.8}$$

where φ ,α>0 are reduced-form parameters that depend on the policy parameters; g_t and u_t are serially uncorrelated stochastic shocks with zero mean. By substituting equation (2.6) in equation (2.7), an aggregate demand (AD) relation between inflation and output gap can be derived[69]

$$\hat{y}_t = -\frac{\varphi\lambda_\pi}{1+\varphi\lambda_y}\pi_t + \frac{1}{1+\varphi\lambda_y}g_t. \tag{2.9}$$

---

63 The reason for this is quite straightforward: considerable deviations from the steady-state level and/or long-lasting adjustment all induce losses and uncertainty in the economy.

64 The rule specified by Taylor (1999) is a more general form of the Taylor (1993) one.

65 Taylor (1993) sets the inflation target to be equal to 2 percent per annum. In Taylor (1999) only π_t enters the policy rule, i.e. $\pi^* = 0$.

66 In Taylor (1993) the output gap denotes the percent deviation of real GDP from a target (trend real GDP). Taylor (1999) defines the output gap as the percentage deviation of real GDP from potential GDP. For the purpose of this work, the latter definition will be used.

67 The steady-state real interest rate is estimated in Taylor (1993) using US data and set at 2 percent per annum.

68 In Taylor (1993), $\lambda_\pi = \lambda_y = 0.5$

69 The stochastic term g_t is left out here.

The slope of the AD curve $-\varphi\lambda_\pi/(1+\varphi\lambda_y)$ is determined by the choice of the policy parameters λ_π and λ_y. For $\lambda_\pi > 0$ (i.e. $\lambda_\pi^* > 1$), the aggregate demand curve is downward-sloping[70] and for $\lambda_\pi < 0$ it is upward-sloping. Figure 2.2 reveals graphically the stability properties of a Taylor rule for an effective inflation response coefficient greater or smaller than unity (the upper two panels) and the resulting AD relations for these two cases (the two lower panels). The horizontal lines in the two lower panels represent the aggregate supply (price adjustment) relation. The zero slope of the AS line is determined by the fact that in equation (2.8) current-period inflation depends in the previous-period output gap, rather than on the contemporaneous one. Changes in $\hat{y}_t$ are thus transmitted to the inflation dynamics with a time lag. The intersection of the two solid lines (the AS and the AD line) in the two lower panels represents a situation when $y_t = \overline{y}$ (actual output is equal to the potential output), i.e. $\hat{y}_t = 0$. The AS line eventually moves up when the output gap is positive and vice versa. A positive supply shock also shifts the line upwards.

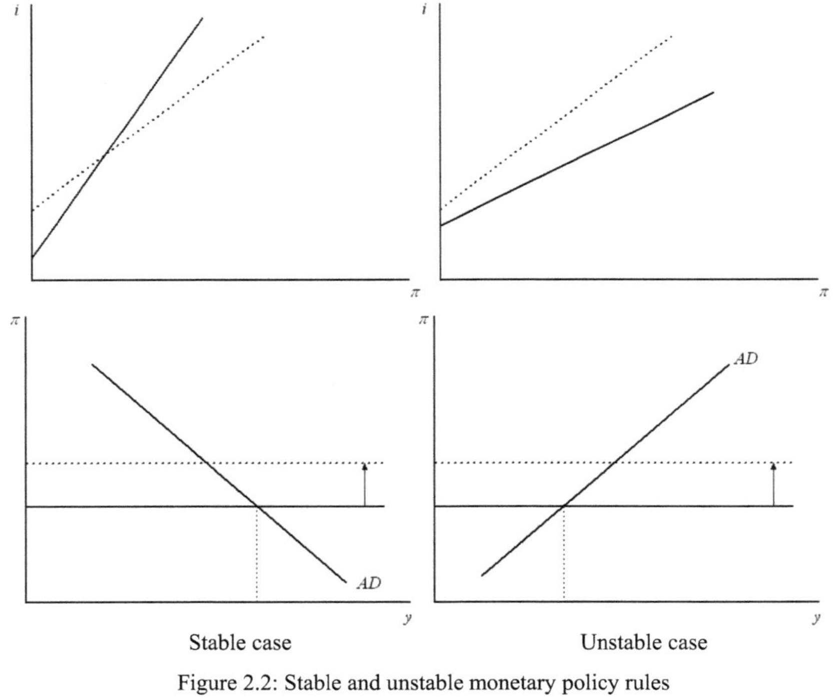

Stable case Unstable case

Figure 2.2: Stable and unstable monetary policy rules

70 As $\lambda_y > 0$.

The two left-hand panels in Figure 2.2 present a rule with $\lambda_{\pi}^{*} > 1$ and the two right-hand panels one with $\lambda_{\pi}^{*} < 1$. The case on the left is stable because an upward shift in the AS line (a positive inflation shock) results in a decline of the output gap below zero, which leads to a downward adjustment of the inflation rate, represented by a downward shift of the price adjustment (AS) line. The case on the right is unstable, as, by contrast to the previous case, a positively sloped AD line implies that an upward shock to inflation leads to a positive output gap and contributes to further increases in inflation. This explosive property of the system has as consequence that supply-side shocks will tend to have a permanent, self-accelerating effect on inflation, bringing the system farther away from its equilibrium.

Algebraically, the above results can be substantiated as follows. The stability question can be expressed in terms of whether shocks will have a permanent, self-accelerating effect on inflation, i.e.

$$\left|\frac{d\pi_t}{d\pi_{t-1}}\right| \lesseqgtr 1 \text{ ?} \qquad (2.10)$$

whereby only under $|d\pi_t / d\pi_{t-1}| < 1$ does the system converge to steady state after a shock occurs. Equivalently, iterating (2.10) one period forward yields

$$\frac{d\pi_{t+1}}{d\pi_t} \lesseqgtr 1 \text{ ?} \qquad (2.10')$$

and $|d\pi_{t+1} / d\pi_t| < 1$ as a condition for stability respectively. The policy-dependence of the stability property of the system becomes evident after one last transformation, this time of the AS relation. One period forward, equation (2.8) becomes

$$\pi_{t+1} = \alpha \hat{y}_t + \pi_t + u_{t+1} \,. \qquad (2.8')$$

Then,

$$\frac{d\pi_{t+1}}{d\pi_t} = 1 + \alpha \frac{d\hat{y}_t}{d\pi_t} \,. \qquad (2.8'')$$

Substituting $d\hat{y}_t / d\pi_t = -\varphi\lambda_{\pi} / 1 + \varphi\lambda_y$ from the AD relation (2.9) into (2.8'') yields

$$\frac{d\pi_{t+1}}{d\pi_t} = 1 - \frac{\alpha\varphi\lambda_{\pi}}{1+\varphi\lambda_y} \,. \qquad (2.8''')$$

Then, for stability,

$$\frac{\alpha\varphi\lambda_{\pi}}{1+\varphi\lambda_y} \overset{!}{>} 1 \,. \qquad (2.11)$$

Equivalently,

$$\lambda_{\pi} \overset{!}{>} 0 \,, \qquad (2.11')$$

and

$$\lambda_\pi^* \overset{!}{>} 1. \tag{2.11”}$$

The relationship between the stability of inflation and the size of the inflation response coefficient in the central bank's monetary policy rule has been reaffirmed by empirical analysis, such as Clarida *et al.* (2000), Judd and Rudebusch (1998) and Wright (1998). Benhabib *et al.* (1999) also argue that real determinacy could be attributed to the degree of activeness of monetary policy and the inflation measure that enters the central bank's interest rule. They find that under sticky prices and an active monetary policy stance (i.e. a policy that aggressively fights inflation by raising the nominal interest rate by more than the registered increase in inflation), a forward-looking component in the intermediate target is more likely to lead to indeterminacy than a backward-looking component. The assumption that the demand for money also plays a role in the monetary-transmission mechanism and that productivity is affected by the cost of funds leads to novel results concerning equilibrium determinacy. A further point is recognising the difference between local and global determinacy of equilibrium. An active policy stance may appear to lead to macroeconomic stability as it ensures locally unique equilibrium, but in fact be destabilizing because it is associated with global indeterminacy and equilibria in which the economy converges to a cycle[71].

Clarida *et al.* (2000) provide empirical analysis of US monetary policy, based on a baseline sticky-prices model[72] with a modified Taylor rule where the Fed responds to expected future deviations of inflation and the output from their target values, instead of to their current values. Their findings support the results of and Kerr and King (1996) concerning the destabilising impact of an excessively weak reaction of the policy instrument to an increase in expected inflation. This is the case of an effective policy reaction coefficient on the inflation gap $\lambda_\pi^* \leq 1$. Values of λ_π^* below unity lead to equilibrium indeterminacy and monotone divergence or fluctuations around the steady-state values of inflation and output, resulting from self-fulfilling changes in expectations. The rise of self-fulfilling changes in expected inflation can be explained by the fact that with $\lambda_\pi^* < 1$, a rise in anticipated inflation is accompanied by a decline in the real interest rate which stimulates aggregate demand and causes a rise in inflation. Thus, due to the accommodating stance of monetary policy, the initial rise in expected inflation becomes “self-confirmed”. As shown by Clarida *et al.* (2000), the unity threshold value of λ_π^* is obtained only in the absence of a systematic policy response to output variations (i.e. $\lambda_y = 0$). For values of the policy reaction coefficient on the output gap $\lambda_y > 0$, the lower bound for λ_π decreases be-

71 For further analysis, see Benhabib et al. (2001).

72 For similar models, see King and Wolman (1996), Woodford (1996, 1998) and Yun (1996).

low unity, although the deviation from unity is quantitatively negligible, and is independent of whether an interesting-smoothing parameter (i.e. the lagged nominal interest rate) enters the rule specification. As far as the upper bound for the unique equilibrium defined by the range of values of λ_{π}^{*} is concerned, Bernanke and Woodford (1997) find that an excessive response to variations in expected inflation may also lead to indeterminacy.

3. Preliminary summary

Since the middle of the last century, the design, transmission channels and outcomes of monetary policy have been the focus of extensive research. The practical experience with "activist" monetary policies in the 1960s and 1970s, motivated by the conviction that in the long run the monetary authority can attain a permanent reduction in the unemployment rate by allowing for a higher rate of inflation, has been disappointing. Parallel to the practical experience with activeist policies, there has also been an academic critique of using monetary policy as a tool to obtain full employment at the expense of a higher inflation rate. Among the most influential arguments are Milton Friedman's monetary critique concerning the uncertain outcomes of monetary policy interventions, the Lucas critique of the optimal control paradigm for monetary policy, the conclusion reached by Friedman (1968) and Phelps (1968) that there is no long-run tradeoff between inflation and unemployment, as well as the warning against the perils of time inconsistency under discretionary policy delivered by Kydland and Prescott (1977), Calvo (1978) and Barro and Gordon (1983).

The experience with time-inconsistent discretionary policy has not only fuelled the debate on the benefits of systematic policy behaviour vs. discretion, but has also given an impetus for extensive research on how monetary policy rules should be designed and assessed. In terms of policy instrument choice, in the last two decades setting the nominal interest rate has generally prevailed over directly controlling money supply in both theory and practice. However, selecting the target variables and their response coefficients in the policy rule currently remains a controversial issue, since the estimated outcomes are to a great extent model-dependent. In order to ensure a comprehensive assessment of the different rule specifications, it is essential to consider not only the aggregate demand, but also the aggregate supply monetary transmission channel, which requires using a comprehensive macroeconomic framework incorporating endogenous capital (as the one used in Chapter III). Under such a framework, the determinacy and shock response properties of different rule specifications, as well as the relevance of the Taylor principle will be examined and assessed in the next two chapters.

III. A New Keynesian model with endogenous capital with adjustment costs

One of the main findings concerning rule-based monetary policy design in Chapter II has been that the assessment of different rule specifications in terms of the criteria presented in Section 2 (determinacy of rational-expectations equilibrium and response to shocks), as well as the evaluation of the relevance of the Taylor principle for fulfilling these criteria are to a great extent dependent on the model used and the inclusion of a supply-side transmission channel in particular.

Therefore, in this chapter I focus on deriving a New Keynesian model with endogenous capital and adjustment costs and proceed with examining the system's determinacy properties under different rule specifications. In terms of the general applicability of the Taylor principle, the findings are non-trivial. In the model with endogenous capital an inflation response coefficient greater than unity is not sufficient *per se* for ensuring a unique rational-expectations equilibrium. Apart from a small value interval of the inflation response coefficient above unity, implying a moderately strong policy reaction, determinacy under an "active" rule requires some degree of output gap response. Moreover, even within the inflation coefficient interval yielding determinacy under a sole inflation target in the rule, adding an output gap term is still associated with a unique equilibrium. In terms of "passive" rules (with an inflation response coefficient below one), the Taylor principle is only partially valid as well. Indeed, if inflation is the only target variable entering the rule, a smaller than one-on-one nominal interest rate response to inflation deviations yields indeterminacy of rational-expectations equilibrium. However, introducing a sufficiently large output gap response can lead to a unique equilibrium even under a passive rule[73].

Thus, modelling endogenous capital provides important new insights and an extension to the baseline formulation of the Taylor principle, namely by adding the requirement of introducing an output gap response in order to guarantee uniqueness of the system's rational-expectations equilibrium.

The chapter is organised as follows. In Sections 1 and 2, I give an overview to the baseline New Keynesian framework and possible approaches to modelling capital and investment. The model with endogenous capital and adjustment costs, which is the basis for the determinacy and impulse response analysis to follow in the next chapters, is presented in Section 3. In this section, I first examine the households' optimisation problem. The resulting first-order conditions describe the aggregate demand side of the model. Then I present the producers' optimisation and derive the aggregate supply curve and the real-wage equation and add an interest rate rule to the system. Dynamics of the whole economy are

73 In fact, as it is evident in the analysis in Section 4, the output gap response required for determinacy increses as the inflation response coefficient decreases.

thus fully characterised by combining equilibrium conditions from both the demand and the supply side. As a next step, in Section 4 these log-linearised equilibrium conditions are used to study the determinacy property of interest rate rules. Then, in Section 4 I present the responses generated under different interest-rate-rule specifications to three types of shocks. Section 5 provides a preliminary summary of results.

1. The New Keynesian framework: an overview

Over the past decade numerous examples of small-scale monetary business cycle optimising models featuring nominal rigidities have appeared in the literature. They are generally known as New Keynesian models. Both their theoretical appeal as micro-founded models, and their ability to explain the short-run effects of monetary policy, have contributed to their popularity among researchers. Taylor (2000) describes New Keynesian models as "...dynamic, stochastic, economy wide models with forward-looking behaviour and some rigidities that make them useful for policy evaluation". This kind of models are also sometimes referred to as "Dynamic New Keynesian" (Bernanke *et al.* (1998)) or New Neoclassical Synthesis (Goodfriend and King (1997)).

New Keynesian models typically integrate standard Keynesian elements (imperfect competition, nominal rigidities in price- and wage-setting) into a dynamic general equilibrium framework with rational expectations of market participants. One substantial improvement in recent research in comparison to the traditional Keynesian framework consists in stronger theoretical and microeconomic foundations. Behavioural functions for aggregate variables are derived from optimal individual behavior of households and firms with simultaneous clearing of all markets. Thus, these models are an appropriate tool for analysing the connection between interest rates, inflation and the business cycle, as well as for comparing the impact of alternative monetary policies.

An important feature of New Keynesian models is the inclusion of rational expectations of market participants. Muth (1961) first formulated the rational expectations hypothesis, which requires that the subjective expectation of economic actors (households and firms) regarding a particular variable be equal to the objective expectation for that variable conditional on the information set available[74]. In the following decade the idea has been further developed, among others, by Lucas (1972, 1973), Sargent (1973), Sargent and Wallace (1975, 1976) and Barro (1976).

Another essential characteristic of New Keynesian models concerns the nature of inflation dynamics under monopolistic competition reflected in the New Keynesian Phillips Curve. Under the widely adopted staggered price specifica-

74 In the original paper, Muth suggested that „...expectations, since they are informed predictions of future events, are essentially the same as the predictions of the relevant economic theory" (1961, p. 316).

tion as in Calvo (1983), inflation has forward-looking character as a result of the assumption that firms face constraints on the frequency of price-adjustment. This means that previously adjusted prices are likely to remain effective for longer than one period, i.e. current price-setting decisions (and therefore current inflation) are based on expectations about future cost and demand developments. Another determinant of inflation dynamics are mark-up variations (or real marginal cost variations) that arise from the monopolistic firms' repeated attempts to adjust actual to desired mark-ups. Roberts (1998) suggests that the aggregate supply equation fits better to empirical data if the rational expectations assumption is replaced by a partially backward-looking model of expected inflation. The output gap is an endogenous variable in the New Keynesian models, related to the ex ante real interest rate and expected output gap in the aggregate demand relation. Frequently the variable enters as an inflation fluctuations determinant the aggregate supply relation[75] and as a policy target the central bank reaction function.

The empirical relevance of New Keynesian models has often been criticised. The dependence of optimising New Keynesian models on a forward-looking decision making process limits their capacity to capture some of the business cycle regularities observed in the data. For instance, most optimising models are not very successful in replicating the delay in the responses of output and inflation to a monetary shock. In particular, an optimising model should explain why, rather than immediately, responses of both output and inflation to a monetary impulse reach their maximal impact several quarters after the shock. This phenomenon has been widely investigated in recent papers using optimising models incorporating frictions in price-setting and/or wage-setting, e.g. in Chari et al. (2000), Christiano et al. (2001) and Giannoni and Woodford (2003).

The canonical New Keynesian model, as well as most of its standard generalisations, abstracts from investment in order to maintain simplicity[76]. One possible explanation is the emphasis on short-run analysis of macroeconomic stabilisation processes that allows abstracting from long-term capital accumulation implications. Moreover, the exclusion of capital is often justified on the grounds that the capital stock is not characterised by substantial volatility at business cycle frequencies and empirically there is a very small correlation between capital

75 As mentioned in the last paragraph, the output gap is sometimes substituted at the place of real marginal cost as inflation determinant. In fact, the Phillips curve relation derived from staggered price-setting as in Calvo (1983) involves the deviation of real marginal cost from its steady-state value. As Galí and Gertler (1999) and Clarida *et al.* (1999) show, certain assumptions about technology, preferences and the labour market structure can be made that infer a proportionate relation between real marginal cost and the output gap.

76 This view has been expressed by McCallum and Nelson (1999b). Examples of New Keynesian models with constant (exogenous) capital and investment include, among others, Kerr and King (1996), Bernanke and Woodford (1997) and Clarida *et al.* (2000).

and aggregate output measures (see McCallum and Nelson (1999a)). Difficulties with empirical measures of the capital stock also discourage developing models that involve capital accumulation.

However, Dennis (2004) argues that abstracting from investment may imply that an important shock propagation mechanism that may have important implications for the design and implementation of an optimal monetary policy is omitted. Woodford (2003) provides a further critique on models with constant capital: "while this has kept our analysis of the effects of interest rates on aggregate demand quite simple, one may doubt the accuracy of the conclusions obtained, given the obvious importance of variations in investment spending both in business fluctuations and in the transmission mechanism for monetary policy in particular." Casares and McCallum (2006) provide a further argument for the inclusion of endogenous capital and investment, as it enables not only studying issues relating to capital formation and growth, but also provides an endogenous explanation for the empirically observed contrasting variability of consumption and investment spending.

When introducing investment within a New Keynesian framework, a crucial choice to make involves modelling the speed of capital stock adjustment in the occurrence of shocks. The case when capital adjusts relatively fast can be represented by modelling endogenous investment with an economy-wide rental market[77] as in Hairault and Portier (1993), Kimball (1995), Yun (1996), King and Watson (1996), King and Wolman (1996) and Chari et al. (2000). A further option consists in introducing a certain degree of inertia in capital accumulation in the model, which, as an additional advantage, seems to match better empirical data on capital stock dynamics. This can be achieved by introducing assumptions that prevent the capital stock from immediately responding to shocks. As already mentioned in Section 1, three possible assumptions about investment and the capital stock could generate an inertial response on part of capital: capital accumulation adjustment costs, a time-to-build requirement and firm-specific capital. As shown by Casares and McCallum (2006), an appropriate possibility to endogenise investment in a less complex manner is to incorporate endogenous investment with capital adjustment costs under sluggish price adjustment in a dynamic model of the IS-LM type with optimising behaviour[78]. This is approach chosen in the next section for deriving the New Keynesian model that is later used for examining the determinacy and shock response properties of different

77 My results obtained under such a specification without adjustment costs (not included here) confirm the intuition that variable responses to shocks in such a case are unrealistically large. This makes the choice of such a modelling option quite unappealing for policy analysis.

78 Such models have been used by Woodford (1995), Kerr and King (1996), Rotemberg and Woodford (1998a, 1998b), Clarida *et al.* (1999) and Galí and Gertler (1999).

interest rate rule specifications in Section 4 (Chapter III) and Sections 2 and 3 (Chapter IV).

2. Modelling capital and investment

Ever since Keynes (1936) and Hicks (1939), the role of investment dynamics in business cycle fluctuations has been highlighted in macroeconomic analysis[79]. Some prominent models include the neoclassical theory of investment, the accelerator model and Tobin's q theory.

The neoclassical theory of investment[80] uses the firm's production function and IS curve to derive demand for capital. Based on the IS curve and production function a relation between a firm's cash flow and its contemporaneous stock of fixed capital (plant and equipment) is obtained. The firm's demand for fixed capital is then set at a level that equates the marginal profit of capital with the user cost of capital[81]. The neoclassical theory of investment postulates that a firm's demand for capital is positively related to the firm's level of output and negatively related to the user cost of capital. Among the more significant empirical results reported by Jorgenson and associates[82] are that (i) investment demand is highly responsive to changes in relative prices, including policy variables such as the interest rate and taxes; (ii) the lag to the investment response to changes in its determinants is relatively long (on the average, about eight to nine quarters) and there is no response in the first few quarters and (iii) the distributed lag structure of investment behavior is bell-shaped; gross investment initially rises at an increasing rate and then increases at a decreasing rate as long-run equilibrium is approached. A more simplistic neoclassical framework, in which the demand for capital is still determined by the output level, but not by the user cost of capital, is the accelerator model of investment[83].

Both the Jorgenson and the accelerator model treat steady-state capital stock as the desired level of capital stock and then impose an adjustment mechanism of actual capital stock towards its desired (steady-state) level[84]. Rather than de-

---

79 Abel (1988) offers a very comprehensive overview of investment literature. The empirical performance of different investment models is studied by Bischoff (1971) and Clark (1979).

80 As in Jorgenson (1963), Jorgenson and Siebert (1968) and Jorgenson and Stephenson (1969).

81 The user cost denotes the cost of using a unit of capital in production over a certain period of time.

82 The studies are based on quarterly postwar time-series for U.S. manufacturing industries.

83 In the accelerator model, no capital-labour substitutability either ex ante or ex post is assumed.

84 This deficit is corrected by the flexible accelerator model of Eisner and Strotz (1963), where dynamic capital adjustment costs are a convex function of the rate of investment. Thus, firms would not find it profitable to adjust instantaneously to long-run equilib-

riving a particular dynamic capital adjustment mechanism in the firm's optimisation problem (for instance, based on an adjustment cost function), these models assume that there exists an exogenous mechanism that determines the speed of the adjustment of actual to desired capital stock.

An alternative approach is to incorporate adjustment costs and the price of investment goods directly into the maximization problem and then to derive the optimal rate of investment in each period. The q theory of investment as in Tobin (1969) explicitly derives the dynamic response of investment to permanent and temporary (as well as anticipated and unanticipated) changes in the underlying determinants. Tobin's q theory of investment builds on a baseline Keynesian idea that the investment decision is influenced by the market value of capital relative to the cost of acquiring additional capital. In case an additional unit of capital would increase the market value of the firm by more than the cost of acquiring the capital and putting it in place, then an optimizing firm should decide in favour of investment[85]. Although the original version of the q theory did not explicitly model the firms' production function and demand curve, it is possible to start with the IS curve and the production function and then derive the q theory as the result of intertemporal maximisation by firms.

Since the beginning of the 1990s, numerous contributions have aimed at incorporating the findings of neoclassical investment theory on the lagged character of capital and investment responses within a forward-looking New Keynesian framework with dynamic adjustment costs, micro-foundation and nominal price and wage rigidities. As Casares (2006) argues, introducing slow capital adjustment over time helps to replicate the delay in the responses of output and inflation to a shock, observed in the data. Several options to model the slow adjustment of the capital stock have been discussed in the recent literature: dynamic capital adjustment costs, time-to-build assumption, restricted capital stock mobility across sectors or firms (firm-specific capital).

The approach of assuming capital adjustment costs reflects the fact that modifying the scale of capital services in a firm generates disruption costs during installation of any new or replacement capital. As a result, costly learning must be incurred as the structure of production may have been changed. Installing new equipment or structures frequently implies delivery lags and time to install/build. The irreversibility of many projects caused by a lack of secondary

rium, because of the increasing marginal costs of doing so. Instead, they would find it optimal to adjust slowly and distribute the adjustment costs over time. This notion has been later expanded by Lucas (1967), Gould (1968), Treadway (1969) and others.

85 Tobin (1969) defined q to be the ratio of the market value of a firm to the capital replacement cost of the firm. This ratio measures the value of fixed capital relative to its cost. A high ratio enhances incentive to acquire the capital and therefore the rate of investment. As the value of the firm is measured using data from financial markets, the link between asset markets and investment expenditure is quite straightforward.

markets for capital goods acts as another form of adjustment cost[86]. Among others, Eisner and Strotz (1963), Lucas and Prescott (1971), and Hayashi (1982) have incorporated the assumption that the process of installing capital goods requires the use of resources. The baseline model in the investment literature has been a standard neoclassical model with convex (often approximated to be quadratic) costs of adjustment[87]. Caballero (1999) shows that this model has not performed well at an aggregate level; besides, some industry studies[88] suggest that both convex and non-convex adjustment costs can be observed in practice. That is why an alternative approach to the standard convex cost model has been advocated recently by Abel and Eberly (1994, 1996), Caballero *et al.* (1995), and Cooper *et al.* (1999), emphasizing that non-convexities and irreversibility play an important role in the investment process. Paez-Farrell (2003) points out that the realistic modeling of adjustment costs is hindered by the fact that they are difficult to quantify.

Still, Caballero and Engel (1999), Thomas (2002) and Cooper and Haltiwanger (2006) find that, despite performing poorly at the plant level, a model with convex costs fits the aggregate data reasonably well[89]. Therefore, despite the inaccuracy problems that are incurred by approximating capital adjustment costs by convex costs, this modeling choice is appealing due to it relative simplicity. The above deficiencies notwithstanding, models with endogenous capital and convex capital adjustment costs still perform better than the ones with endogenous capital only. This is confirmed by Casares and McCallum (2006) who argue that models with endogenous capital/investment choices but no adjustment costs imply highly unrealistic responses to monetary-policy shocks under the assumption of sticky prices and wages.

A second option of modelling the slow adjustment of capital over time, consistent with the empirical data, is to introduce lags to the investment process, for instance by adopting a time-to-build assumption. This approach can be traced back to Kydland and Prescott (1982) who construct a one-sector optimal growth model with persistent technology shocks. In order to design a more complex propagation mechanism for such shocks and to incorporate the co-movement of output and investment over time in a more realistic manner, they introduce a time-to-build lag in capital stock adjustment and achieve a good match of the

86 McDonald and Siegel (1986) argue that if investment is irreversible (e.g. building a plant), the optimal decision of firms might be to forego some investments whose present value exceeds their cost. Then the correct calculation involves comparing the value of investing today with the (present) value of investing at all possible times in the future.

87 A detailed overview of convex adjustment cost models and numerous references to the motivation and results of the literature are provided by Hamermesh and Pfann (1996).

88 See, for example, Holt *et al.* (1960) and Peck (1974).

89 However, they also find that convex cost models tend not to track investment at turning points well.

simulation results to quarterly U.S. postwar business cycle data. In a similar line, Taylor (1983) calculates optimal investment cost-reducing policy rules to offset investment fluctuations in a model with dynamic investment optimisation at firms' level. In the Taylor (1983) model, investment dynamics are generated by heterogeneous gestation lags between the start and completion of investment projects rather than by introducing capital adjustment costs. A more recent paper by Paez-Farrell (2003) highlights that, by introducing the time-to-build assumption, two key difficulties surrounding basic sticky price models can be overcome, namely, the high volatility of the variables and the immediate impact of monetary policy shocks.

Other recent contributions study the responses to monetary shocks under a time-to-build assumption in a more elaborated framework. Casares (2006) examines the effects of a monetary policy shock across two alternative time-to-build specifications and a model with no time-to-build feature and finds that the inclusion of the time-to-build assumption matters for the response of investment, output and inflation to an interest rate shock. The multiple-period time-to-build model reports realistic (u-shaped) responses of the above mentioned variables, while the models with no or a one-period time-to-build structure fail to replicate empirical developments. Edge (2007) also develops a model with several time-to-build requirements for household capital accumulation but without imposing a time-to-build constraint on the demand for capital of the production sector. His findings provide further arguments in favour of the introduction of a time-to-build feature in order to replicate the adjustment pattern as a result of a monetary shock, evident in the data. He concludes that the assumptions that capital takes time to build and to plan, and that investment plans are costly to change once they are underway act to reduce the response of investment following a monetary shock.

On the other hand, Rouwenhorst (1991) criticizes the conclusion that the time-to-build feature can actually be crucial to the explanation of business cycles. By comparing models with and without this assumption, he finds that time-to-build can introduce cyclical behaviour to the dynamic adjustment of consumption, output and investment only as a result of the stochastic processes for the shocks that hit the economy and concludes: "Time to build, by itself, contains only relatively weak material-propagation mechanisms for transferring real shocks, in terms of effects on output, labour input, and consumption. For persistent deviations of output and investment to occur in the neoclassical model, it is required that the time series of shocks that hit the economy behave very much like the fluctuations which the model aims to explain… Thus the paper concludes that time to build does not seem to be central to the explanation of business cycles" (p. 242). A more general critique is provided by Blanchard and Fischer (1989) who argue that the time-to-build approach becomes much less tractable once no capital rental markets are assumed[90]. In this case, when making an investment decision, the firm must also assess the probability that the conditions could change in the meantime and cause it to want to stop the project.

The notion that capital can be firm-specific in the Blanchard and Fischer (1989) critique above has been further highlighted by more recent research. Woodford (2005) finds that the assumption of a competitive rental market for capital services in which at every point in time the shadow cost of capital is equal across firms and sectors is unrealistic, as it could imply that a substantial part of the aggregate capital stock shifts each period from low-demand to high-demand producers. He also argues that the rental market feature has non-trivial implications for the evolution of marginal cost at the firm level and hence for price-setting and inflation dynamics. He finds that, in terms of price stickiness, incorporating a rental market for capital results in a substantial exaggeration of the infrequency of price adjustment, while assuming exogenous capital instead results in a smaller underestimate. The insight that firm-specific capital leads to a lower estimate of the degree of price stickiness has been confirmed in a framework with constant firm-specific capital by Sbordone (1998) and Galí *et al.* (2001). Later Eichenbaum and Fisher (2004), as well as Altig et al. (2005), building on the research by Woodford[91] have analysed the consequences of endogenous firm-specific capital for the estimated frequency of price adjustment in empirical versions of the New Keynesian Phillips curve in order to allow a closer fit to U.S. empirical data. Woodford (2005) highlights that the introducetion of firm-specific capital solves the "micro/macro" conflict, i.e. the differing parameter values required to explain the co-movement between aggregate inflation and aggregate output (as estimated by Phillips curve time series) and the parameter values consistent with microeconomic observations. He argues that the discrepancy between the frequency of price adjustment required to explain the aggregate inflation/output co-movements and the one that is suggested by microeconomic data disappears once certain more realistic assumptions are introduced to the model (such as firm-specific capital, industry-specific labour markets, intermediate inputs entering production, non-constant elasticity of substitution among differentiated consumption and investment goods).

As far as aggregate inflation dynamics is concerned, Sveen and Weinke (2004), as well as Woodford (2005) find that the introduction of firm-specific endogenous capital does not alter the results under constant (exogenous) capital stock. Woodford (2005) argues that the same form of equilibrium relation between inflation dynamics and the evolution of average real marginal cost can be derived under firm-specific capital. Moreover, he finds that the relation between the slope of the Phillips curve and the frequency of price adjustment that can be

90 See Chapter 6, p. 297.

91 The first version of Woodford (2005) with form-specific endogenous capital dates back to 2003 (see Chapter 5 in "Interest and Prices").

derived under the simpler assumption of an exogenously given capital stock for each firm seems to be fairly accurate as an approximation to the correct relation in the case of firm-specific capital with an empirically realistic size of investment adjustment costs. In addition, Sveen and Weinke (2004) provide an elaborate explanation of the similarity in terms of inflation dynamics resulting from a monetary shock between the model with endogenous firm-specific capital and the baseline version with exogenous capital stock. Under firm-specific capital, there are two opposite effects on marginal costs[92]. In the first place, the additional output generated by investment demand raises marginal costs; on the other hand, the additionally accumulated capital stock enhances the economy's productive capacity and thus reduces marginal costs. In terms of the output response, Sveen and Weinke (2004) find that, both on impact and during the transition period, the response of output is higher under the assumption of firm-specific capital than in a model with exogenous capital.

3. The model with endogenous capital and adjustment costs

3.1. Household utility function and optimality conditions

Under the assumption of identical capital and non-capital wealth in the initial period, complete financial markets and homogenous factor prices, all households make identical consumption, investment and factor supply decisions. Thus the household sector of the economy can be characterised by a representative household that is both a consumer and an owner of production factors. It seeks to optimise the intertemporal utility function

$$E_t\sum_{j=0}^{\infty}\beta^j U(c_{t+j},l_{t+j},m_{t+j},\upsilon_{t+j},\varsigma_{t+j}) \qquad (3.1)$$

where c_t, l_t, and m_t are consumption, leisure and the stock of real money balances, E_t is the expectation operator conditional on information available at t and $\beta=(1+\rho_U)^{-1}$, $\rho_U>0$ is the household's discount factor. The terms υ_t and ς_t denote two preference shocks, affecting consumption and the household's holdings of the economy's medium of exchange, respectively. On the supply side, the representative household is engaged in producing specialised output. The household's production is described by a homogenous Cobb-Douglas production function of degree 1:

$$f(A_t n_t^d,k_t)=(A_t n_t^d)^{1-\alpha_{PF}}k_t^{\alpha_{PF}}, \quad 0<\alpha_{PF}<1 \qquad (3.2)$$

92 Here the plural form used reflects the fact that, under firm-specific capital, due to the absence of an economy-wide rental market, there exist as many quantitatively differing marginal costs as there are individual producers in the economy.

where α_{PF} is the elasticity of substitution between capital and labour, A_t is a (labour-augmenting) technology shock, n_t^d and k_t denote the household's labour demand and capital stock at time t. Sales of the household's specialised output are constrained by the demand function

$$Y_t^A \left(\frac{P_t}{P_t^A} \right)^{-\theta}, \tag{3.3}$$

where Y_t^A, P_t and P_t^A denote aggregate demand, the price of the household's product and the aggregate price level. The elasticity of substitution across differentiated consumption goods is denoted by θ. In addition, the representative household supplies differentiated labour services on the monopolistically competitive labour market. The quantity demanded is given by

$$n_t^A \left(\frac{W_t}{W_t^A} \right)^{-\theta_W}, \tag{3.4}$$

where aggregate labour is denoted by n_t^A, W_t is the household's nominal wage, W_t^A is the aggregate nominal wage and θ_W is the elasticity of substitution for the differentiated labour services. At the same time, the representative household buys time units of a Dixit-Stiglitz composite labour input at the real wage rate $\omega_t = W_t^A / P_t^A$. The household's budget constraint in t is given by[93]

$$Y_t^A \left(\frac{P_t}{P_t^A} \right)^{1-\theta} - tx_t - \omega_t \left\{ n_t^d - n_t^A \left(\frac{W_t}{W_t^A} \right)^{1-\theta_W} \right\} = c_t + k_{t+1} - (1-\delta)k_t + m_t - (1+\pi_t)^{-1} m_{t-1} + (1+r_t)^{-1} b_{t+1} - b_t \tag{3.5}$$

where $\pi_t = \left(P_t^A / P_{t-1}^A \right) - 1$ is the inflation rate, b_{t+1} denotes one-period government bonds purchased in t with real price $(1+r_t)^{-1}$, tx_t stands for lump-sum taxes (net of transfers) paid by the household and k_t is the capital stock and δ is the capital depreciation rate. Next, I introduce two equilibrium conditions for the representative household's production and labour supply. Production is equal to the quantity that is demanded as in

$$f(A_t n_t^d, k_t) = Y_t^A \left(\frac{P_t}{P_t^A} \right)^{-\theta}. \tag{3.6}$$

Labour supply is determined by the labour demand in the monopolistic competition labour market and is equal to

$$n_t^A \left(\frac{W_t}{W_t^A} \right)^{-\theta_W} + l_t = 1. \tag{3.7}$$

93 If constant labour input is assumed, (3.5) is reduced to $Y_t^A \left(P_t / P_t^A \right)^{1-\theta} - t.inv_t - \omega_t (n_t - 1) = c_t + k_{t+1} - (1-\delta)k_t + m_t - (1+\pi_t)^{-1} m_{t-1} + (1+r_t)^{-1} b_{t+1} - b_t$.

The household's optimality conditions consist of (3.5) - (3.7), together with[94]

$$U_1(c_t, m_t, l_t, \upsilon_t, \varsigma_t) - \lambda_t = 0 \tag{3.8}$$

$$U_2(c_t, m_t, l_t, \upsilon_t, \varsigma_t) - \lambda_t + \beta E_t\left[\lambda_{t+1}(1+\pi_{t+1})^{-1}\right] = 0 \tag{3.9}$$

$$U_3(c_t, m_t, l_t, \upsilon_t, \varsigma_t) - \varsigma_t = 0 \tag{3.10}$$

$$-\lambda_t \omega_t + \vartheta_t A_t f_1(A_t n_t^d, k_t) = 0 \tag{3.11}$$

$$-\lambda_t + \beta E_t \lambda_{t+1}(1-\delta) + \beta E_t\left[\vartheta_{t+1} f_2(A_{t+1} n_{t+1}^d, k_{t+1})\right] = 0 \tag{3.12}$$

$$-\lambda_t (1+r_t)^{-1} + \beta E_t \lambda_{t+1} = 0 \tag{3.13}$$

$$\lambda_t Y_t^A (1-\theta) P_t^{-\theta} / (P_t^A)^{1-\theta} + \vartheta_t Y_t^A \theta P_t^{-(\theta+1)} / (P_t^A)^{-\theta} = 0 \tag{3.14}$$

$$\lambda_t \omega_t n_t^A (1-\theta_W) W_t^{-\theta_W} / (W_t^A)^{1-\theta_W} + \varpi_t n_t^A \theta_W W_t^{-(\theta_W+1)} / (W_t^A)^{-\theta_W} = 0 \tag{3.15}$$

whereby λ_t, ϑ_t and ϖ_t are the Lagrange multipliers to (3.5), (3.6) and (3.7) respectively. The marginal product of labour and capital are denoted by mpl_t and mpk_t: $f_1(A_t n_t^d, k_t) = mpl_t$ and $f_2(A_t n_t^d, k_t) = mpk_t$.

Equations (3.5)- (3.15) determine the paths of c_t, m_t, l_t, n_t^d, k_{t+1}, b_{t+1}, P_t, W_t, λ_t, ϑ_t and ϖ_t given π_t, ω_t, r_t, P_t^A, W_t^A and tx_t. For general equilibrium, there are two market clearing conditions:

$$n_t^A = \sum n_t^d \tag{3.16}$$

$$m_t = \frac{M_t}{P_t^A}, \tag{3.17}$$

the identity

$$\pi_t = \frac{P_t^A}{P_{t-1}^A} - 1 \tag{3.18}$$

and the government's budget constraint

$$g_t - tx_t = m_t - (1+\pi_t)^{-1} m_{t-1} + (1+r_t)^{-1} b_{t+1} - b_t, \tag{3.19}$$

whereby M_t and g_t denote the nominal money supply and government consumption of goods and services per household, while r_t is the real interest rate. Without nominal rigidities, $P_t = P_t^A$ and $W_t = W_t^A$. Altogether, equations (3.5)-(3.19) determine the paths of c, m, l, n^A, n^d, k, b, P, W, λ, ϑ, ϖ, ω, r and π in response to the exogenous paths of M_t, g_t and tx_t. Alternatively, it can be assumed that the government sets the path of b_t instead of g_t or tx_t. By analogy, the central bank can implement monetary policy by determining the nominal interest rate i_t, instead of using M_t as an instrument. The latter option will be pursued further in Subsection 3.5.

---

94 Here $f_i(.)$ denotes the partial derivative of the function $f(.)$ with respect to its i-th argument.

3.2. The "IS sector"

Having presented the model's micro-foundations in Subsection 3.1, some of the "IS sector" relations will be derived in this subsection, including the consumption equation and the overall resource constraint. The equations relating to capital and investment will be presented in Subsection 3.3. In order to derive the consumption relation for the "IS block", (3.8) and (3.13) can be combined to yield

$$U_1(c_t, m_t, l_t, \upsilon_t, \varsigma_t) = \beta E_t\left[U_1(c_{t+1}, m_{t+1}, l_{t+1}, \upsilon_{t+1}, \varsigma_{t+1})\right](1+r_t) \tag{3.20}$$

Then, combining (3.8), (3.9) and (3.13) yields

$$U_2(c_t, m_t, l_t, \upsilon_t, \varsigma_t) = U_1(c_t, m_t, l_t, \upsilon_t, \varsigma_t)\frac{i_t}{1+i_t} \tag{3.21}$$

with $1+i_t = (1+r_t)(1+E_t\pi_{t+1})$.

The period utility function is approximated by[95]

$$U(c_t, m_t, l_t, \upsilon_t, \varsigma_t) = \Upsilon \exp(\upsilon_t)\frac{c_t^{1-\sigma}}{1-\sigma} + (1-\Upsilon)\exp(\varsigma_t)\frac{m_t^{1-\gamma}}{(1-\gamma)} + \Lambda\frac{l_t^{1-\tau}}{1-\tau} \tag{3.22}$$

or

$$\exp(\upsilon_t)c_t^{-\sigma} = E_t\left[exp(\upsilon_{t+1})c_{t+1}^{-\sigma}\right]\beta(1+r_t), \tag{3.23}$$

with $U_1(c_t, m_t, l_t, \upsilon_t, \varsigma_t) = \Upsilon\exp(\upsilon_t)c_t^{-\sigma}$, $U_2(c_t, m_t, l_t, \upsilon_t, \varsigma_t) = (1-\Upsilon)\exp(\varsigma_t)m_t^{-\gamma}$, $0 < \Upsilon < 1$ and $\sigma, \gamma, \tau, \Lambda > 0$. Equation (3.23) can be transformed to yield

$$\hat{c}_t = E_t\hat{c}_{t+1} - \sigma^{-1}(r_t - \bar{r}) - \sigma^{-1}(E_t\upsilon_{t+1} - \upsilon_t), \tag{3.24}$$

whereby the "hat" variables denote logarithmic fractional deviations from the respective steady-state values, i.e. $\hat{c}_t = \log\left(c_t / \bar{c}\right)$. Assuming that the consumption preference shock follows the AR (1) process $\upsilon_t = \rho_\upsilon \upsilon_{t-1} + \varepsilon_{\upsilon_t}$ and also substituting $r_t = i_t - E_t\pi_{t+1}$ in (3.24) yields the following consumption equation:

$$\hat{c}_t = E_t\hat{c}_{t+1} - \sigma^{-1}(i_t - E_t\pi_{t+1} - \bar{r}) + \sigma^{-1}(1-\rho_\upsilon)\upsilon_t. \tag{3.25}$$

Next, the log-linear approximation to the overall resource constraint can be written as

$$\hat{y}_t = \omega_c\hat{c}_t + \omega_g\hat{g}_t + \omega_{inv}\widehat{inv}_t, \tag{3.26}$$

where the value of the coefficient ω_{inv} depends on the share of investment in total output in steady-state, i.e. $\omega_{inv} = \overline{inv}(1 + f(\overline{inv}, \bar{k})) / \bar{y}$. By analogy, the steady-state shares in output of consumption and government expenditure are given by $\omega_c = \bar{c} / \bar{y}$ and $\omega_g = \bar{g} / \bar{y}$.

95 The period utility function is separable in terms of consumption and real money balances.

3.3. Capital accumulation adjustment costs

In order to specify realistic movements of capital and investment, it is necessary to add investment adjustments costs to the model. As already discussed in Section 1, some plausible ways of achieving this would include adopting the assumption that capital investment (or capital good "installation") creates certain costs or adding exogenous "time to build" constraints. Here I choose to endogenise the sluggishness of capital stock adjustments and adopt the adjustment-cost specification as in Hayashi (1982) and Casares and McCallum (2006). Gross investment is given by:

$$inv_t = k_{t+1} - (1-\delta)k_t \tag{3.27}$$

Adjustment costs take the form

$$C(inv_t, k_t) = inv_t \, f\left(\frac{inv_t}{k_t}\right) \tag{3.28}$$

where the unit capital installation cost depends on the investment-capital ratio inv_t / k_t according to

$$\frac{C(inv_t, k_t)}{inv_t} = f\left(\frac{inv_t}{k_t}\right), \tag{3.28'}$$

with $f'(.) > 0$ and $2f'(.) + \delta f''(.) > 0$. Within this specification, total adjustment cost of investment in t varies with both inv_t and k_t. The production function with adjustment costs $f(A_t n_t^d, k_t) - C(inv_t, k_t)$ is assumed to be homogeneous of degree 1, implying constant returns to scale[96], i.e. the size of the plant has no influence on the steady-state ratio of adjustment cost to output $C(\overline{inv}, \overline{k}) / \overline{y}$. If the functional form $f(inv_t / k_t) = \Theta_1 (inv_t / k_t)^{\Theta_2}$ is assumed, total adjustment costs are given by

$$C(inv_t, k_t) = \Theta_1 \frac{inv_t^{\Theta_2 + 1}}{k_t^{\Theta_2}}. \tag{3.29}$$

If adjustment costs for investment are introduced, the household's budget constraint (3.5) from Subsection 3.1 becomes

---

96 Another possibility is to specify adjustment costs as in Abel (1983), where total adjustment cost of investment in t varies only with gross investment according to $C(inv_t) = \xi inv_t^{\eta}$ where the scale parameter $\xi > 0$ represents adjustment costs and $\eta > 1$ is the elasticity of total adjustment costs with respect to investment. Then, the values of the parameters ξ and η imply increasing marginal adjustment costs as result of a rise in gross investment. Under a homogeneous production function of degree 1, subtracting adjustment costs from the production function $f(A_t n_t^d, k_t) - C(inv_t)$ implies decreasing returns to scale.

$$Y_t^A\left(\frac{P_t}{P_t^A}\right)^{1-\theta}-tx_t-\omega_t\left\{n_t^d-n_t^A\left(\frac{W_t}{W_t^A}\right)^{1-\theta_W}\right\}-C(inv_t,k_t)=c_t+k_{t+1}-(1-\delta)k_t+m_t-(1+\pi_t)^{-1}m_{t-1}+(1+r_t)^{-1}b_{t+1}-b_t\,.$$

(3.5')

After introducing capital adjustment costs of the form (3.29), the capital stock first-order optimality condition in $t+1$[97] takes the form

$$-\lambda_t\left[1+C_1(inv_t,k_t)\right]+\beta E_t\lambda_{t+1}\left[1-\delta-C_2(inv_{t+1},k_{t+1})\right]+\beta E_t\left[\vartheta_{t+1}mpk_{t+1}\right]=0\,. \qquad (3.12')$$

Marginal adjustment costs in t and $t+1$ are given by $C_t=C_1(inv_t,k_t)$ and $C_{t+1}=C_2(inv_{t+1},k_{t+1})$. After substituting for next period's real marginal cost $rmc_{t+1}=\omega_{t+1}/A_{t+1}mpl_{t+1}$ from (3.11), (3.12') takes the form

$$\lambda_t(1+C_t)=\beta E_t\lambda_{t+1}(1-\delta-C_{t+1})+\beta E_t\lambda_{t+1}\left(rmc_{t+1}mpk_{t+1}\right). \qquad (3.12'')$$

Substituting $\beta E_t\lambda_{t+1}=\lambda_t(1+r_t)^{-1}$ from (3.13) into (3.12'') yields

$$1+r_t=\frac{1-\delta-E_tC_{t+1}+E_t\left(rmc_{t+1}mpk_{t+1}\right)}{1+C_t}, \qquad (3.30)$$

where $1+r$ is the return on the financial asset (the opportunity cost for investment). The right-hand side denotes the expected net marginal return on investment in the real asset. After substituting C_t and E_tC_{t+1}, the marginal cost in t and the marginal cost expected in $t+1$, from (3.29), (3.30) becomes

$$1+r_t=\frac{1-\delta+(1-\delta)\Theta_1(\Theta_2+1)\left(\frac{E_tinv_{t+1}}{k_{t+1}}\right)^{\Theta_2}+\Theta_1\Theta_2\left(\frac{E_tinv_{t+1}}{k_{t+1}}\right)^{\Theta_2+1}+E_t\left(rmc_{t+1}mpk_{t+1}\right)}{1+\Theta_1(\Theta_2+1)\left(\frac{inv_t}{k_t}\right)^{\Theta_2}}$$

(3.31)

Using the log approximation, (3.31) yields the following semi-log-linear expectational investment equation[98]:

$$\widehat{inv}_t=\frac{1}{1+\delta}E_t\widehat{inv}_{t+1}+\frac{\overline{rmc}*\overline{mpk}}{(1+\delta)\Theta_2\overline{C}_1}E_t\widehat{rmc}_{t+1}+\frac{1}{(1+\delta)\Theta_2\overline{C}_1}\left(E_tmpk_{t+1}-\delta-r_t\right)+\frac{\delta}{(1+\delta)}\hat{k}_t,$$

(3.32)

where $\widehat{inv}_t=inv_t/\overline{inv}$, with $\overline{C}_1=\Theta_1(\Theta_2+1)\delta^{\Theta_2}$. Steady-state adjustment costs are denoted by $\overline{C}_1$; $\overline{rmc}$, $\overline{mpk}$ and $\overline{inv}$ are the steady-state values of real marginal cost, marginal product of capital and investment respectively. The gap between the expected net return on capital and the return on the financial asset is denoted by $E_tmpk_{t+1}-\delta-r_t$. Equation (3.32) shows that current investment depends not only on current, but also on the expected future premiums on investment in real

97 See equation (3.12) in Subsection 3.1.

98 For steady-state analysis, see Appendix.

assets because of the inclusion of the forward-looking term $E_t\widehat{inv}_{t+1}$. For simplicity, a parameter Ξ denoting the semi-elasticity of investment with respect to the real asset's premium in (3.32) can be introduced as $\Xi = 1/(1+\delta)\Theta_2\overline{C}_1$. Thus, investment behaviour is described by

$$\widehat{inv}_t = \frac{1}{1+\delta}E_t\widehat{inv}_{t+1} + \Xi\left(\overline{rmc} * \overline{mpk} * E_t\widehat{rmc}_{t+1} + E_t mpk_{t+1} - \delta - r_t\right) + \frac{\delta}{1+\delta}\hat{k}_t . \tag{3.32'}$$

Thus, under endogenous capital and investment adjustment costs, the model consists of an "IS sector" in the form

$$\hat{c}_t = E_t\hat{c}_{t+1} - \sigma^{-1}(r_t - \bar{r}) + \sigma^{-1}(1-\rho_\upsilon)\upsilon_t \tag{3.25}$$

$$\widehat{inv}_t = \frac{1}{1+\delta}E_t\widehat{inv}_{t+1} + \Xi\left(\overline{rmc} * \overline{mpk} * E_t\widehat{rmc}_{t+1} + E_t mpk_{t+1} - \delta - r_t\right) + \frac{\delta}{1+\delta}\hat{k}_t \tag{3.32'}$$

$$\widehat{rmc}_t = \hat{\omega}_t - \frac{\alpha_{PF}}{1-\alpha_{PF}}\left(\hat{k}_t - \hat{y}_t\right) - A_t \tag{3.33}$$

$$mpk_t = \overline{mpk}(\hat{y}_t - \hat{k}_t) \tag{3.34}$$

$$\hat{k}_{t+1} = (1-\delta)\hat{k}_t + \delta\widehat{inv}_t \tag{3.35}$$

$$\hat{y}_t = \omega_c\hat{c}_t + \omega_g\hat{g}_t + \omega_{inv}\widehat{inv}_t \tag{3.26}$$

where (3.25) describes consumption decisions made by the households as derived in Subsection 3.2, (3.32') represents investment behaviour by firms, (3.33) and (3.34) are log-linear approximations to real marginal cost and the marginal product of capital for the Cobb-Douglas production function (3.2), (3.35) is a log-linearisation around the steady state of the investment specification (3.27) and (3.26) is the overall resource constraint with investment from Subsection 3.2. The technology shock A_t and the consumption preference shock υ_t are modelled as AR(1) processes, with $A_t = \rho_A A_{t-1} + \varepsilon_{A_t}$ and $\upsilon_t = \rho_\upsilon\upsilon_{t-1} + \varepsilon_{\upsilon_t}$.

3.4. Inflation and real wage equations under sticky prices and wages

In this section, I derive the inflation and real wage relations under sticky prices and wages, which will be used in the subsequent determinacy and impulse response analysis. For illustration, the corresponding equations under flexible prices and wages are presented in Appendix. As a first step, I assume that η_P is the fixed probability that households cannot adjust their price as in Calvo (1983), so that the first-order condition on price-setting (3.14) becomes

$$E_t\sum_{i=0}^{\infty}\beta^i\eta_P^i\left[\lambda_{t+i}Y_{t+i}^A(1-\theta)P_t^{-\theta}/(P_{t+i}^A)^{1-\theta} + \vartheta_{t+i}Y_{t+i}^A\theta P_t^{-(\theta+1)}/(P_{t+i}^A)^{-\theta}\right] = 0 , \tag{3.14'}$$

which can be log-linearised to yield an equation describing sluggish price adjustment[99]

$$\pi_t - \bar{\pi} = \beta\left(E_t\pi_{t+1} - \bar{\pi}\right) + \frac{(1-\beta\eta_P)(1-\eta_P)(1-\alpha_{PF})}{\eta_P(1-\alpha_{PF}+\alpha_{PF}\theta)}\widehat{rmc}_t. \qquad (3.36)$$

Similarly to prices, for nominal wages it may be assumed that they cannot be adjusted with a fixed probability η_W, so that the nominal wage first-order condition (3.15) is transformed into

$$E_t\sum_{i=0}^{\infty}\beta^i\eta_W^i\left[\lambda_{t+i}\omega_{t+i}n_{t+i}^A(1-\theta_W)W_t^{-\theta_W}/(W_{t+i}^A)^{1-\theta_W} + \varpi_{t+i}n_{t+i}^A\theta_W W_t^{-(\theta_W+1)}/(W_{t+i}^A)^{-\theta_W}\right] = 0. \qquad (3.15')$$

Log-linearising (3.15') yields an expression for the dynamic real wage behaviour under sticky prices of the form

$$\hat{\omega}_t = \frac{1}{1+\beta}\hat{\omega}_{t-1} + \frac{\beta}{1+\beta}E_t\hat{\omega}_{t+1} - \frac{1}{1+\beta}\left(\pi_t - \bar{\pi}\right) + \frac{\beta}{1+\beta}\left(E_t\pi_{t+1} - \bar{\pi}\right) + \frac{a}{1+\beta}\hat{d}_t$$

(3.37)

with $a = (1-\beta\eta_W)(1-\eta_W)/\eta_W\left[1+\theta_W\tau\left(\bar{n}/\bar{l}\right)\right]$ and $\hat{d}_t$ denoting the log deviations from steady state of the ratio of the average leisure-consumption marginal rate of substitution over the real wage or the left-hand side in (A3.10)[100].

3.5. Interest-rate rule specifications

This subsection concludes the derivation of the New Keynesian model with endogenous capital and capital adjustment costs by adding a monetary policy rule. For the sake of realism, monetary policy is assumed to be implemented through a nominal interest rate instrument, so that money supply becomes an endogenous variable[101]. Policy behaviour can be specified in terms of a Taylor rule as in Taylor (1993):

$$i_t = \bar{r} + \pi_t + \lambda_\pi\left(\pi_t - \pi^*\right) + \lambda_y\hat{y}_t + \varepsilon_{i_t}, \qquad (3.38)$$

$$\lambda_\pi, \lambda_y > 0,$$

where i_t is the nominal interest rate, π_t denotes the inflation rate, $\hat{y}_t$ is the deviation of actual output from its steady-state (potential) level, $\bar{r}$ is the steady-

99 For a more detailed derivation of the New Keynesian Phillips curve, see Sbordone (2002) Sveen and Weinke (2004) and Woodford (2005).

100 See Appendix. Sbordone (2001) offers a detailed derivation of this real wage equation under sticky wages.

101 The money-demand relation is derived in Appendix. However, with the nominal interest rate chosen as a monetary policy instrument and with a separable period utility function (3.22), the LM equation can be excluded from the model relations that will be calibrated in Subsection 4.1 and used for the subsequent determinacy and impulse response analysis.

state real interest rate and π^* is the central bank's target inflation rate[102]. The term ε_{i_t} stands for is a monetary policy unit shock[103]. The reaction coefficients λ_π and λ_y determine how strongly the monetary authority stresses inflation and output stabilisation respectively. The response to inflation deviations in (3.38) is actually $\lambda_\pi^* = 1 + \lambda_\pi > 1$ for $\lambda_\pi > 0$. Thus, in the classification of Leeper (1991), the Taylor rule as in (3.38) is an "active" monetary policy rule, describing a more than one-on-one increase in the policy instrument as a result of deviation of the actual inflation rate from the target (steady-state) rate. Another possible specification of policy behaviour is given by a rule proposed by Casares and McCallum (2006)

$$i_t - \bar{i} = (1-\lambda_i)\left[(1+\lambda_\pi)\left(\pi_t - \bar{\pi}\right) + \lambda_y \widehat{y}_t\right] + \lambda_i\left(i_{t-1} - \bar{i}\right) + \varepsilon_{i_t}, \tag{3.39}$$

and

$$\lambda_\pi^* = (1-\lambda_i)(1+\lambda_\pi);\ \lambda_y^* = (1-\lambda_i)\lambda_y, \tag{3.40}$$

whereby λ_π^* and λ_y^* are the effective inflation and output gap response coefficients implied by the policy rule. Additionally, the real interest rate equals the difference between the nominal interest rate and next period's expected inflation in accordance with the Fisher equation, i.e.

$$r_t = i_t - E_t \pi_{t+1}. \tag{3.41}$$

Equations (3.25), (3.26), (3.32') and (3.33)-(3.35), together with (3.36), (3.37), (3.39) or (3.38) and (3.41) determine time paths for the ten endogenous variables in the model: $\widehat{c}_t$, $\widehat{inv}_t$, mpk_t, $\widehat{rmc}_t$, $\widehat{k}_{t+1}$, $\widehat{y}_t$, r_t, π_t, $\widehat{\omega}_t$ and i_t.

4. Determinacy analysis

After the New Keynesian model with endogenous capital and adjustment costs has been derived in the previous section, I proceed with studying the system's determinacy properties under several policy rule specifications. Since, when deriving the model's reduced forms, the ten system equations yield quite complex coefficients, it is not possible to use the analytical approach to assessing the system's determinacy properties. Thus, as a second-best solution, the eigenvalues

102 In the following subsections instead of the target rate π^* the steady-state inflation rate $\bar{\pi}$ enters the Taylor rule, reflecting the assumption that the central bank correctly assesses the steady-state inflation rate and uses it as a target value.

103 The term ε_{i_t} is not included in the original Taylor (1993) version, but is added here in order to enable analysis of the impact of a monetary policy shock on the system under different policy specifications. The monetary policy shock term captures nominal interest rate changes that are not a result of the central bank's response to the target variables as prescribed by the rule. The monetary policy unit shock is modelled as an upward blip of 1 percent in the shock term ε_{i_t} in the policy rules (3.38) and (3.39) that is transmitted to the policy instrument, causing it to rise.

of the system are examined after substituting the coefficients with the numerical values provided in Subsection 4.1. Then, I offer some preliminary insights to the relevance of the Taylor principle using the calibration in the previous subsection for active and passive rules with and without an output target. Finally, in the last subsection a more global perspective to determinacy outcomes under a wide range of inflation and output gap response coefficients is provided.

4.1. Calibration

In order to enable quantitative analysis of the model's properties it should be specified in numerical terms. Table 3.1 presents the values of the model parameters[104], used for the determinacy analysis in Subsection 4.2 and the impulse responses in Chapter IV. In addition, some of the calibration choices should be considered in detail. For equation (3.25), $\sigma = 5$ implies an intertemporal elasticity of substitution in consumption $\sigma^{-1} = 0.2$ as in Hall (1988) and Fuhrer (2000). The value of the steady-state real interest rate $\bar{r} = 0.005$ corresponds to an annual value of 2 percent. In equation (3.32'), $\Theta_1 = 5363$ and $\Theta_2 = 3.14$ yield $\bar{C} = \Theta_1 \delta^{\Theta_2} = 0.05$, implying that the unit adjustment cost in steady state equals 5 percent of investment. The marginal adjustment cost in steady state is then $\bar{C_1} = \Theta_1(\Theta_2 + 1)\delta^{\Theta_2} = 0.21$. The steady-state values of real marginal cost are derived from the relation for the steady-state marginal product of capital (A3.6)[105]. In equations (3.25) and (3.33), the autocorrelation coefficients assigned to the preference and technology shocks $\upsilon_t = \rho_\upsilon \upsilon_{t-1} + \varepsilon_{\upsilon_t}$ and $A_t = \rho_A A_{t-1} + \varepsilon_{A_t}$ are $\rho_\upsilon = 0.3$ and $\rho_A = 0.95$.

Table 3.1: Parameter values (in order of appearance)

"IS sector": Equations (3.25), (3.26), (3.32'), (3.33)- (3.35)	$\sigma = 5$ $\rho_\upsilon = 0.3$ $\bar{r} = 0.005$ $\delta = 0.025$ $\Theta_1 = 5363$ $\Theta_2 = 3.14$ $\Xi = 1.5$ $\overline{rmc} = 0.83$ $\overline{mpk} = 0.04$ $\alpha_{PF} = 0.36$

104 The parameter values chosen are based on the calibration in Casares and McCallum (2006).

105 See Appendix.

	$\rho_A = 0.95$ $\omega_c = 0.78$ $\omega_g = 0$ $\omega_{inv} = 0.22$
Aggregate supply (3.36):	$\bar{\pi} = 0.005$ $\beta = 0.99$ $\theta = 6$ $\eta_P = 0.75$
Real wage equation (3.37):	$\theta_W = 4$ $\eta_W = 0.75$ $\tau = 2$ $\bar{n}/\bar{l} = 0.5$
Monetary policy rule (3.38), active	$\lambda_\pi = 0.5$ $\lambda_\pi^* = 1.5$ $\lambda_y = \lambda_y^* = 0.5$
Monetary policy rule (3.38), passive	$\lambda_\pi^* = 0.5$ $\lambda_y = \lambda_y^* = 0.5$; $\lambda_y = \lambda_y^* = 0.1$ [106]
Monetary policy rule (3.39):	$\lambda_\pi = 1.5$ $\lambda_\pi^* = 0.3$ $\lambda_y = 0.1$ $\lambda_y^* = 0.02$ $\lambda_i = 0.8$

In the aggregate supply equation (3.36) $\bar{\pi} = 0.005$ corresponds to an annual value of steady-state inflation of 2 percent. The degree of price and wage stickiness is represented by the probability that the representative household is not able to adjust its price or wage; $\eta_P = \eta_W = 0.75$ implies that prices and wages are reset once a year on average107. The value of the elasticity of substitution between differentiated consumption goods $\theta = 6$ is frequently assigned in the business-cycle literature. Thus some simple calculations show that in (3.36) the coeffi-

106 In Chapter III, Subsection 4.2 the value $\lambda_y = \lambda_y^* = 0.1$ has been used for the determinacy analysis. Based on the finding that such a value of the output gap coefficient cannot yield a determinate rational-expectations equilibrium, the value $\lambda_y = \lambda_y^* = 0.5$ has been chosen for the impulse-response analysis in Chapter IV, Subsections 3.2 and 3.3.

107 As in Erceg et al. (1999).

cient $(1-\beta\eta_P)(1-\eta_P)(1-\alpha_{PF})/\eta_P(1-\alpha_{PF}+\alpha_{PF}\theta)$ is equal to 0.02, i.e. the deviations of real marginal cost have a relatively modest impact on inflation dynamics, especially in comparison to the influence of inflation expectations. In the wage adjustment equation (3.37) the leisure relative risk aversion coefficient $\tau=2$ implies that in the steady state leisure is twice the labour hours ($\bar{n}/\bar{l}=0.5$). When calibrating the monetary policy rule specifications (3.38) and (3.39), I have included for convenience the terms λ_π^* and λ_y^*, which denote the effective inflation and output gap response coefficients implied by the policy rule.

In the forthcoming determinacy and shock response analysis two main simple monetary rule specifications will be tested, namely an "active" and a "passive" monetary policy rule. The former possibility can be illustrated by a baseline Taylor rule that incorporates an active policy stance with regard to the inflation objective and a more moderate response to output fluctuations as in (3.38). The latter option can be represented by a passive Taylor rule with a reaction coefficient assigned to inflation smaller than unity (for instance, 0.5) and no interest-rate smoothing as in (3.38). The passive policy stance can also be illustrated by a rule of the form (3.39), proposed by Casares and McCallum (2006), where the effective coefficients assigned to inflation and output deviations are considerably smaller than in the previous case (0.3 and 0.02 respectively) and interest-rate smoothing has a considerable weight for setting the policy instrument.

The above mentioned options for the design of a simple monetary policy rule can be reduced to three main issues to be explored. Firstly, whether the Taylor principle requiring an active policy stance with respect to inflation still needs to be adhered to in a framework with endogenous capital, capital adjustment costs and sticky prices and wages. Secondly, whether the introduction of output-targeting ensures determinacy of rational expectations equilibrium (REE) and/or can alleviate the negative effects of shocks. Thirdly, whether interest-rate smoothing can compensate for the impact of non-compliance with the Taylor principle in the case of passive policy stance or, alternatively, improve the results attained by active policy. In order to enable comparability of the results concerning the effect of the degree of "activism", response to output fluctuations and interest-rate smoothing, six cases will be considered: active rule with inflation-targeting only, active rule with inflation- and output-targeting and no interest-rate smoothing (as in the Taylor rule), active rule with inflation- and output-targeting and interest-rate smoothing, passive rule with inflation-targeting only, passive rule with inflation- and output-targeting and no interest-rate smoothing (as in the Taylor rule) and finally a passive rule with inflation- and output-targeting and interest-rate smoothing[108]. In the case of passive policy, experi-

108 In order to limit the dimensions of the reduced-form system, in the determinacy analysis in Chapter III, Subsection 4.2 interest-rate smoothing is abstracted from. Later on, for the impulse-response analysis in Chapter IV the interest-rate smoothing option is included.

menting with the size of the inflation and output response coefficients provides additional insights to whether the magnitude of the monetary authority's response when passive policy is pursued has a significant impact on the results obtained. For this purpose, in Chapter IV, Subsection 3.3 I include impulse response results under both (3.38) entailing a relatively stronger passive response with inflation and output coefficients of 0.5 each and (3.39) implying a weaker reaction , with parameter values of 0.3 and 0.02 respectively.

4.2. Determinacy and the Taylor principle: some numerical examples

The structural equations (3.25), (3.26), (3.32') and (3.33)-(3.35), together with (3.36), (3.41), (3.39) or (3.38) and (3.41) can be reduced to a system of four equations[109], expressed in terms of inflation, consumption, capital and the real wage. Unfortunately, when deriving the four reduced forms, the ten system equations yield quite complex coefficients, which makes the analytical approach to assessing the system's determinacy properties impossible. Thus, as a second-best solution, the eigenvalues of the system will be studied after substituting the coefficients with the numerical values included in the previous subsection. First, in the next two subsections I offer some preliminary insights using the calibration in the previous subsection for active and passive rules with and without an output target. Then, in Subsection 4.2.3 a more global perspective to determinacy outcomes under a wide range of inflation and output gap response coefficients is provided.

For convenience, the system's reduced forms are presented as:

$$\widehat{k_{t+2}} = a_1\widehat{k_{t+1}} + a_2\hat{k}_t - a_3\pi_t - a_4\hat{c}_t - a_5\hat{\omega}_t + a_6\hat{\omega}_{t-1} \tag{A3.13}$$

$$E_t\pi_{t+1} = -a_7\widehat{k_{t+1}} + a_8\hat{k}_t + a_9\pi_t - a_{10}\hat{c}_t - a_{11}\omega_t \tag{A3.14}$$

$$E_t\hat{\omega}_{t+1} = a_{12}\widehat{k_{t+1}} - a_{13}\hat{k}_t + a_{14}\hat{c}_t + a_{15}\hat{\omega}_t - a_{16}\hat{\omega}_{t-1} \tag{A3.15}$$

$$E_t\hat{c}_{t+1} = a_{17}\widehat{k_{t+1}} - a_{18}\hat{k}_t + a_{19}\pi_t + a_{20}\hat{c}_t + a_{21}\hat{\omega}_t \tag{A3.16}$$

The system (A3.13)- (A3.16) can be written in the vector form $E_tX_{t+1} = AX_t$. If the identities $\hat{k}_{t+1} = \hat{k}_{t+1}$ and $\hat{\omega}_t = \hat{\omega}_t$ are added to the system, vector X_t contains the six elements $\hat{k}_{t+1}$, $\hat{k}_t$, π_t, $\hat{c}_t$, $\hat{\omega}_t$ and $\hat{\omega}_{t-1}$ of which only the capital stock k is a pre-determined state variable:

109 The step-by-step derivation, as well as the analytical form of the reduced forms' coefficients, are included in Appendix.

$$\begin{bmatrix} \hat{k}_{t+2} \\ \hat{k}_{t+1} \\ E_t\pi_{t+1} \\ E_t\hat{c}_{t+1} \\ E_t\hat{\omega}_{t+1} \\ \hat{\omega}_t \end{bmatrix} = \begin{bmatrix} a_1 & a_2 & -a_3 & -a_4 & -a_5 & a_6 \\ 1 & 0 & 0 & 0 & 0 & 0 \\ -a_7 & a_8 & a_9 & -a_{10} & -a_{11} & 0 \\ a_{17} & -a_{18} & a_{19} & a_{20} & a_{21} & 0 \\ a_{12} & -a_{13} & 0 & a_{14} & a_{15} & -a_{16} \\ 0 & 0 & 0 & 0 & 1 & 0 \end{bmatrix} \begin{bmatrix} \hat{k}_{t+1} \\ \hat{k}_t \\ \pi_t \\ \hat{c}_t \\ \hat{\omega}_t \\ \hat{\omega}_{t-1} \end{bmatrix} \tag{3.42}$$

Under the parameter values chosen in Chapter III, Subsection 4.1[110],

$a_1 = 1.99+0.33\lambda_y^*$,

$a_2 = -(0.98+0.32\lambda_y^*)$,

$a_3 = 0.04-0.04\lambda_\pi^*$,

$a_4 = 0.001-0.03\lambda_y^*$,

$a_5 = 0.002$,

$a_6 = 0.001$,

$a_7 = 0.1$,

$a_8 = 0.11$,

$a_9 = 1.01$,

$a_{10} = 0.01$,

$a_{11} = 0.02$,

$a_{12} = 0.1$,

$a_{13} = 0.11$,

$a_{14} = 0.01$,

$a_{15} = 2.03$,

$a_{16} = a_9 = 1.01$,

$a_{17} = 0.02+1.76\lambda_y^*$,

$a_{18} = 0.02+1.72\lambda_y^*$,

$a_{19} = 0.2\lambda_\pi^*-0.2$,

$a_{20} = 1.002+0.16\lambda_y^*$,

$a_{21} = 0.004$.

110 Here the parameters $a5 = 0.002$, $a6 = 0.001$ and $a21 = 0.004$ will be taken as equal to zero, as all three of them are significantly smaller than 0.01.

4.2.1. Active rule

The case with inflation-targeting only

For an active interest rate rule with inflation-targeting only with $\lambda_\pi^* = 1.5$ and $\lambda_y^* = 0$, the coefficient matrix F is given by:

$$F = \begin{bmatrix} 1.99 & -0.98 & 0.02 & 0 & 0 & 0 \\ 1 & 0 & 0 & 0 & 0 & 0 \\ -0.1 & 0.11 & 1.01 & -0.01 & -0.02 & 0 \\ 0.02 & -0.02 & 0.1 & 1 & 0 & 0 \\ 0.1 & -0.11 & 0 & 0.01 & 2.03 & -1.01 \\ 0 & 0 & 0 & 0 & 1 & 0 \end{bmatrix}.$$

Again, only $\hat{k}_t$ is a pre-determined state variable, which implies that for determinacy of rational expectations equilibrium F should have exactly one eigenvalue inside the unit circle and the remaining five eigenvalues should be greater than unity. In order to guarantee methodical consistence, coefficient values are represented with a 0.01 accuracy as in the previous subsection. Thus $a_5 = 0.002$, $a_6 = 0.001$ and $a_{21} = 0.004$ are set to equal zero and $a_{20} = 1.002$ is taken to be equal to 1. Since after this procedure the dynamics of the capital stock, inflation and consumption are independent of the realisations of the real wage in t-1 and one eigenvalue of F is given by $a_{16} > 1$, stability of the system is completely determined by the 5x5 submatrix $\widehat{F}$:

$$\widehat{F} = \begin{bmatrix} 1.99 & -0.98 & 0.02 & 0 & 0 \\ 1 & 0 & 0 & 0 & 0 \\ -0.1 & 0.11 & 1.01 & -0.01 & -0.02 \\ 0.02 & -0.02 & 0.1 & 1 & 0 \\ 0.1 & -0.11 & 0 & 0.01 & 2.03 \end{bmatrix}.$$

The eigenvalues of $\widehat{F}$ are given by $(0.91,\ 0.997-0.03i,\ 0.997+0.03i,\ 1.1,\ 2.03)$, of which the first three eigenvalues of the system are within the unit circle. Thus, an active rule satisfying the Taylor principle under inflation-targeting only does not necessarily yield determinacy of rational expectations equilibrium in a model with endogenous capital and investment under the parameter values chosen.

The case with inflation- and output-targeting

For an active interest rate rule with $\lambda_\pi^* = 1.5$ and $\lambda_y^* = 0.5$[111], the coefficient matrix G is given by:

111 The same parameter values are assigned in Taylor (1993).

$$G=\begin{bmatrix} 2.16 & -1.14 & 0.02 & -0.01 & 0 & 0 \\ 1 & 0 & 0 & 0 & 0 & 0 \\ -0.1 & 0.11 & 1.01 & -0.01 & -0.02 & 0 \\ 0.9 & -0.88 & 0.1 & 1.08 & 0 & 0 \\ 0.1 & -0.11 & 0 & 0.01 & 2.03 & -1.01 \\ 0 & 0 & 0 & 0 & 1 & 0 \end{bmatrix}.$$

As in the system of equations (3.42) only $\hat{k}_t$ is a pre-determined state variable, the necessary and sufficient condition for determinacy of rational expectations equilibrium is that G should have exactly one eigenvalue inside the unit circle and the remaining five eigenvalues greater than unity. By analogy to the previous case, since the dynamics of the capital stock, inflation and consumption are independent of the realisations of the real wage in *t-1* and one eigenvalue of G is given by $a_{16} > 1$, stability of the system is completely determined by the 5x5 submatrix $\widehat{G}$:

$$\widehat{G}=\begin{bmatrix} 2.16 & -1.14 & 0.02 & -0.01 & 0 \\ 1 & 0 & 0 & 0 & 0 \\ -0.1 & 0.11 & 1.01 & -0.01 & -0.02 \\ 0.9 & -0.88 & 0.1 & 1.08 & 0 \\ 0.1 & -0.11 & 0 & 0.01 & 2.03 \end{bmatrix}.$$

The eigenvalues of $\widehat{G}$ are given by $(0.94,\ 1.01,\ 1.52-0.02i,\ 1.52+0.02i,\ 2.03)$, of which only the first eigenvalue of the system is within the unit circle. Thus, an active rule satisfying the Taylor principle can yield a determinate rational expectations equilibrium when both inflation and output enter the interest rate rule.

4.2.2. Passive rule

The case with inflation-targeting only

For a passive interest rate rule with inflation-targeting only with $\lambda_\pi^* = 0.5$ and $\lambda_y^* = 0$, the coefficient matrix H is given by:

$$H=\begin{bmatrix} 1.99 & -0.98 & -0.02 & 0 & 0 & 0 \\ 1 & 0 & 0 & 0 & 0 & 0 \\ -0.1 & 0.11 & 1.01 & -0.01 & -0.02 & 0 \\ 0.02 & -0.02 & -0.1 & 1 & 0 & 0 \\ 0.1 & -0.11 & 0 & 0.01 & 2.03 & -1.01 \\ 0 & 0 & 0 & 0 & 1 & 0 \end{bmatrix}.$$

Again, only $\hat{k}_t$ is a pre-determined state variable, which implies that for determinacy of rational expectations equilibrium H should have exactly one eigenvalue inside the unit circle and the remaining five eigenvalues greater than unity. In order to guarantee methodical consistence coefficient values are represented with an 0.01 accuracy as in the previous subsection. Thus $a_5 = 0.002$, $a_6 = 0.001$ and $a_{21} = 0.004$ are set to equal zero and $a_{20} = 1.002$ is taken to be equal to 1. Since after this procedure the dynamics of the capital stock, inflation and consumption are independent of the realisations of the real wage in *t-1* and one eigenvalue of *H* is given by $a_{16} > 1$, stability of the system is completely determined by the 5x5 submatrix $\widehat{H}$:

$$\widehat{C} = \begin{bmatrix} 1.99 & -0.98 & -0.02 & 0 & 0 \\ 1 & 0 & 0 & 0 & 0 \\ -0.1 & 0.11 & 1.01 & -0.01 & -0.02 \\ 0.02 & -0.02 & -0.1 & 1 & 0 \\ 0.1 & -0.11 & 0 & 0.01 & 2.03 \end{bmatrix}.$$

The eigenvalues of $\widehat{H}$ are given by $(0.88,\ 0.98,\ 1.05,\ 1.1,\ 2.03)$, of which the first and the second eigenvalues of the system are within the unit circle. Thus, a passive rule under inflation-targeting only yields indeterminacy of rational expectations equilibrium under the parameter values chosen.

The case with inflation- and output-targeting

For a passive interest rate rule with $\lambda_\pi^* = 0.5$ and $\lambda_y^* = 0.1$ [112], the coefficient matrix *J* is given by:

$$J = \begin{bmatrix} 2.02 & -1.01 & -0.02 & 0 & 0 & 0 \\ 1 & 0 & 0 & 0 & 0 & 0 \\ -0.1 & 0.11 & 1.01 & -0.01 & -0.02 & 0 \\ 0.2 & -0.2 & -0.1 & 1.02 & 0 & 0 \\ 0.1 & -0.11 & 0 & 0.01 & 2.03 & -1.01 \\ 0 & 0 & 0 & 0 & 1 & 0 \end{bmatrix}.$$

Again, as in the system of equations (3.42) only $\widehat{K}_t$ is a pre-determined state variable, the necessary and sufficient condition for determinacy of rational expectations equilibrium is that *J* should have exactly one eigenvalue inside the unit circle and the remaining five eigenvalues greater than unity. Since the dynamics of the capital stock, inflation and consumption are independent of the realisations of the real wage in *t-1* and one eigenvalue of *J* is given by $a_{16} > 1$, stability of the system is completely determined by the 5x5 submatrix $\widehat{J}$:

$$\widehat{J} = \begin{bmatrix} 2.02 & -1.01 & -0.02 & 0 & 0 \\ 1 & 0 & 0 & 0 & 0 \\ -0.1 & 0.11 & 1.01 & -0.01 & -0.02 \\ 0.2 & -0.2 & -0.1 & 1.02 & 0 \\ 0.1 & -0.11 & 0 & 0.01 & 2.03 \end{bmatrix}.$$

112 See the calibration of a passive rule under (3.38).

The eigenvalues of $\hat{J}$ are given by $(0.89,\ 0.99,\ 1.05,\ 1.11,\ 2.03)$, of which the first and the second eigenvalues of the system are within the unit circle[113]. Thus, a passive rule with $\lambda_\pi^* = 0.5$ and $\lambda_y^* = 0.1$, cannot yield a determinate rational expectations equilibrium when both inflation and output enter the interest rate rule.

4.2.3. Interest-rate rule response coefficient values and determinacy: a global perspective

The previous numeric examples reveal differing stability properties of the system when certain numeric values of the monetary policy response coefficients are assumed. Subsection 4.2.1 shows that adherence to the Taylor principle alone does not guarantee determinacy of rational expectations equilibrium under endogenous capital, as the output gap coefficient also plays an important role. Therefore, it is necessary to examine the results for a greater number of parameter values within a plausible interval, in order to identify the stability regions for the values of λ_π^* and λ_y^*.

More generally, the system's coefficient matrix can be represented in terms of both policy parameters from the interest rate rule as:

$$\begin{bmatrix} 1.99+0.33\lambda_y^* & -0.98-0.32\lambda_y^* & 0.04\lambda_\pi^*-0.04 & 0.03\lambda_y^*-0.001 & 0 \\ 1 & 0 & 0 & 0 & 0 \\ -0.1 & 0.11 & 1.01 & -0.01 & -0.02 \\ 1.76\lambda_y^*+0.02 & -1.72\lambda_y^*-0.02 & 0.2\lambda_\pi^*-0.2 & 0.16\lambda_y^*+1.002 & 0 \\ 0.1 & -0.11 & 0 & 0.01 & 2.03 \end{bmatrix}.$$

Fig. 3.1 shows in three-dimensional space the determinacy results for values of the policy response parameters λ_π^* and λ_y^* from 0 to 2[114]. The vertical axis represents the unit circle. Whenever only one eigenvalue of the system is smaller than unity, the respective combination of values of λ_π^* and λ_y^* is marked in blue. Alternatively, the cases when the parameter values generate less or more than one eigenvalue within the unit circle are denoted by blank space. The intersection of the λ_π^* and λ_y^* axes with the unit circle (1.0) plane is represented from a two-dimensional perspective on Fig. 3.2, where the black regions stand for indeterminacy of rational expectations equilibrium (none or two or more eigenvalues within the unit circle) and the white areas correspond to parameter values inducing a unique convergence path with a single eigenvalue smaller than unity.

Figures 3.1 and 3.2 reveal a picture that is consistent with the numeric results in the previous section. With endogenous capital, the introduction of output-targeting is crucial for the determinacy of rational expectations equilibrium.

---

113 The exact value of the second eigenvalue of the system is 0.99341, i.e. very close to unity, but still within the unit circle.

114 For the purpose of the analysis, the values of λ_π^* and λ_y^* are being altered with a 0.05 step.

What is more, adherence to the Taylor principle alone does not necessary guarantee a unique convergence path of the system when capital is endogenous. Only within a very limited value interval of the inflation reaction coefficient between 1.0 and 1.3 does an active rule with no output gap response yield determinacy. For all other values of λ_π^* above 1.3 and under 1.0, setting $\lambda_y^* = 0$ leads to more than one eigenvalue within the unit circle, i.e. to multiple rational expectations equilibria. Still, bearing in mind the above mentioned findings on output-targeting, an active policy in terms of inflation (i.e. $\lambda_\pi^* > 1$) is more likely to lead to a unique equilibrium, as the required intensity of the output response in this case is significantly smaller than under a passive rule. For example, for $\lambda_\pi^* = 2$, any λ_y^* higher than 0.1 yields determinacy; for values of the inflation coefficient significantly smaller than unity, a much stronger output gap response is needed, e.g. an inflation parameter $\lambda_\pi^* = 0.5$ requires an output response of an equal size ($\lambda_y^* = 0.5$).

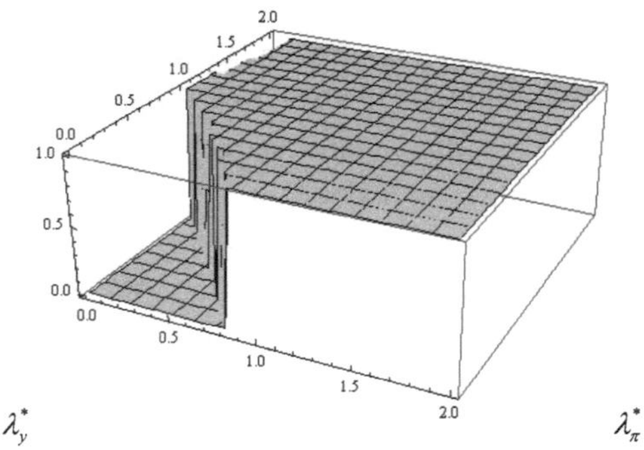

Figure 3.1: Determinacy regions (3D)

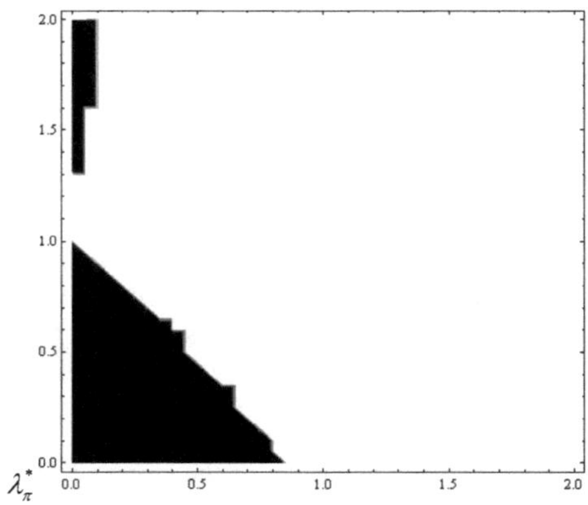

Figure 3.2: Determinacy regions (2D)

Apart from the requirement that some small degree of output-targeting should be introduced when λ_π^* is above 1.3 in order to guarantee determinacy of rational expectations equilibrium, the above findings in general reaffirm adherence to the Taylor principle as a policy recommendation. Except for a small indeterminacy region, active policy in fact generates determinacy and even unconditionally so for the interval $1 < \lambda_\pi^* < 1.3$. The second, more controversial, conclusion refers to the implications of passive policy. Contrary to the results of Taylor (1993), in a model specification with endogenous capital $\lambda_\pi^* < 1$ does not necessarily induce indeterminacy of rational expectations equilibrium. With a sufficient (ever-increasing as λ_π^* decreases) degree of an output gap response, a determinate equilibrium may still be obtained even if $\lambda_\pi^* < 1$.

Generally, the results plotted on Figures 3.1 and 3.2 show that an active interest rate rule might be more advantageous as it is associated with a wider range of response coefficients' values inducing a unique equilibrium. Determinacy of rational expectations equilibrium is a highly desirable quality, as it assures that, after some disturbance has occurred, the system will converge to steady state following a unique, predictable path. Still, the exact unique adjustment path of the economy and especially the size and the persistence of deviations from steady state also play a crucial role in monetary policy decision-making. For example, a monetary policy stance that guarantees a faster convergence to steady state with smaller and less fluctuating deviations in variables such as interest rates, inflation, the output gap, consumption and investment (to name a few) will clearly be preferred to scenarios generating more uncertainty and distress in the economy. The adjustment paths induced by several different interest rate rule specifications will be presented and discussed in the next chapter.

5. Preliminary summary of results

In Sections 1 and 2, I gave an overview to the baseline New Keynesian framework and possible approaches to modelling capital and investment. Then, in Section 3 I derived a model with endogenous capital, sticky prices and wages and capital adjustment costs. As a next step, different specifications of the interest rate rule with respect to the degree of activeness of the rule (measured by the inflation coefficient) and the target variables included were assessed based on the existence of a determinate rational expectations equilibrium.

The numerical experiments pertaining to the specification of the central bank's interest rate rule were illustrated by Figures 3.1 and 3.2 that plot determinacy and indeterminacy regions for each combination of values for the inflation and the output gap reaction coefficients λ_π^* and λ_y^* in the interval $[0,2]$. The determinacy analysis in Section 4 led to the conclusion that, under the assumption of endogenous capital and investment with capital adjustment costs and calibration of the model parameters consistent with the existing literature[115], adherence to the Taylor principle alone does not guarantee determinacy of rational expectations equilibrium under endogenous capital, as the output gap coefficient also plays an important role. Even under an active rule, some degree of output-targeting is needed to guarantee determinacy (except for the very limited value interval of the inflation reaction coefficient between 1.0 and 1.3). Secondly and more interestingly, a passive interest rate rule does not necessarily yield indeterminacy of rational expectations equilibrium. With a significantly strong response of monetary policy to the output gap (ever-increasing as λ_π^* decreases), a determinate equilibrium may still be obtained even if the inflation response coefficient is smaller than unity.

The general conclusion from the numerical experiments in Subsection 4.2.3 that an output target improves the performance of policy rules irrespective of the degree of the inflation response is a useful starting point for assessing the results from the shock impulse responses in the next chapter.

115 See, for example, Casares and McCallum (2006).

IV. Shock impulse responses

In Chapter III, I studied the determinacy properties of different interest rate rule specifications with respect to the degree of activeness of the rule (measured by the inflation coefficient) and the target variables included were assessed within a New Keynesian framework with endogenous capital and adjustment costs. Based on the results obtained, I will now assess the characteristics of the convergence path back to steady state after a shock occurs, implied by active and passive rules under three possible specifications for each class: (i) rules with a sole inflation target; (ii) rules with an inflation and output target and (iii) rules with inflation and output gap target and interest-rate smoothing. The types of shocks entering the impulse responses are threefold: (i) a monetary policy unit shock; (ii) a technology unit shock and (iii) a consumption preference shock. In the subsequent analysis, policy rule specifications that yield determinacy of rational-expectations equilibrium (REE) and in addition involve quantitatively smaller deviations and fast, monotonic convergence path after a shock occurs would be preferred.

The chapter is organised as follows. Section 1 provides some general preliminary insights to the adjustment mechanisms in the system as a result of three types of shocks (monetary policy unit shock, technology unit shock and consumption preference unit shock) and identifies the two main transmission channels in the model (the real interest rate and the real marginal cost channel). Then in Sections 2 and 3 the adjustment paths of consumption, investment, the capital stock, real marginal cost, the output gap, the marginal product of capital, inflation, real wages and the nominal and real interest rate are traced for the case of active and passive rule specifications. Section 4 summarises the impulse response results.

1. Some preliminary remarks on the adjustment mechanisms in the system

In this subsection, I will offer some general preliminary insights to the adjustment mechanisms in the system as a result of three types of shocks (monetary policy unit shock, technology unit shock and consumption preference unit shock). As it will be further revealed in more detail, the deviations registered as a result of the occurrence of shocks within each of the two main group of rules (active vs. passive) share the same sign. The differences observed under the different interest-rate rule specifications within each group pertain rather to the magnitude of the responses and the period convergence to the steady-state level takes. More generally, a comparison between active and passive specifications reveals the crucial role of the real-rate response that is the determinant of differing dynamics of the remaining variables. A second initial transmission channel pertains to real marginal cost (i.e. in the case of a technology shock)[116]. A closer look at the ten system equations reveals a common pattern of adjustment dynamics that can be anticipated before assigning numerical values to the reaction coefficients in the monetary policy specification.

1.1. Monetary policy unit shock

In accordance with the theoretical framework presented, a monetary policy unit shock is modelled as an upward blip of 1 percent in the shock term ε_{i_t} in the policy rules (3.38) and (3.39) that is transmitted to the policy instrument, causing it to rise. The monetary policy shock term captures nominal interest rate changes that are not a result of the central bank's response to the target variables as prescribed by the rule. Under rational expectations, expected inflation will sink.

Investment, consumption and output gap dynamics as evident by (3.32'), (3.25) and (3.26) are all triggered by the impulse to the real interest rate. The Fisher equation $r_t = i_t - E_t\pi_{t+1}$ postulates that the dynamics of the real interest rate is approximated by the difference between the deviations of expected inflation and the nominal interest rate. Due to the expected rise in the real interest rate as a result of the shock under both active and passive policy[117], negative spikes of differing magnitude depending on the policy rule specification selected occur in investment, consumption and the output gap immediately after the shock, followed by a gradual return to the steady-state level[118]. The stronger deviation in investment compared to consumption is straightforward in the case of a monetary policy shock as the real interest rate enters (3.32') with a coefficient $\Xi = 1.5$ and (3.25) with a coefficient $\sigma^{-1} = 0.2$. Since according to equation (3.26) the output gap is a weighted average of consumption and investment, its immediate response can be expected to have an intermediate value. The magnitude of the output gap response reveals the significance of the endogenous capital assumption for the model's quantitative results: under constant capital, the output gap response to a monetary policy unit shock would still be negative, but of a considerably smaller magnitude, as it would only incorporate the relatively more moderate fall in consumption. Still, because of assigning a higher weight to consumption ($\omega_c = 0.78$) than to investment ($\omega_{inv} = 0.22$) in (3.26), the adjustment path of the output gap can be anticipated to match the dynamics in consumption more closely than that of investment.

---

116 Real marginal cost dynamics determine the inflation response. Under sticky prices, the real marginal cost channel plays a quantitatively modest role, as firms cannot adjust their prices immediately after the shock occurs. Changes in expected inflation, however, play a crucial role and are transmitted nearly one-to-one to current inflation (as $\beta = 0.99$).

117 The rise in the real interest rate as a result of the positive blip in the nominal interest rate can only be circumvented if an immediate positive spike of comparable magnitude in inflation expectations occurs.

118 As the shock is assumed to be of temporary nature.

The impact on investment is transmitted to capital with a one-period lag as evident from (3.35). The value assigned to the rate of depreciation $\delta = 0.025$ in the capital accumulation equation determines the significantly smaller maximum response of capital compared to the initial deviation in investment. The speed of adjustment of the capital stock to its steady-state level can be anticipated as being slower than that of investment. This result is a logical consequence of the fact that capital is a predetermined variable as specified in equation (3.35). By contrast, investment according to equation (3.32') does not depend on the past realisations of any of its determinants and can therefore respond immediately and in full magnitude as soon as the shock occurs.

In comparison to the response of capital and the output gap the magnitude of the deviation of the marginal product of capital will be of a considerably smaller magnitude, due to the relatively small value of the steady-state marginal product of capital ($\overline{mpk} = 0.04$) that enters equation (3.34) as a coefficient. The assumption of a steady-state real interest rate of 2 percent p.a., depreciation rate of 0.025, steady-state unit adjustment cost and steady-state marginal adjustment cost of 0.05 and 0.21 respectively in (A3.6) $\overline{mpk} = \rho(1+\overline{C}_1) + \delta(1+\overline{C}\ ) / \overline{rmc}$ imply a relatively weaker response of marginal product of capital to deviations in output and capital.

The assumption of sticky wages in (3.37), modelled by the inclusion of a fixed probability η_W ($\eta_W = 0.75$) that nominal wages cannot be adjusted in the current quarter (which implies that on average wages are re-set once a year) and the partial history-dependence of the variable determines the sluggish adjustment of the real wage. The transmission of the shock to real wages occurs through the adjustment of the inflation expectations $E_t\pi_{t+1} - \overline{\pi}$ and through the dynamics of the inflation differential $\pi_t - \overline{\pi}$. Quantitatively, with $\beta = 0.99$, the coefficient on the inflation differential $1/(1+\beta)$ is only slightly higher than the coefficient on expected inflation $\beta/(1+\beta)$. As the two terms enter (3.37) with opposite signs, the inflation transmission channel plays a role only as long as the changes in expected inflation are not countervailed by a proportional blip in actual inflation. In the initial period after the shock such a development can be assumed, with a subsequent disappearance of the effect leading to a gradual convergence of the real wage to steady state.

The responses of capital, the output gap and real wage determine the dynamics of real marginal cost, as evident from equation (3.33). Compared to the output gap dynamics, the path of real marginal cost is expected to show a lengthier adjustment process due to its partial dependency on the dynamics of the capital stock. A more moderate maximum response compared to output seems also plausible for the same reason.

A monetary policy unit shock can be anticipated to have a quantitatively small and non-persistent impact on inflation. As evident from equation (3.36), the monetary impulse is transmitted by real marginal cost. Under sticky prices, even with a strong response of real marginal cost to the shock, inflation remains hardly affected, as the value of the fixed probability that households cannot adjust their price $\eta_P = 0.75$ (i.e. priced adjusted once a year on average) implies that the coefficient $(1-\beta\eta_P)(1-\eta_P)(1-\alpha_{PF})/\eta_P(1-\alpha_{PF}+\alpha_{PF}\theta)$ equals 0.02. Thus, the initial negative blip in inflation is significantly smaller than the unit shock. Until the effect subsides completely, the path of inflation will continue to mimic the deviation of real marginal cost on a smaller scale.

Although the direct impact of the monetary policy unit shock on the nominal interest rate is straightforward, the final adjusted outcome is worth further discussion. As far as the nominal interest rate is concerned, its final response depends essentially on three factors. Firstly, the choice of an active or a passive rule with respect to inflation plays quite logically a significant role. Secondly, under output-gap targeting, the response of the policy instrument depends on the change in inflation in (3.38) and (3.39) and of the output gap. Since the impulse to inflation is expected to be quite moderate, the effect of decline in actual output will prevail. A fall in actual output would motivate decreasing the nominal interest rate, thus (at least partly) offsetting the initial shock impulse. Thirdly, the magnitude of the interest-rate change depends on whether interest-rate smoothing is added to the monetary policy rule and on the size of the interest-rate coefficient λ_i. In the calibration of in Chapter III, Subsection 4.1 the choice of $\lambda_i = 0.8$ implies that under interest-rate smoothing the path of the nominal interest rate is to a significant extent history-dependent. Thus the maximum response of the nominal interest rate will remain modest and its adjustment will be characterised by a lengthy, graduate convergence to steady state.

1.2. Technology unit shock

In accordance with the theoretical framework presented, a technology unit shock is modelled as an upward blip of 1 percent in the shock term ε_{A_t} in the AR(1) process $A_t = \rho_A A_{t-1} + \varepsilon_{A_t}$ that enters the real marginal cost condition (3.33).

The initial transmission of the technology unit shock occurs through the immediate and quantitatively large effect on real marginal cost in (3.33). This negative initial impulse is then transmitted to inflation as evident from (3.36). The assumption of sticky prices, reflected in the reaction coefficient $0 < (1-\beta\eta_P)(1-\eta_P)(1-\alpha_{PF})/\eta_P(1-\alpha_{PF}+\alpha_{PF}\theta) \ll 1$ determines a relatively modest negative deviation of inflation from steady state.

The negative spike in inflation induces a partial response of the real wage. The initial impulse on the real wage bears the opposite sign of the inflation deviation- thus, real wage is characterised by a positive deviation from its steady-state value as a result of the labour-augmenting technology unit shock. The response is initially triggered by the inflation expectations and then sustained by the inflation differential and the history-dependence on own past realisations of the real wage. The latter property implies a more gradual adjustment in time.

As a result of the negative blip in actual inflation, the nominal interest rate is reduced in accordance with the policy rule. Of course, under a passive rule and/or under interest-rate smoothing the response of the policy instrument is quantitatively smaller as under an active rule and/or no history-dependence of the nominal interest rate. As far as the impact of output-targeting is concerned, the results in the case of a technology shock differ from those under a monetary policy shock. A technology unit shock typically induces a positive spike in actual output, thus ceteris paribus requiring an increase in the nominal interest rate. A negative blip in the policy instrument as a response to the shock can therefore be expected with certainty only in the case when inflation is the only target variable in the policy rule. Under inflation- and output-targeting the path of the nominal interest rate is more difficult to predict. Since under a rule of the form (3.38) or (3.39) a fall in inflation requires reducing the nominal interest rate, whereas increased actual output implies raising it, it can be expected that under inflation- and output-targeting the monetary policy response will be weaker under both active and passive policy than in the case of inflation-targeting only. The sign of the initial impulse depends on the magnitude of the inflation and the output responses, as well as the values of the reaction coefficients λ_π and λ_y.

The responses of investment, consumption, the output gap, capital and the marginal product of capital to a technology unit shock all are triggered by the dynamics of the real interest rate. Again, differing magnitudes of the maximum responses of investment and consumption can be anticipated due to the values of the coefficients assigned to the real interest rate in (3.32') and (3.25), $\Xi = 1.5$[119] and $\sigma^{-1} = 0.2$ respectively. Since according to equation (3.26) the output gap is a weighted average of consumption and investment, its immediate response will have an intermediate maximum value. Again, the response of the real interest rate is determined by the Fisher equation $r_t = i_t - E_t\pi_{t+1}$. Because, as explained above, the nominal interest rate response cannot be predicted with certainly, the initial impulse on the real interest rate can also vary depending on the interest-rate rule specification entering the system. What can be concluded even without explicit knowledge of the numerical results, however, is that under quantitatively too weak a response of the nominal interest rate that is not sufficient to offset the change in the inflation expectations determined by (3.36) the real interest rate can actually increase. Alternatively, under a sufficiently strong response of the nominal interest rate the deviations of both the nominal and the real interest rate will bear the same sign. Thus, a more moderate response to inflation (passive rule) in the case of a technology shock acts counter-cyclically; a

119 The value of Ξ, the semi-elasticity of investment in the investment function (4.27'), is yielded by substituting for the depreciation rate δ, the scale parameter of the adjustment-cost function Θ_2 and marginal adjustment cost in steady state $\overline{C_1}$ in $\Xi = 1/(1+\delta)\Theta_2\overline{C_1}$.

stronger response to inflation (active rule), on the other hand, reinforces the effect of the shock.

As far as capital and the marginal product of capital are concerned, the technology shock is channelled through its impact on investment and the output gap respectively. It can therefore be expected that the paths of capital and the marginal product of capital will be characterised by a weaker initial response and a lengthier convergence process. In addition, the deviations in investment are channelled with a time lag to the dynamics of capital. In comparison to the response of capital and the output gap the magnitude of the deviation of the marginal product of capital is quite modest, due to the inclusion of steady-state unit and marginal adjustment costs.

1.3. Consumption preference unit shock

In accordance with the theoretical framework presented, a consumption preference unit shock is modelled as an upward blip of 1 percent in the shock term ε_{υ_t} in the AR(1) process $\upsilon_t = \rho_\upsilon \upsilon_{t-1} + \varepsilon_{\upsilon_t}$ that enters the consumption equation (3.25). The consumption preference shock denotes a shift of the household's preferences towards consumption in the utility function (3.1).

The initial transmission of the shock occurs through the immediate effect on consumption as in (3.25), causing a positive blip observed immediately after the shock. Under the parameter values chosen, the initial impulse to consumption can be assessed as being quite moderate (0.14 times the shock). Through its effect on consumption, the preference shock is channelled to the output gap (see equation (3.26)) which is also expected to register a positive spike. The magnitude of the output reaction can be predicted as smaller than the initial impulse to consumption in (3.25), based on the value of the consumption coefficient $\omega_c = 0.78$ in the output identity (3.26). For a clear-cut prediction of the sign of the output deviation, the sign and size of the investment response should also be taken into account.

In order to determine the adjustment path of investment as a result of the consumption preference shock, the response of the real interest rate should be given detailed consideration. For a prediction about the real-interest rate response, the adjustment of the nominal interest rate and of expected inflation are to be examined. If the consumption-enhancing effect prevails in (3.26) and a positive output gap is registered, the nominal interest rate should be increased in accordance with the policy rules (3.38) or (3.39) if output-targeting is pursued. As far as inflation is concerned, according to (3.36) the triggering impulse is given by the adjustment of real marginal cost. The history-dependence of capital in (3.35) and the real wage in (3.33) imply that at least initially after the shock the path of the real marginal cost will mimic the dynamics of the output gap on a smaller scale, given by the coefficient $0 < \alpha_{PF} / (1 - \alpha_{PF}) < 1$. Thus, if actual output is characterised by a positive deviation from steady state, real marginal cost will also register a positive spike, inducing a rise in inflation as given by (3.36). Increased inflation has two main impact mechanisms to the system. Firstly, it is an additional impulse for the monetary authority to raise the nominal interest rate, so that the effect of the positive output gap in the policy rule is reinforced. In other words, when both inflation- and output targeting are pursued, it could be expected that under an output-boosting scenario the response of the nominal interest rate is likely to be stronger than in the case of inflation-targeting only for both an active and a passive policy stance. The second influence channel of increased inflation can be sought in terms of the real interest rate dynamics. According to (3.36), changes in expected inflation play a comparatively more significant role for the dynamics of actual inflation than the deviations of real marginal cost, as reflected by the size of the coefficients $\beta = 0.99$ and $(1-\beta\eta_P)(1-\eta_P)(1-\alpha_{PF}) / \eta_P(1-\alpha_{PF}+\alpha_{PF}\theta) = 0.02$.

The rise in the real interest rate releases an initial fall in investment, followed by a monotonic adjustment to its steady-state level. Capital as a predetermined variable responds with a time lag. The deviations of capital and the output gap from steady state, entering the term $(\widehat{y}_t - \widehat{k}_t)$ in equations (3.34) and (3.33) determine the responses of marginal product of capital and real marginal cost respectively. A positive, however quantitatively weaker response can be expected for both the marginal product of capital and the real marginal cost.

The positive initial effect on real marginal cost is transmitted to inflation as evident from (3.36), whereby the maximum impact on inflation is expected to be quantitatively small Finally, as in (3.37) the real wage response is driven by the dynamics of inflation expectations and the positive inflation differential and then sustained by the and the history-dependence on own past realisations of the real wage.

2. Active rule

2.1. The case of inflation-targeting only

This subsection shows the impulse responses of $\widehat{c}_t$, $\widehat{inv}_t$, $\widehat{y}_t$, $\widehat{rmc}_t$, $\widehat{k}_t$, $\widehat{mpk}_t$, $\widehat{\omega}_t$, π_t, r_t and i_t as for three shocks: the random component of monetary policy ε_{i_t}, the technology shock ε_{A_t} and the preference shock ε_{υ_t} when monetary policy is defined in terms of a slightly modified Taylor rule of the form (3.38)[120]. Here no output-targeting and no interest-rate smoothing enter the monetary policy rule and the effective response coefficient to inflation deviations takes the value of 1.3[121]. As already mentioned, the "hat" variables denote deviations of the

120The difference to the baseline Taylor specification (3.38) is the exclusion of the output gap target.

121 As it is evident from the determinacy analysis in Chapter III, Subsection 4.2.3, for an active rule without an output gap target, only inflation coefficient values in the interval $[1.0, 1.3]$ guarantee determinacy of REE. The choice of the coefficient value at 1.3 has

actually registered variable values from their steady-state levels. The magnitude of a variable response to a one-percent shock is measured on the vertical axis of each impulse response figure- thus, a value of 0.5 for example means that the variable's response is half as large as the shock.

2.1.1. Monetary policy unit shock

In accordance with the theoretical framework presented, a monetary policy unit shock is modelled as an upward blip of 1 percent in the shock term ε_{i_t} in the policy rule (3.38). Figure 4.1 reports impulse responses to a monetary policy unit shock for the model specification with sticky prices and wages, endogenous capital and adjustment costs.

Variable deviations, caused by a monetary unit shock, are as in the case of a standard Taylor rule with output-targeting again characterised by a relatively fast convergence to the steady state. All variables, including capital, converge within 60 quarters. The main distinction from the impulse responses under a Taylor specification with output-targeting[122] lies in the magnitude of the maximum deviation from steady state induced by the monetary policy unit shock. For all variables, when inflation is the only target variable entering the policy rule, the shock generates a stronger response that is up to twice as strong as under an active rule with both inflation- and output-targeting. The reason for these differences lies in the dynamics of the nominal interest rate (that also influence the real interest rate adjustment path) under the specification (3.38). The strongest deviations are reported for investment, the output gap, the nominal and the real interest rate. Except for the exact values of the maximum deviations registered, the results in the case of inflation-targeting only comply with those under the standard Taylor specification[123].

Again, negative spikes in investment, consumption and the output gap are observed immediately after the shock, followed by a gradual return to the steady-state level. Here the investment response is characterised by the sharpest fall (3 times as large as the shock). Compared to investment, consumption shows a more moderate response (about 0.5 times the shock) and a fast adjustment to its steady-state value. As a weighted average of consumption and investment, the immediate response of the output gap has an intermediate value equal to the size of the monetary policy unit shock. The paths of consumption, investment and output gap plotted on Fig. 4.1 reveal the significance of the endogenous capital assumption for the model's quantitative results. Under constant capital, the output gap response to a monetary policy unit shock would still be negative, but of a smaller magnitude, as it would only incorporate the fall in consumption.

---

been motivated by the intention to analyse Taylor-like specifications as close to the original as possible, while ruling out the option of multiple adjustment paths.

122 See Chapter IV, Subsection 2.2.

123 I.e. bear the same sign.

The maximum negative response of capital (approximately 0.15 times the size of the shock) is significantly smaller than the initial fall in investment. Again, it takes about 6 quarters until capital reaches its largest negative response. As a predetermined variable, capital is also characterised by a longer-lasting adjustment to its steady-state level than investment, taking about 60 quarters.

The deviation of the marginal product of capital (-0.04 times the shock at its minimum) is twice as strong as when output enters the central bank reaction function. Algebraically this is determined by the relatively small value of the steady-state marginal cost (0.04) that enters equation (3.34) as a coefficient. The assumption of a steady-state real interest rate of 2 percent p.a., depreciation rate of 0.03, steady-state unit adjustment cost and steady-state marginal adjustment cost of 0.05 and 0.21 respectively in (A3.6)[124] $\overline{mpk} = \rho(1+\overline{C}_1)+\delta(1+\overline{C}\ )/\overline{rmc}$ imply a relatively weaker response of marginal product of capital to deviations in output and capital. The initial negative blip in the marginal product of capital is triggered by the fall in actual output and further sustained by the longer-lasting adjustment of capital.

The sluggish adjustment of the real wage over the entire 60 quarters is determined by the partial history-dependence of the variable as seen from (3.37) and by the assumption of sticky wages. The latter is modelled by the inclusion of a fixed probability η_W ($\eta_W = 0.75$) that nominal wages cannot be adjusted in the current quarter, which implies that on average wages are re-set once a year.

The responses of capital, the output gap and real wage determine the dynamics of real marginal cost, as evident from equation (3.33). Compared to the output gap dynamics, the path of real marginal cost reaches a more moderate maximum negative value (0.5 times the shock), but does not adjust monotonically to its steady-state value. Instead, 4 quarters after the shock real marginal cost overshoots the steady-state value, reaching a maximum positive value of 0.08 about 7 quarters after the initial impulse. After that, real marginal cost converges monotonically to the steady—state level. While the initial negative impulse to real marginal cost is mainly a result of the immediate decline of the output gap after the shock, the overshooting part is essentially explained by the slow and lasting response of capital and the real wage.

A monetary policy unit shock has a quantitatively small and non-persistent impact on inflation. As evident from equation (3.36), the monetary impulse is transmitted by real marginal cost. Under sticky prices, despite the strong response of real marginal cost to the shock, inflation remains hardly affected, as the value of the fixed probability that households cannot adjust their price $\eta_P = 0.75$ (i.e. priced adjusted once a year on average) implies that the coefficient $(1-\beta\eta_P)(1-\eta_P)(1-\alpha_{PF})/\eta_P(1-\alpha_{PF}+\alpha_{PF}\theta)$ equals 0.02. Thus, the initial negative blip in inflation is negligibly small. Until the effect subsides completely after 16

124 See Appendix.

quarters, the path of inflation includes overshooting dynamics in the fourth quarter before steady-state value is reached.

As far as the nominal interest rate is concerned, according to the policy rule (3.38) its deviation depends on the unit shock itself and the responses of the target variable (the inflation differential). The monetary authority's reaction to the unit shock involves an increase in the nominal interest rate equal to the unit shock, followed by a gradual convergence to the steady-state level. The effect of the monetary impulse disappears completely after 10 quarters. The Fisher equation $r_t = i_t - E_t\pi_{t+1}$ postulates that the dynamics of the real interest rate is approximated by the difference between the paths of expected inflation and the nominal interest rate. Due to the quantitatively weak response of actual and expected inflation, the real interest rate response (a positive blip with a maximum value as large as the shock itself, followed by a monotonic decrease) matches the nominal interest rate dynamics.

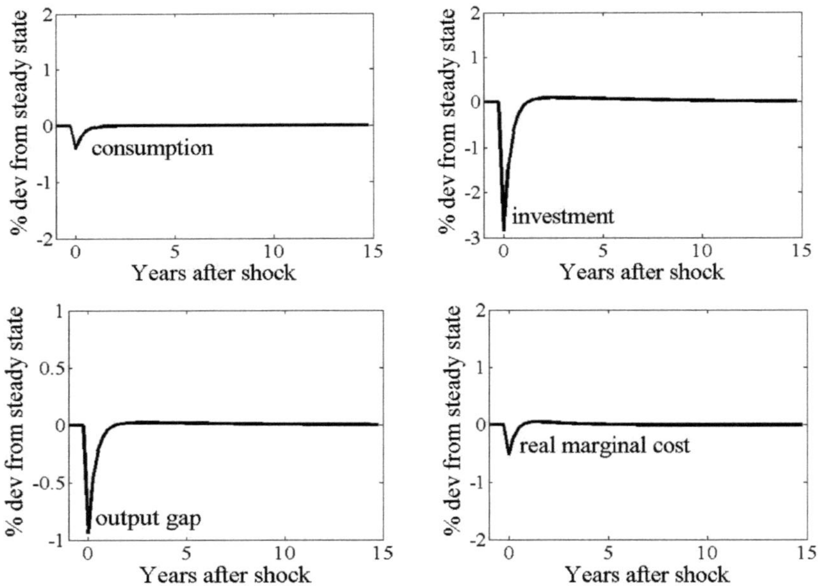

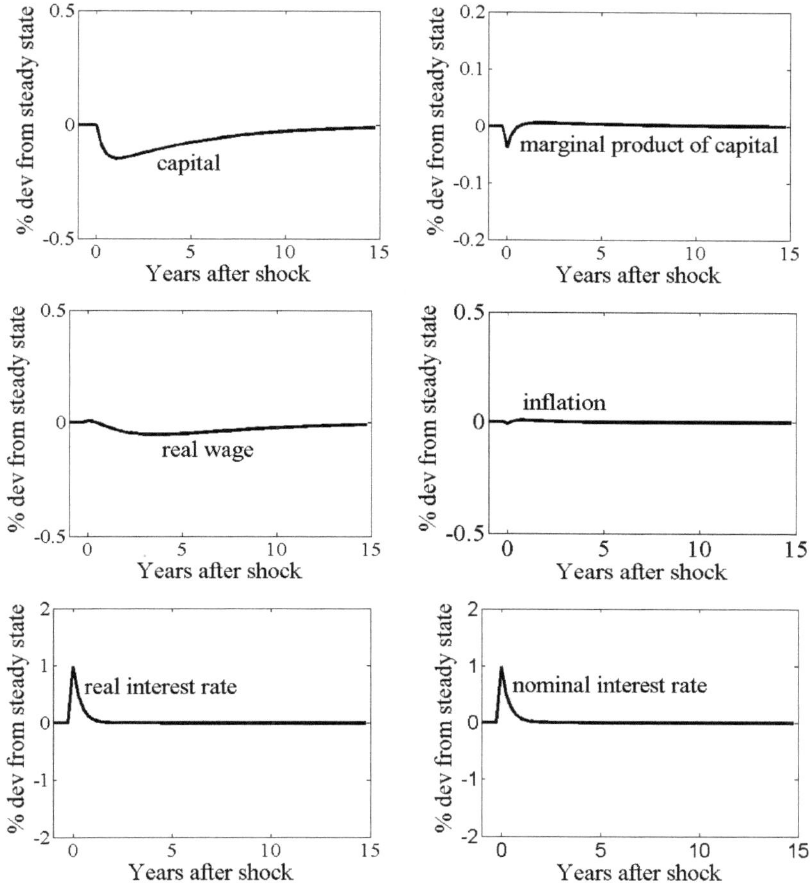

Figure 4.1: Responses to a monetary policy unit shock under an active rule with inflation-targeting only

In conclusion, the analysis of the impact of a monetary policy unit shock in a model with sticky prices and wages, endogenous capital and adjustment costs and a standard Taylor specification for monetary policy shows that the only long-lasting deviations from steady-state values concern the capital stock and the real wage, which take almost 60 quarters to converge. Consumption, the output gap, the real and the nominal interest rate, on the other hand, all return to their steady-state values within a maximum of 10 quarters. These results basically confirm the long-run monetary neutrality of the model.

2.1.2. Technology unit shock

In accordance with the theoretical framework presented, a technology unit shock is modelled as an upward blip of 1 percent in the shock term ε_{A_t} in the AR(1) process $A_t = \rho_A A_{t-1} + \varepsilon_{A_t}$ that enters the real marginal cost condition (3.33). Figure 4.2 reports impulse responses to a technology unit shock for the model specification with sticky prices and wages, endogenous capital and adjustment costs.

Variable deviations, caused by a technology unit shock, are generally of a much smaller magnitude that those occurring as a result of a monetary policy unit shock and in each case of a lower value than the shock itself. In the case of a sole inflation target in the monetary policy rule, adjustment of all model variables considered reveals oscillatory paths. A further distinction in the case of a technology shock compared to the monetary policy unit shock's impact is the slower adjustment to the steady-state values of all variables. The strongest deviations are reported for real marginal cost, real wage and investment.

The initial transmission of the shock occurs through the immediate effect on real marginal cost. A large negative spike of nearly 0.9 times the shock is observed immediately after the shock, followed by a gradual return to the steady-state level within the next 20 quarters. This negative initial impulse is then transmitted to inflation as evident from (3.36). As evident from the coefficient $0 < (1-\beta\eta_P)(1-\eta_P)(1-\alpha_{PF}) / \eta_P(1-\alpha_{PF} + \alpha_{PF}\theta) \ll 1$ the assumption of sticky prices determines the negative, but relatively modest (0.1 times the shock) deviation of inflation from steady state. As a result of the negative inflation differential, the nominal interest rate is reduced in accordance with the policy rule (3.38), followed by overshooting dynamics between the twelfth and the sixtieth quarter. The path of the real interest rate mimics on a smaller scale that of the nominal interest rate. Due to the negative response of inflation, the initial negative blip in the real interest rate is more moderate than the nominal interest decrease, as explained by the Fisher equation $r_t = i_t - E_t\pi_{t+1}$.

Investment, consumption, the output gap, capital and the marginal product of capital all reveal an initial positive response to the technology shock, followed by a countervailing negative deviation of a comparatively larger magnitude before their steady-state values are reached. The strongest deviations in consumption, the output gap and the marginal product of capital all occur within the first 12 quarters, while it takes about 35 quarters until the maximum impact of the shock on capital unfolds. The technology shock is channelled to consumption and investment through its impact on the real interest rate; the considerably differing magnitudes of the maximum responses of investment and consumption can be traced to the values of the coefficients assigned to the real interest rate in (3.32') and (3.25), $\Xi = 1.5$[125] and $\sigma^{-1} = 0.2$ respectively. Again, since according to

125 The value of Ξ, the semi-elasticity of investment in the investment function (4.32'), is yielded by substituting for the depreciation rate δ, the scale parameter of the adjust-

equation (3.26) the output gap is a weighted average of consumption and investment, its immediate response has an intermediate largest positive and negative value of about 0.1 and –0.1 times the size of the technology shock respecttively.

The largest positive and negative responses of capital (approximately 0.02 and –0.08 times the size of the shock respectively) are significantly smaller than the strongest deviations in investment. In addition, the deviations in investment are channelled with a time lag to the dynamics of capital. It takes the capital stock a whole 35 quarters until it reaches its largest negative deviation. Once again, capital is also characterised by a longer-lasting adjustment to its steady-state level than investment- even after 60 quarters, capital remains under its steady-state level.

In comparison to the response of capital and the output gap the magnitude of the deviation of the marginal product of capital (about 0.003 times the shock in both directions) is again quite modest, due to the inclusion of steady-state unit and marginal adjustment costs. Both the sluggish adjustment of marginal product of capital over more than 60 quarters and the undershooting path registered after the forth quarter following the shock can be traced back to the different adjustment dynamics of capital and output gap discussed above.

Finally, the impulse response of the real wage is worth some consideration. As a result of the labour-augmenting technology shock, the variable reaches a quantitatively significant[126] maximum positive deviation from steady state of nearly 0.5 times the shock after 12 quarters and converges monotonically to its steady-state value thereafter. The response is initially triggered by the inflation differential and then sustained by the dynamics of inflation expectations and the history-dependence on own past realisations of the real wage.

---

ment-cost function Θ_2 and marginal adjustment cost in steady state $\overline{C}_1$ in $\Xi = 1/(1+\delta)\Theta_2\overline{C}_1$.

126 The magnitude of the impulse response of real wage is significant especially compared to the magnitude of the responses of the other model variables.

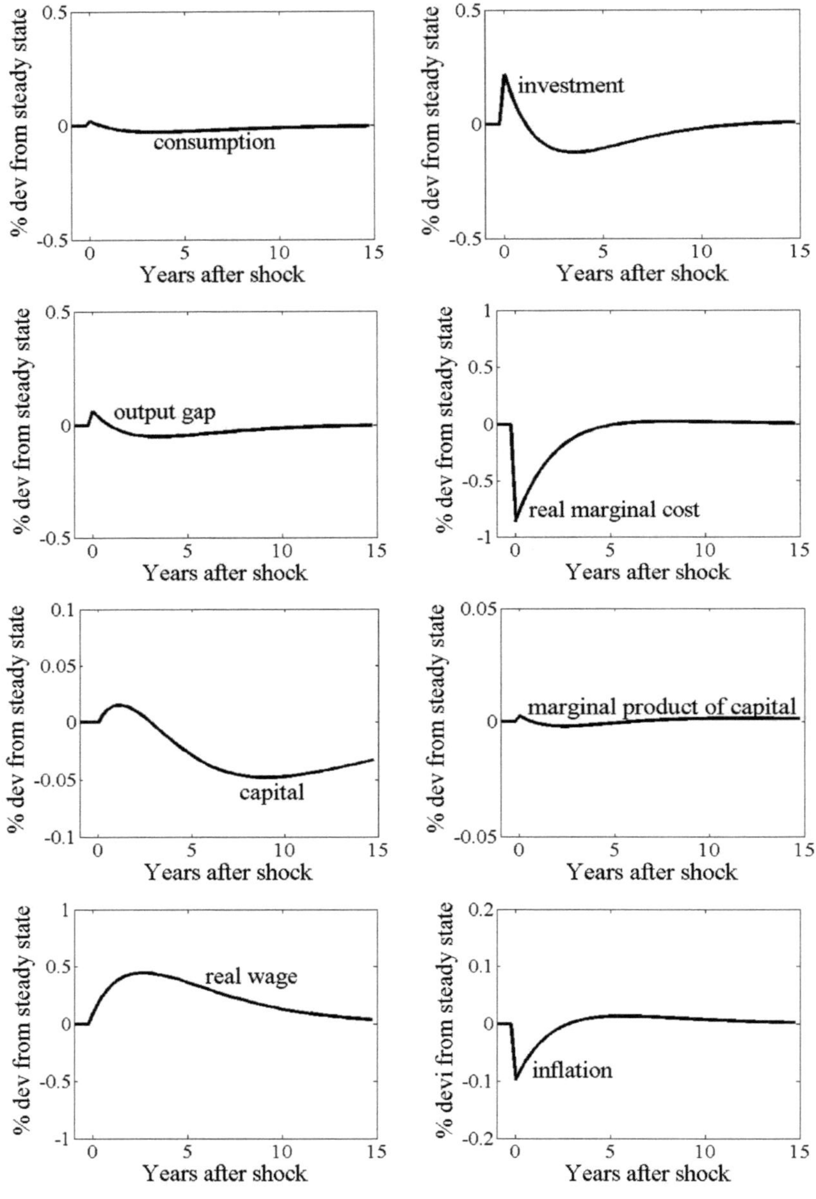
% dev from steady state
0.5
0
-0.5
consumption
0
5
10
15
Years after shock
investment
output gap
real marginal cost
1
-1
capital
0.1
0.05
-0.05
-0.1
marginal product of capital
real wage
inflation
% devi from steady state
0.2
0.1
-0.1
-0.2

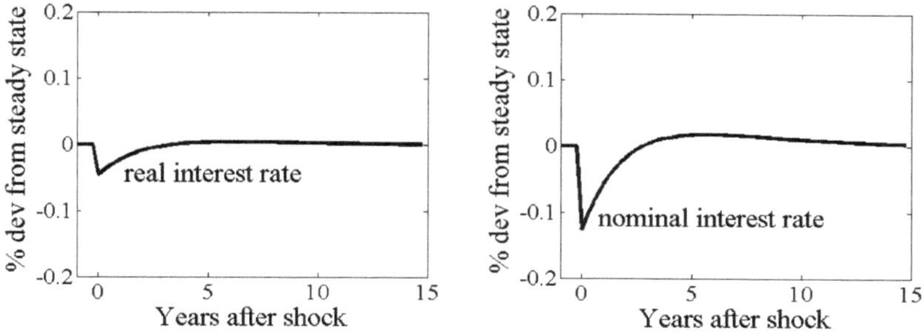

Figure 4.2: Responses to a technology unit shock under an active rule with inflation-targeting only

In conclusion, the analysis of the impact of a technology unit shock in a model with sticky prices and wages, endogenous capital and adjustment costs shows that the only long-lasting deviations from steady-state values concern the capital stock that takes more than 60 quarters to converge. Compared to the impact of a monetary policy shock convergence to the steady-state values generally appears to be a longer-lasting process. For most variables (except inflation, real marginal cost and real wage) the magnitude of the observed deviations is relatively smaller than in the case of a monetary policy unit shock. The reason for the milder impact of a technology unit shock is that in the model it induces a more moderate response of the nominal interest rate cuts as a reaction to the inflation differential that quantitatively exceed the latter and thus generate a moderate real-interest rate response. Through the real-interest-rate channel investment and consumption report initial positive deviations significantly smaller than the size of the shock.

2.1.3. Consumption preference unit shock

In accordance with the theoretical framework presented, a consumption preference unit shock is modelled as an upward blip of 1 percent in the shock term ε_{υ_t} in the AR(1) process $\upsilon_t = \rho_\upsilon \upsilon_{t-1} + \varepsilon_{\upsilon_t}$ that enters the consumption equation (3.25). Figure 4.3 reports impulse responses to a consumption preference unit shock for the model specification with sticky prices and wages, endogenous capital and adjustment costs.

Variable deviations, caused by a technology unit shock, are of a very small magnitude and in each case of a much lower value than the shock itself. Another distinction in the case of a preference shock is that the adjustment to the steady-state values for all variables occurs much faster than in the case of a technology or a monetary policy shock. Within approximately 16 quarters after the initial impulse all variables apart from capital and the real wage have returned to their steady-state values. The strongest deviations as a result of the shock are reported for consumption, the output gap and real marginal cost.

The initial transmission of the shock occurs through the immediate effect on consumption as in (3.25). A positive blip of 0.2 percent is observed immediately after the shock, followed by a fast return to the steady-state level within the first 4 quarters. Through its effect on consumption, the preference shock is channelled to the output gap (see equation (3.26)) which also reports a sharp rise by 0.15 percent, followed by a rapid convergence to steady state.

The positive output gap transmits the impulse to the real marginal cost which shows an initial positive spike of almost 0.09 times the shock, followed by a gradual convergence to steady state within the first 4 quarters. The positive initial effect on real marginal cost is transmitted to inflation as evident from (3.36), whereby the maximum impact on inflation occurs immediately after the shock and is quantitatively small (an increase of 0.002 times the shock). The impulse disappears in less than 4 quarters. As a result of the inflation differential, the nominal interest rate is increased in accordance with the policy rule (3.38), but the response is of a smaller magnitude (0.003 times the shock at its peak). After the first quarter, the nominal interest rate is gradually decreased and reaches its steady-state value in the fourteenth quarter. The path of the real interest rate mimics that of the nominal interest rate.

The rise in the real interest rate releases an increase in investment of a very small magnitude, followed by a gradual adjustment within 12 quarters. Capital initially responds to the increase in investment by a gradual increase, reaching a maximum positive deviation from its steady-state level 10 quarters after the shock. After that, capital converges to steady state after approximately 60 quarters. The deviations of capital and the output gap from steady state, entering the term $(\widehat{y}_t - \widehat{k}_t)$ in equation (3.34) determine the responses of marginal product of capital. Due to the combined impact of the output gap and the capital fluctuations, the maximum response of marginal product of capital (0.006 times the shock) is stronger than that of capital.

Finally, as in (3.37) the real wage response is driven by the positive inflation differential and then sustained by the dynamics of inflation expectations and the history-dependence on own past realisations of the real wage. Unlike inflation, the real wage takes about 2 quarters to reach its highest negative deviation of 0.002 times the shock.

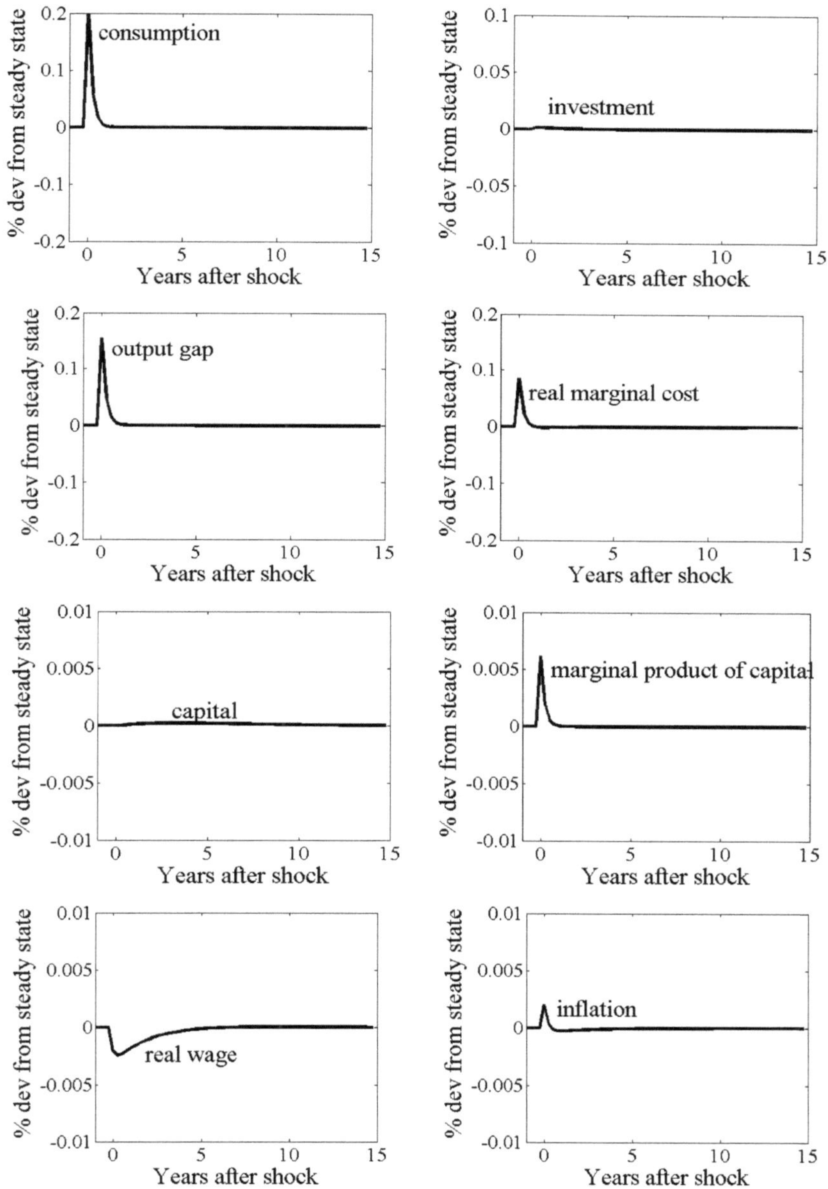
consumption
investment
output gap
real marginal cost
capital
marginal product of capital
real wage
inflation
% dev from steady state
Years after shock

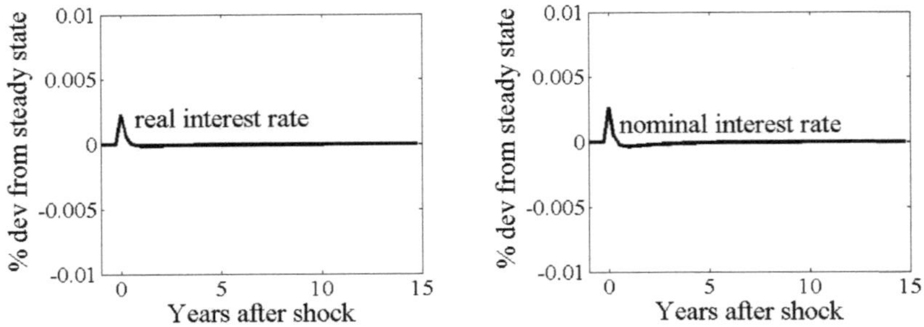

Figure 4.3: Responses to a consumption preference unit shock
under an active rule with inflation-targeting only

In conclusion, a consumption preference unit shock has quantitatively a relatively modest effect on the model variables. Its initial impact on consumption, the output gap and investment is alleviated by the increase in the real interest rate (caused by the nominal interest rate hike). The moderate responses of all other variables are determined by the magnitude of the deviations in the two latter variables in particular.

2.2. The case of inflation- and output-targeting

This subsection shows the impulse responses of $\widehat{c}_t$, $\widehat{inv}_t$, $\widehat{y}_t$, $\widehat{rmc}_t$, $\widehat{k}_t$, $\widehat{mpk}_t$, $\widehat{\omega}_t$, π_t, r_t and i_t as for three shocks: the random component of monetary policy ε_{i_t}, the technology shock ε_{A_t} and the preference shock ε_{υ_t} when monetary policy is defined in terms of a baseline Taylor rule of the form (3.38). Here no interest-rate smoothing enters the monetary policy rule and the effective response coefficients to inflation and output deviations take the values of 1.5 and 0.5 respectively.

2.2.1. Monetary policy unit shock

In accordance with the theoretical framework presented, a monetary policy unit shock is modelled as an upward blip of 1 percent in the shock term ε_{i_t} in the policy rule (3.38). Figure 4.4 reports impulse responses to a monetary policy unit shock for the model specification with sticky prices and wages, endogenous capital and adjustment costs.

Variable deviations, caused by a monetary policy unit shock, are characterised by a relatively fast convergence to the steady state. Only as far as capital is concerned the shock impulse is still present after 60 quarters. The strongest deviations are reported for investment, the output gap, the nominal and the real interest rate.

Negative spikes in investment, consumption and the output gap are observed immediately after the shock, followed by a gradual return to the steady-state level. Here the investment response is characterised by the sharpest fall (2 times as large as the shock). Compared to investment, consumption shows a more moderate response (about 0.3 times the shock) and a fast adjustment to its steady-state value. The output gap's immediate response has an intermediate value of about 0.7 times the size of the monetary policy unit shock. It takes investment, consumption and the output gap less than 8 quarters until the effect of the monetary policy unit shock subsides completely.

The maximum negative response of capital (approximately 0.1 times the size of the shock) is significantly smaller than the initial fall in investment. Contrary to the immediate impact of the shock on investment, it takes about 6 quarters until capital reaches its maximum negative response. Moreover, capital is also characterised by a longer-lasting adjustment to its steady-state level than investment- even after 60 quarters, capital remains slightly under its steady-state level. These results are a logical consequence of the fact that capital is a predetermined variable as specified in equation (3.35). Investment according to equation (3.32'), however, does not depend on the past realisations of any of its determinants and can therefore respond immediately and in full magnitude as soon as the shock occurs. As in the case of inflation-targeting only, once again the marginal product of capital responds moderately (-0.02 times the shock).

The sluggish adjustment of the real wage over the entire 60 quarters is determined by the partial history-dependence of the variable as seen from (3.37) and by the assumption of sticky wages. The responses of capital, the output gap and real wage determine the dynamics of real marginal cost, as evident from equation (3.33). Compared to the output gap dynamics, the path of real marginal cost reaches a more moderate maximum negative value (0.4 times the shock), but does not adjust monotonically to its steady-state value. Instead, 4 quarters after the shock real marginal cost overshoots the steady-state value, reaching a maximum positive value of 0.05 about 7 quarters after the initial impulse. After that, real marginal cost converges monotonically to the steady—state level. While the initial negative impulse to real marginal cost is mainly a result of the immediate decline of the output gap after the shock, the overshooting part is essentially explained by the slow and lasting response of capital and the real wage.

A monetary policy unit shock has a quantitatively small and non-persistent impact on inflation. As evident from equation (3.36), the monetary impulse is transmitted by real marginal cost. Under sticky prices, despite the strong response of real marginal cost to the shock, inflation remains hardly affected. Thus, the initial negative blip in inflation is less than 0.005 times the shock. Until the effect subsides completely after 16 quarters, the path of inflation includes overshooting dynamics (a maximum of 0.006 in the fourth quarter) before steady-state value is reached.

According to the policy rule (3.38), the nominal interest rate response depends on the unit shock itself and on the responses of the target variables (inflation differential and output gap). The monetary authority's reaction to the unit shock involves an increase in the nominal interest rate of 0.7 times the shock, followed by a gradual convergence to the steady-state level. The effect of the monetary impulse disappears completely after 10 quarters. The Fisher equation $r_t = i_t - E_t\pi_{t+1}$ postulates that the dynamics of the real interest rate is approximated by the difference between the paths of expected inflation and the nominal interest rate. Due to the quantitatively weak response of actual and expected inflation, the real interest rate response (a positive blip with a maximum value of about 0.7 percent, followed by a monotonic decrease) matches the nominal interest rate dynamics.

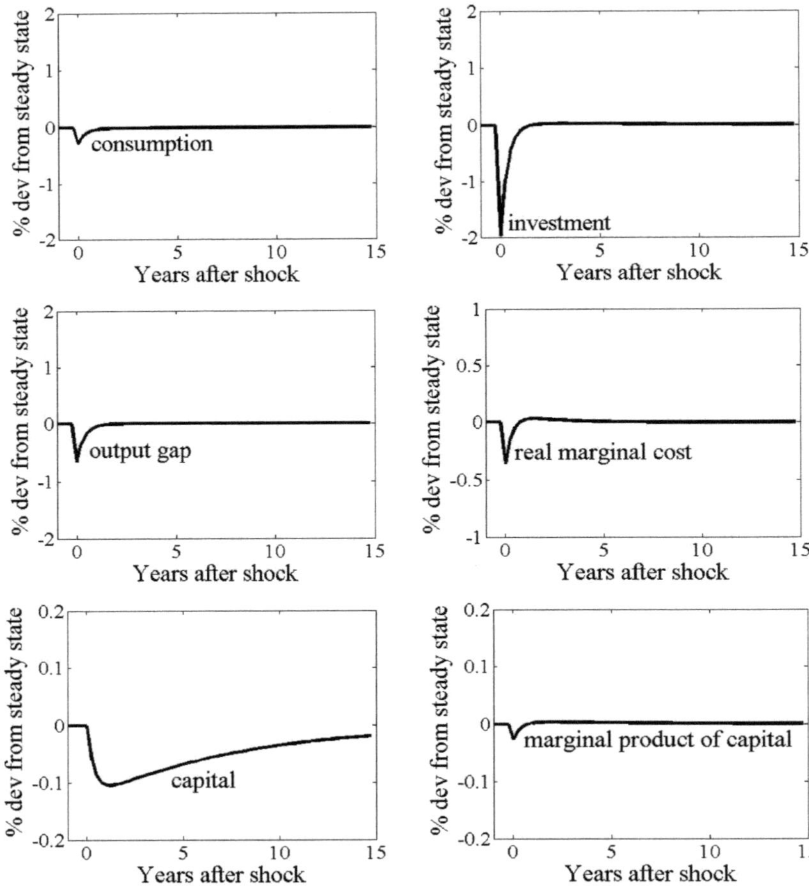

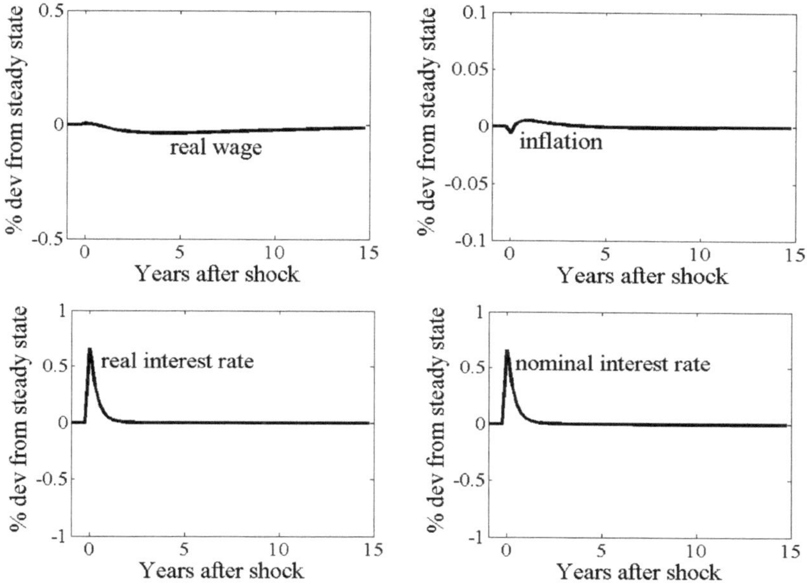

Figure 4.4: Responses to a monetary policy unit shock under an active rule with inflation- and output-targeting

In conclusion, the analysis of the impact of a monetary policy unit shock in a model with sticky prices and wages, endogenous capital and adjustment costs and a standard Taylor specification for monetary policy shows that the only long-lasting deviations from steady-state values concern the capital stock and the real wage, which take at least 60 quarters to converge. Consumption, investment, the output gap, the real and the nominal interest rate, on the other hand, all return to their steady-state values within a maximum of 10 quarters.

2.2.2. Technology unit shock

In accordance with the theoretical framework presented, a technology unit shock is modelled as an upward blip of 1 percent in the shock term ε_{A_t} in the AR(1) process $A_t = \rho_A A_{t-1} + \varepsilon_{A_t}$ that enters the real marginal cost condition (3.33). Figure 4.5 reports impulse responses to a technology unit shock for the model specification with sticky prices and wages, endogenous capital and adjustment costs.

Again, the strongest deviations are reported for real marginal cost, real wage and investment. The initial transmission of the shock occurs through the immediate effect on real marginal cost. A large negative spike of almost 0.9 percent is observed immediately after the shock, followed by a gradual return to the steady-state level within the next 20 quarters. This negative initial impulse is then transmitted to inflation as evident from (3.36).

As a result of the increased inflation differential, the nominal interest rate is reduced in accordance with the policy rule (3.38), reaching a minimum value of slightly above 0.1 times the shock. As the output gap also enters the monetary policy rule, the increase in actual output as a result of the technology shock implies that the actual nominal interest rate hike will eventually be of a smaller magnitude than under an active rule incorporating inflation-targeting only. Nevertheless, as a result of the large reaction coefficient assigned to inflation and the quantitatively small impact of the shock on the output gap , the path of the nominal interest rate mimics that of actual inflation.

For the model specification chosen, a Taylor rule with no interest-rate smoothing induces a negative blip in the real interest rate of approximately 0.03 percent immediately after the shock occurs, followed by a gradual convergence to the steady-state value within the next 20 quarters. The real-interest rate response induced by the nominal interest rate fall additionally reinforces the positive deviations of investment, consumption and the output gap and acts procyclically. This effect can be offset by a stronger emphasis on output-targeting in the monetary policy rule, measured by the value of the coefficient λ_y.

Investment, consumption, the output gap, capital and the marginal product of capital all reveal an initial positive response to the technology shock, followed by a countervailing negative deviation of a comparatively smaller magnitude before their steady-state values are reached. The strongest deviations in consumption, the output gap and the marginal product of capital all occur immediately after the shock, while it takes 9 quarters until the maximum impact of the shock on capital unfolds. The technology shock is channelled to consumption and investment through its impact on the real interest rate; the considerably differing magnitudes of the maximum responses of investment (0.23 times the shock) and consumption (0.03 times the shock) can be traced to the values of the coefficients assigned to the real interest rate in (3.32') and (3.25), respectively. Again, since according to equation (3.26) the output gap is a weighted average of consumption and investment, its immediate response has an intermediate maximum value of about 0.08 times the size of the technology shock.

The maximum positive response of capital (approximately 0.03 times the size of the shock) is significantly smaller than the strongest increase in investment. In addition, the deviation in investment is channelled with a time lag to the dynamics of capital. It takes the capital stock whole 9 quarters until it reaches its highest positive deviation from its steady-state level. Once again, capital is also characterised by a longer-lasting adjustment than investment-even after 60 quarters, capital remains under its steady-state level.

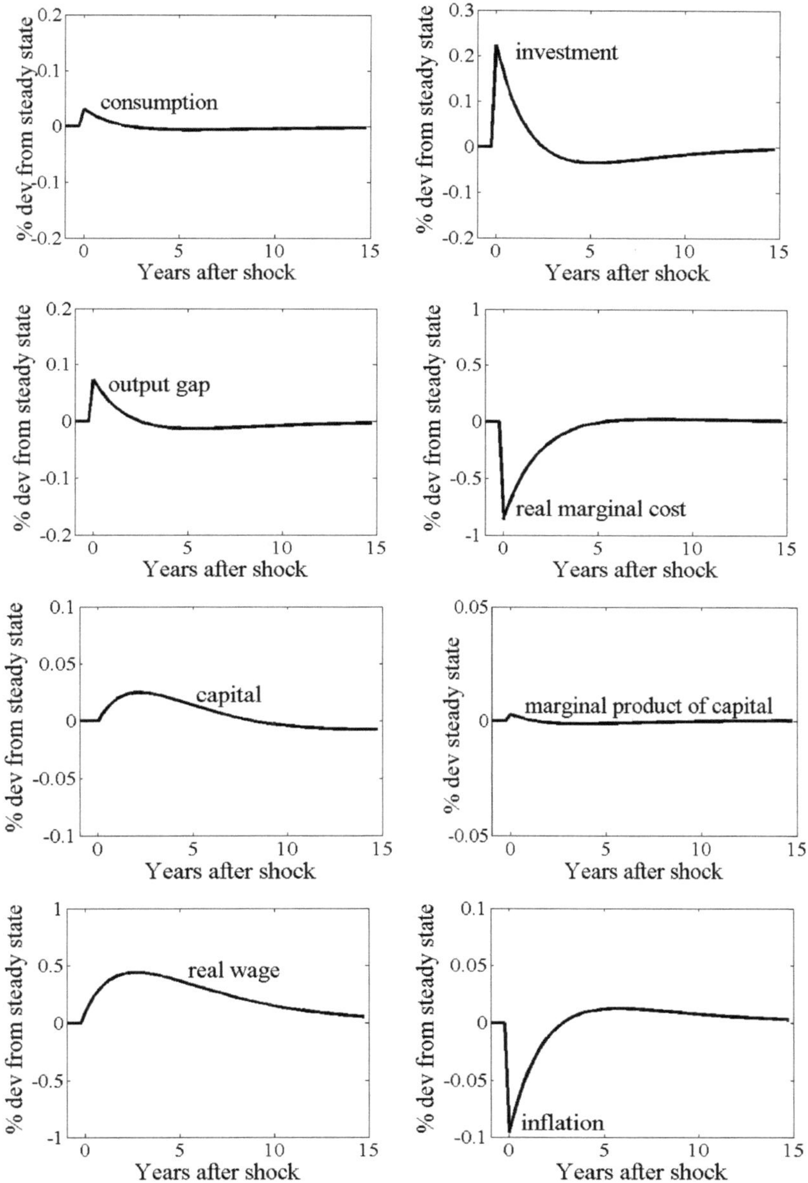
consumption
investment
output gap
real marginal cost
capital
marginal product of capital
real wage
inflation
% dev from steady state
Years after shock

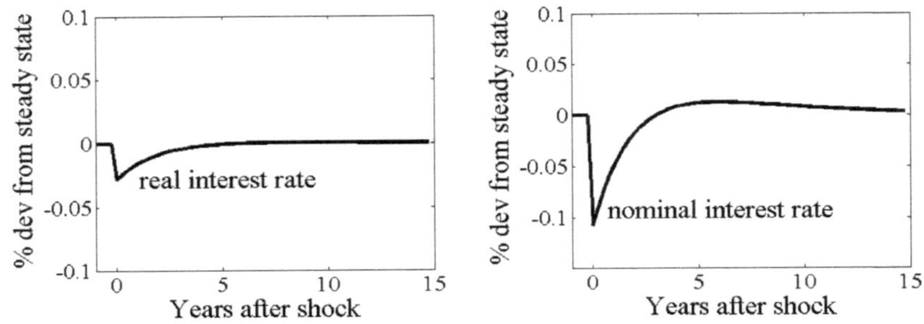

Figure 4.5: Responses to a technology unit shock under an active rule with inflation- and output-targeting

In comparison to the response of capital and the output gap the magnitude of the deviation of the marginal product of capital (about 0.004 times the shock) is again quite modest, due to the inclusion of steady-state unit and marginal adjustment costs. Finally, as a result of the labour-augmenting technology shock, the variable reaches a quantitatively significant[127] maximum positive deviation from steady state of 0.4 times the shock after 11 quarters and converges monotonically to its steady-state value thereafter. The response is initially triggered by the inflation differential and then sustained by the dynamics of inflation expectations and the history-dependence on own past realisations of the real wage.

In conclusion, the analysis of the impact of a technology unit shock in a model with sticky prices and wages, endogenous capital and adjustment costs and a standard Taylor specification of the monetary policy rule shows that the only long-lasting deviations from steady-state values concern the capital stock that takes more than 60 quarters to converge. Compared to the impact of a monetary policy shock, convergence to the steady-state values generally appears to be a longer-lasting process. In addition, the inclusion of an output gap target causes a smaller initial response of the nominal interest rate compared to the case with inflation-targeting only. As a result, deviations in the real nominal rate, investment, capital and the output gap turn out to be of a relatively smaller magnitude. Moreover, output-targeting limits the oscillations in the adjustment paths of consumption, investment, capital and the output gap.

2.2.3. Consumption preference unit shock

In accordance with the theoretical framework presented, a consumption preference unit shock is modelled as an upward blip of 1 percent in the shock term ε_{υ_t} in the AR(1) process $\upsilon_t = \rho_\upsilon \upsilon_{t-1} + \varepsilon_{\upsilon_t}$ that enters the consumption equation (3.25). Figure 4.6 reports impulse responses to a consumption preference unit shock for

127 The magnitude of the impulse response of real wage is significant especially compared to the magnitude of the responses of the other model variables.

the model specification with sticky prices and wages, endogenous capital and adjustment costs.

Variable deviations, caused by a consumption preference unit shock, are of a very small magnitude and in each case of a much lower value than the shock itself. Another distinction in the case of a preference shock is that the adjustment to the steady-state values of nearly all variables (except for the capital stock and the real wage) occurs much faster than in the case of a technology or a monetary policy shock. Within approximately 16 quarters after the initial impulse all variables apart from capital and the real wage have returned to their steady-state values. The strongest deviations as a result of the shock are reported for consumption, the output gap and investment.

The initial transmission of the shock occurs through the immediate effect on consumption as in (3.25). A positive blip of almost 0.2 is observed immediately after the shock, followed by a fast return to the steady-state level within the first 5 quarters. Through its effect on consumption, the preference shock is channelled to the output gap (see equation (3.26)) which also reports a sharp rise by 0.12, followed by a rapid convergence to steady state.

As a result of the positive output gap, the nominal interest rate is increased in accordance with the policy rule (3.38), but the response is of a smaller magnitude (0.06 times the shock at its peak). After the initial blip, the nominal interest rate is gradually decreased and reaches its steady-state value in the forth quarter. The path of the real interest rate mimics that of the nominal interest rate.

The rise in the real interest rate releases an initial fall in investment of 0.12 times the shock, followed by a monotonic adjustment within 4 quarters. Capital initially responds to the negative blip in investment by a gradual decrease, reaching a maximum negative deviation from its steady-state level 3 quarters after the shock. After that, the negative dynamics is reversed and capital converges to steady state after approximately 60 quarters. The deviations of capital and the output gap from steady state determine the responses of marginal product of capital and real marginal cost respectively. The maximum response of marginal product of capital (0.005 times the shock) occurs immediately after the shock. After the initial positive blip, the marginal product of capital converges to steady state within 4 quarters. The response in real marginal cost shows a similar path – an initial positive spike of 0.07 times the shock, followed by a gradual convergence to steady state within the first 4 quarters.

The positive initial effect on real marginal cost is transmitted to inflation as evident from (3.36), whereby the maximum impact on inflation occurs immediately after the shock and is quantitatively small (an increase of 0.002). The impulse disappears in about 4 quarters. The real wage response is driven by the dynamics of inflation expectations and then sustained by the positive inflation differential and the history-dependence on own past realisations of the real wage. Unlike inflation, the real wage takes about 2 quarters to reach its highest negative deviation of slightly above 0.002 times the shock. This negative deviation persists until about 60 quarters after the initial impulse.

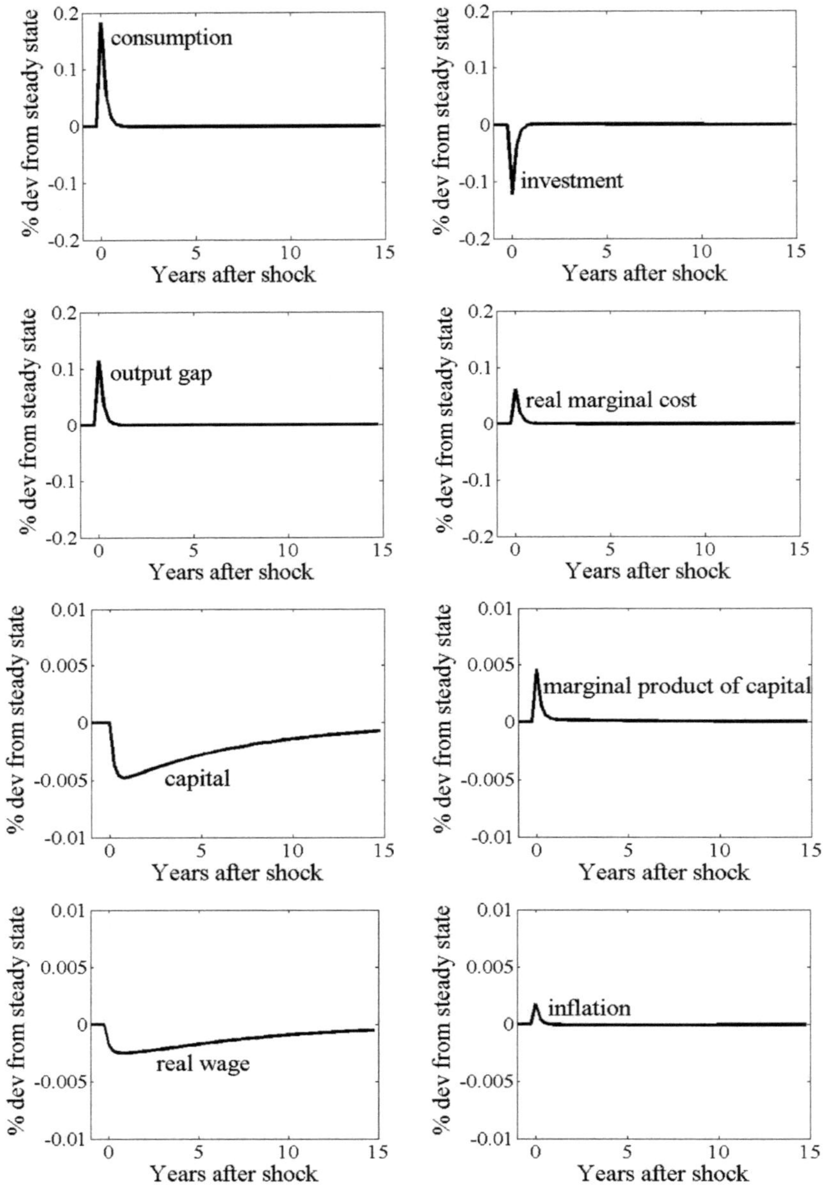

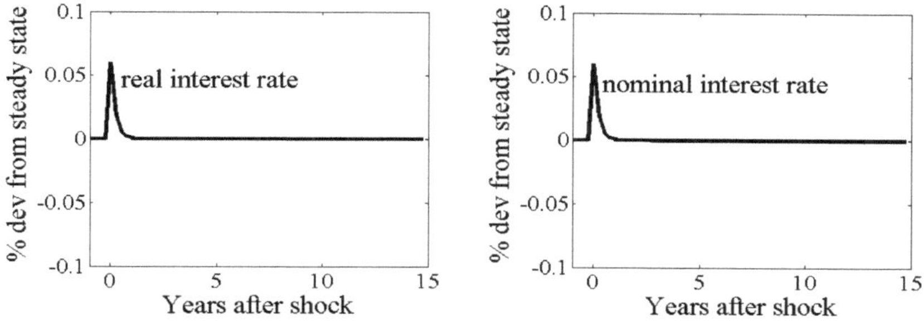

Figure 4.6: Responses to a consumption preference unit shock under an active rule with inflation- and output-targeting

In conclusion, a consumption preference unit shock has a modest effect on the model variables. Its initial impact on consumption, the output gap and investment is alleviated by the increase in the real interest rate (caused by the nominal interest rate hike). The moderate responses of all other variables are determined by the magnitude of the deviations in the two latter variables in particular. Compared to the case with inflation-targeting only, output-targeting induces a stronger response of the nominal interest rate, which in turn leads to a higher positive spike in the real interest rate. The latter result explains the strong negative impulse to investment and the capital stock. The fall in investment partly offsets the initial positive blip in consumption, thus generating a more moderate intermediate positive output gap response. In other words, the monetary policy stance under an active baseline Taylor rule specification plays a stabilising role in the case of a consumption preference unit shock.

2.3. The case of inflation- and output-targeting with interest-rate smoothing

This subsection shows the impulse responses of $\hat{c}_t$, $\widehat{inv}_t$, $\hat{y}_t$, $\widehat{rmc}_t$, $\hat{k}_t$, $\widehat{mpk}_t$, $\hat{\omega}_t, \pi_t$, r_t and i_t as for three shocks: the random component of monetary policy ε_{i_t}, the technology shock ε_{A_t} and the preference shock ε_{υ_t} when monetary policy is defined in terms of an active rule of the form (3.38). Here interest-rate smoothing enters the monetary policy rule ($\lambda_i = 0.8$) and the effective response coefficients to inflation and output deviations take the values of 1.5 and 0.5 respectively.

2.3.1. Monetary policy unit shock

In accordance with the theoretical framework presented, a monetary policy unit shock is modelled as an upward blip of 1 percent in the shock term ε_{i_t} in the policy rule (3.38). Figure 4.7 reports impulse responses to a monetary policy unit shock for the model specification with sticky prices and wages, endogenous capital and adjustment costs.

Large negative spikes in investment, consumption and the output gap are observed immediately after the shock, followed by a gradual return to the steady-state level. Investment response is characterised by the sharpest fall (three times as large as the shock) and relatively quick adjustment (12 quarters). Compared to investment, consumption shows a more moderate response (-0.4). The output gap's immediate response is of a comparable value to the shock itself. It takes both consumption and the output gap approximately 12 quarters until the effect of the monetary policy unit shock subsides completely.

The maximum negative response of capital (approximately 0.2 times the size of the shock) is significantly smaller than the initial fall in investment. Contrary to the immediate impact of the shock on investment, it takes about 6 quarters until capital reaches its maximum negative response. Capital is also characterised by a longer-lasting adjustment to its steady-state level than investment- only after 60 quarters capital tends to reach its steady-state level. As in the previous two subsections, the deviation of the marginal product of capital remains moderate and tends to persist for most of the period observed. The sluggish adjustment of the real wage is also familiar from the previous two experiments.

The responses of capital, the output gap and real wage determine the dynamics of real marginal cost, as evident from equation (3.33). Compared to the output gap dynamics, the path of real marginal cost reaches a more moderate maximum negative value (0.6 the shock), but does not adjust monotonically to its steady-state value. Instead, 7 quarters after the shock real marginal cost overshoots the steady-state value, reaching a maximum positive value of slightly under 0.1 about 8 quarters after the initial impulse. After that, real marginal cost converges monotonically to the steady—state level. While the initial negative impulse to real marginal cost is mainly a result of the sharp immediate decline of the output gap after the shock, the overshooting part is essentially explained by the slow and lasting response of capital and the real wage. A monetary policy unit shock has a quantitatively small and non-persistent impact on inflation. As evident from equation (3.36), the monetary impulse is transmitted by real marginal cost. Under sticky prices, despite the strong response of real marginal cost to the shock, inflation remains hardly affected. The effect subsides completely after 16 quarters.

As far as the nominal interest rate is concerned, according to the policy rule (3.38) its deviation depends on the unit shock itself, the responses of the target variables (inflation differential and output gap) and the past deviation of the variable from its steady-state value. The monetary authority's reaction to the unit shock involves a more gradual increase in the nominal interest rate compared to the cases without interest-rate smoothing- it takes two quarters until the maximum response unfolds. Another distinction from the responses of the nominal (and real) interest rate to a monetary unit shock when no lagged nominal interest rate enters the central bank's rule (see Chapter IV, Subsections 2.1 and 2.2) is that under interest-rate smoothing the maximum response of both variables remains more moderate (0.5 times the shock). After the initial positive deviation, monotonic convergence to the steady-state value occurs within 16 quarters. Again, due to the quantitatively weak response of inflation, the real interest rate response (a positive blip with a maximum value of 0.5, followed by a monotonic decrease) matches the nominal interest rate dynamics.

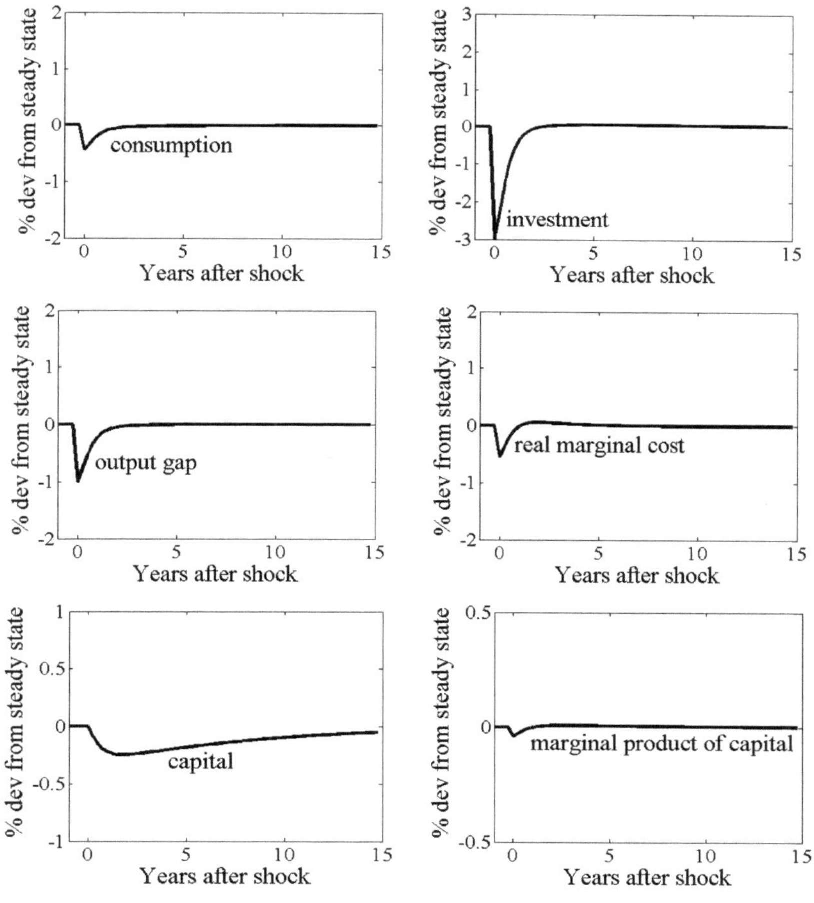

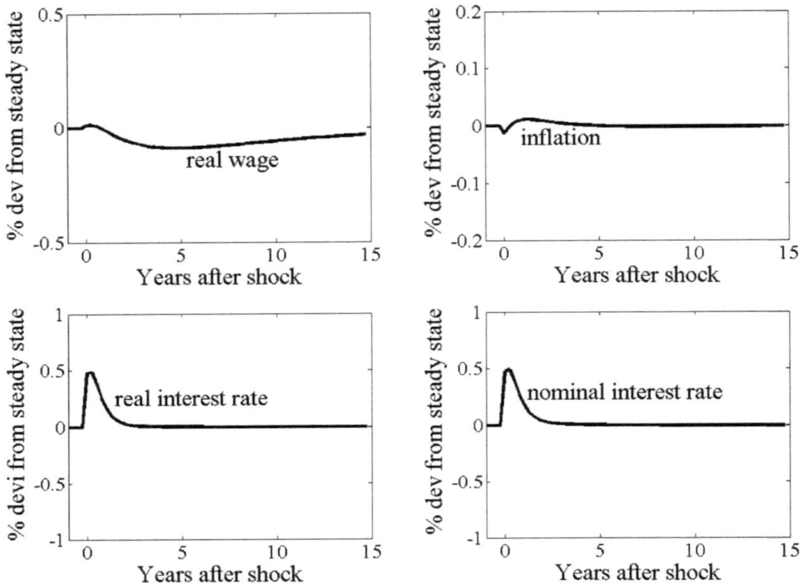

Figure 4.7: Responses to a monetary policy unit shock
under an active rule with inflation- and output-targeting and interest-rate smoothing

In conclusion, the analysis of the impact of a monetary policy unit shock in a model with sticky prices and wages, endogenous capital and adjustment costs shows that the only long-lasting deviations from steady-state values concern the capital stock and the real wage, which take more than 60 quarters to converge. Consumption, the output gap, the real and the nominal interest rate, on the other hand, all return to their steady-state values within approximately 16 quarters. Compared to the results under a baseline Taylor rule in Subsection 2.2, all variables except the nominal and the real interest rate are characterised by larger deviations from their steady-state values when interest-rate smoothing is introduced. The history-dependence of the nominal and real interest rate explains the smoother adjustment paths of both variables, as well as the quantitatively smaller but longer-lasting impact of the shock.

2.3.2. Technology unit shock

A technology unit shock is modelled as an upward blip of 1 percent in the shock term ε_{A_t} in the AR(1) process $A_t = \rho_A A_{t-1} + \varepsilon_{A_t}$ that enters the real marginal cost condition (3.33). Figure 4.8 reports impulse responses to a technology unit shock for the model specification with sticky prices and wages, endogenous capital and adjustment costs.

Variable deviations, caused by a technology unit shock, are generally of a much smaller magnitude that those occurring as a result of a monetary policy unit shock and in each case of a lower value than the shock itself. Adjustment to the steady-state values of all variables (except for real marginal cost) is longer-lasting than in the case of a monetary shock. An interesting result differing from the cases without interest-rate smoothing is the fact that the impact on investment, the output gap and consumption does not unfold immediately after the occurrence of the technology shock. Instead, the largest deviations from steady state are registered only after 2 quarters. The strongest deviations are reported for real marginal cost, investment and the real wage.

The initial transmission of the shock occurs through the immediate effect on real marginal cost. A large negative spike of almost 0.9 percent is observed immediately after the shock, followed by a gradual return to the steady-state level within the next 20 quarters. This negative initial impulse is then transmitted to inflation as evident from (3.36). As a result of the inflation differential, the nominal interest rate is reduced in accordance with the policy rule (3.38), but the response is more gradual. The largest decrease in the nominal interest rate is registered after 3 quarters and is 0.09 times as large as the shock, followed by oscillatory convergence to the steady-state value within more than 60 quarters. The initial positive blip of the real interest rate in the first quarter is explained by the immediate sharp decrease in inflation (and expected inflation) and the initially quantitatively smaller decrease in the nominal rate. After that, the nominal interest rate effect prevails and path of the real interest rate mimics on a smaller scale that of the nominal interest rate.

Investment, consumption, the output gap, capital and the marginal product of capital all reveal an initial positive response to the technology shock, followed by a countervailing negative deviation of a comparatively smaller magnitude before their steady-state values are reached. The strongest deviations in consumption, the output gap and the marginal product of capital all occur within the first four quarters, while it takes about 12 quarters until the maximum impact of the shock on capital unfolds. The technology shock is again channelled to consumption and investment through its impact on the real interest rate. The maximum response of investment (0.5 times the shock) is significantly stronger than that of consumption and consumption (0.08 times the shock). The output gap responds by a positive blip of about 0.17 times the size of the technology shock.

The maximum positive response of capital (approximately 0.08 times the size of the shock) is significantly smaller than the strongest increase in investment. In addition, the deviations in investment are channelled with a time lag to the dynamics of capital. It takes the capital stock a whole 12 quarters until it reaches its highest positive deviation. Once again, capital is also characterised by a longer-lasting adjustment to its steady-state level than investment- even after 60 quarters, capital remains under its steady-state level.

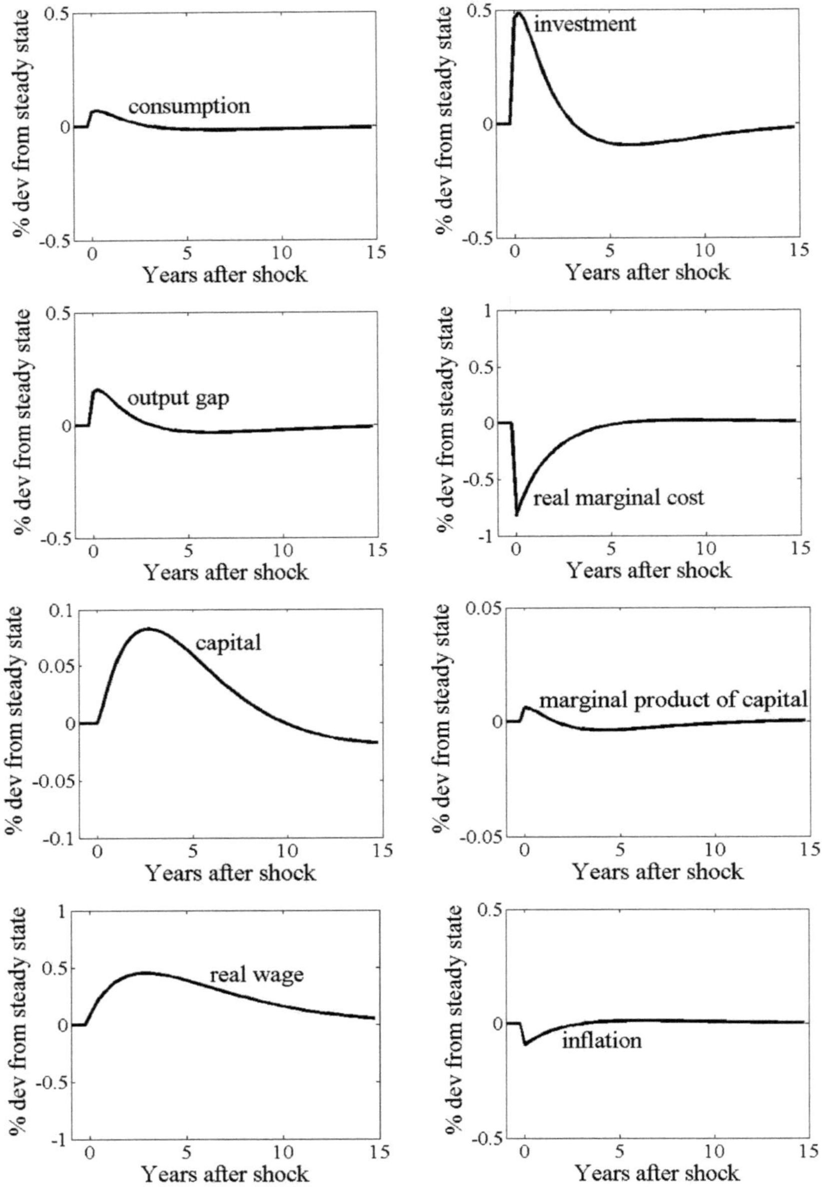

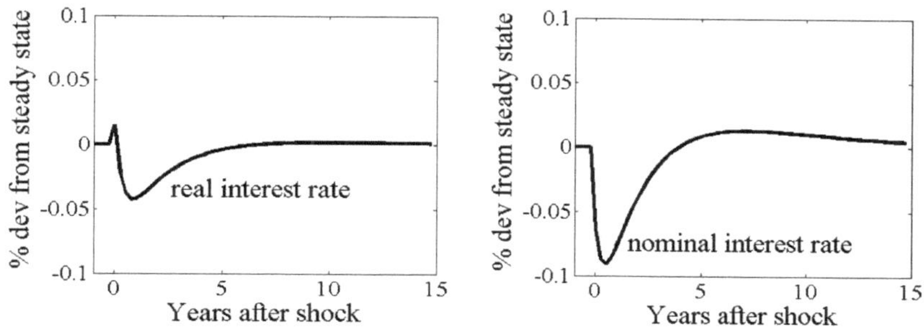

Figure 4.8: Responses to a technology unit shock
under an active rule with inflation- and output-targeting and interest-rate smoothing

In comparison to the response of capital and the output gap the magnitude of the deviation of the marginal product of capital in both directions is again quite modest, due to the inclusion of steady-state unit and marginal adjustment costs. Both the sluggish adjustment of marginal product of capital over 40 quarters and the undershooting path registered after the eight quarter following the shock can be traced back to the different adjustment dynamics of capital and output gap discussed above. Finally, the real wage reaches a maximum positive deviation from steady state of 0.45 times the shock after 12 quarters and converges monotonically to its steady-state value thereafter. The response is initially triggered by the inflation differential and then sustained by the dynamics of inflation expectations and the history-dependence on own past realisations of the real wage.

In conclusion, the analysis of the impact of a technology unit shock in a model with sticky prices and wages, endogenous capital and adjustment costs shows that the long-lasting deviations from steady-state values concern numerous model variables (the capital stock, real wage, inflation, the nominal interest rate and investment) that take more than 60 quarters to converge. Compared to the impact of a monetary policy shock convergence to the steady-state values generally appears to be a longer-lasting process. For all variables the magnitude of the observed deviations is relatively smaller than in the case of a monetary policy unit shock. A monetary policy unit shock under a Taylor rule with interest-rate smoothing generates the largest initial deviations in consumption, investment and the output gap of all active rule specifications considered. The largest negative response of the nominal interest rate is more modest here than in the two cases without interest-rate smoothing and, after the first quarter is quantitatively not sufficient to offset a pro-cyclical fall in the real interest rate.

2.3.3. Consumption preference unit shock

A consumption preference unit shock is modelled as an upward blip of 1 percent in the shock term ε_{υ_t} in the AR(1) process $\upsilon_t = \rho_\upsilon \upsilon_{t-1} + \varepsilon_{\upsilon_t}$ that enters the consumption equation (3.25). Figure 4.9 reports impulse responses to a consumption preference unit shock for the model specification with sticky prices and wages, endogenous capital and adjustment costs.

Variable deviations, caused by a consumption preference unit shock, are again of a very small magnitude and in each case of a much lower value than the shock itself. Moreover, in the case of a preference shock is that the adjustment to the steady-state values for all variables occurs much faster than in the case of a technology or a monetary policy shock. Within approximately 16 quarters after the initial impulse all variables apart from capital, the real wage and the marginal product of capital have returned to their steady-state values. The strongest deviations as a result of the shock are reported for consumption, investment and the output gap.

The initial transmission of the shock occurs through the immediate effect on consumption as in (3.25). A positive blip of 0.17 percent is observed immediately after the shock, followed by a fast return to the steady-state level within the first 4 quarters. Through its effect on consumption, the preference shock is channelled to the output gap (see equation (3.26)) which also reports a sharp rise by 0.09 percent, followed by a rapid convergence to steady state.

As a result of the positive output gap, the nominal interest rate is increased in accordance with the policy rule (3.38), but the response is of a smaller magnitude (0.004 times the shock at its peak). After the first quarter, the nominal interest rate is gradually decreased and reaches its steady-state value in the fourteenth quarter. Because of the negligibly small impact of the shock on inflation, the path of the real interest rate mimics that of the nominal interest rate.

The rise in the real interest rate releases an initial fall in investment of 0.2 times the shock, followed by a monotonic adjustment within 8 quarters. Capital initially responds to the negative blip in investment by a gradual decrease, reaching a maximum negative deviation from its steady-state level 8 quarters after the shock. After that, the negative dynamics is reversed and capital converges to steady state after approximately 60 quarters. The deviations of capital and the output gap from steady state determine the responses of marginal product of capital and real marginal cost respectively. Due to the combined impact of the output gap and the capital fluctuations, the maximum response of marginal product of capital (0.004 times the shock) is stronger than that of capital. The response in real marginal cost shows an initial positive spike of almost 0.5 times the shock.

The positive initial effect on real marginal cost is transmitted to inflation as evident from (3.36), whereby the maximum impact on inflation occurs immediately after the shock and is quantitatively small (an increase of 0.001 percent). The impulse disappears in 12 quarters. Finally, as in (3.37) the real wage response takes about 12 quarters to reach its highest negative deviation of 0.003

times the shock. This negative deviation persists until about 60 quarters after the initial impulse.

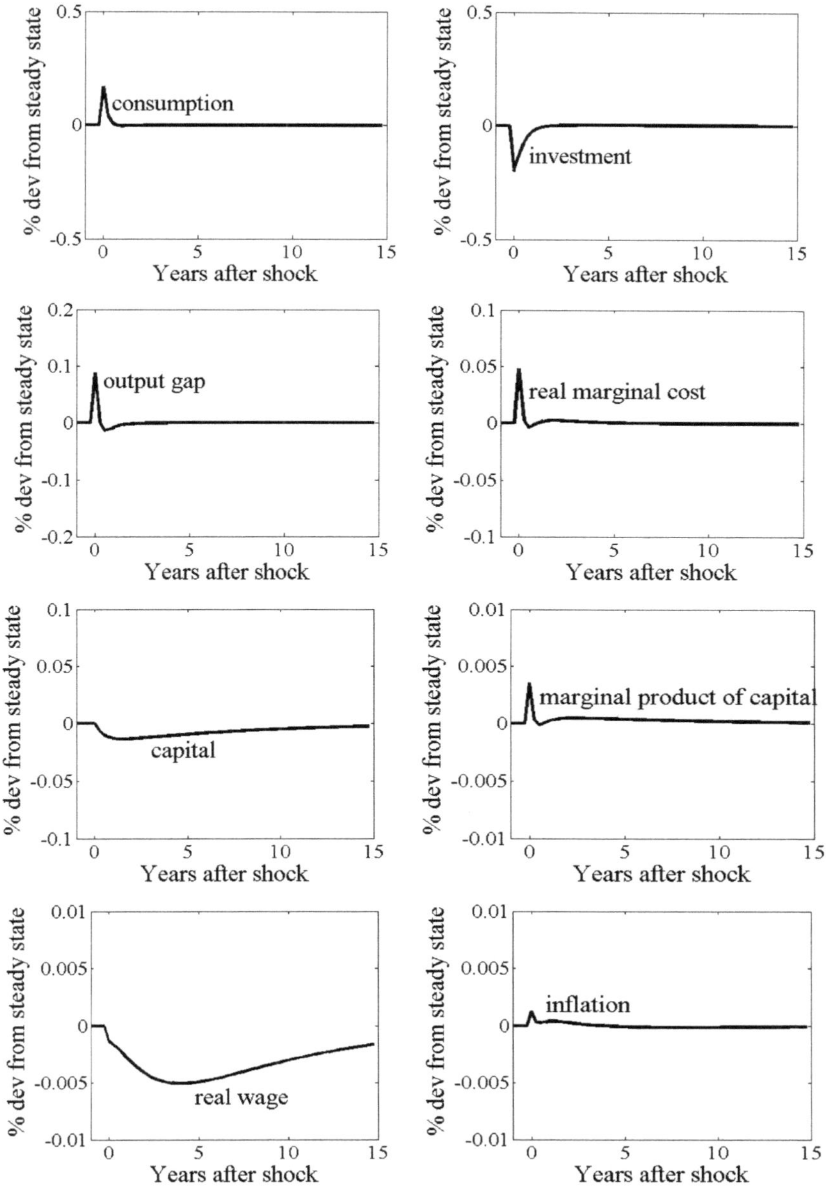

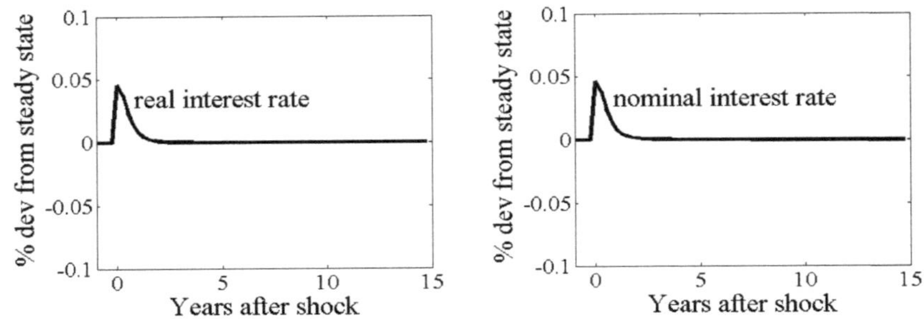

Figure 4.9: Responses to a consumption preference unit shock under an active rule with inflation- and output-targeting and interest-rate smoothing

In conclusion, a consumption preference unit shock has quantitatively a relatively modest effect on the model variables. Its initial impact on consumption, the output gap and investment is alleviated by the increase in the real interest rate (caused by the nominal interest rate hike). The moderate responses of all other variables are determined by the magnitude of the deviations in the two latter variables in particular. The results for a consumption preference unit shock for a Taylor rule with interest-rate smoothing are comparable to these under a baseline Taylor specification. The major difference pertains to the more moderate and gradual responses of the nominal and real interest rate. The induced negative deviation in investment is stronger than under a baseline Taylor rule; thus, the positive output gap impulse is smaller under interest-rate smoothing and the monetary policy stance acts stabilising.

3. Passive rule

3.1. The case of inflation-targeting only

As it is evident from the determinacy analysis in Chapter III, Subsection 4.2.3, an interest-rate rule with $\lambda_\pi^* < 1$ and $\lambda_y^* = 0$ does not yield determinacy of rational-expectations equilibrium for any value of the inflation coefficient under unity. Thus, the impulse response of each variable under a passive rule with a sole inflation target would reveal one adjustment path among several possible, generated by picking the smallest eigenvalue of the system within the unit circle. Still, alternative scenarios cannot be ruled out and therefore no reliable shock analysis can be carried out.

3.2. The case of inflation- and output-targeting

This subsection shows the impulse responses of $\widehat{c}_t$, $\widehat{inv}_t$, $\widehat{y}_t$, $\widehat{rmc}_t$, $\widehat{k}_t$, $\widehat{mpk}_t$, $\widehat{\omega}_t$, π_t, r_t and i_t as for three shocks: the random component of monetary policy ε_{i_t}, the technology shock ε_{A_t} and the preference shock ε_{υ_t}. Monetary policy is defined in terms of a passive Taylor rule with inflation and output coefficients both equal to 0.5[128].

3.2.1. Monetary policy unit shock

Figure 4.10 reports impulse responses to a monetary policy unit shock (an upward blip of 1 percent in the shock term ε_{i_t} in the policy rule (3.38) for the model specification with sticky prices and wages, endogenous capital and adjustment costs.

The variable responses to a monetary policy unit shock under a passive rule with inflation- and output-targeting do not differ substantially from the results under a baseline active Taylor rule. Compared with the case of a passive rule with a sole inflation target, more moderate negative spikes are observed in investment, consumption and the output gap immediately after the shock, followed by a gradual return to the steady-state level. Investment response reports by the sharpest fall (twice the shock). Compared to investment, consumption shows a more moderate response (0.25) and a faster adjustment to its steady-state value. As a weighted average of consumption and investment, the immediate response of the output gap has an intermediate value of about -0.7 times the size of the monetary policy shock. It takes both consumption and the output gap approximately 6 quarters until the effect of the monetary policy unit shock subsides completely.

The maximum negative response of capital (approximately 0.1 times the size of the shock) is significantly smaller than the initial fall in investment. Contrary to the immediate impact of the shock on investment, it takes about 6 quarters until capital reaches its maximum negative response. As a predetermined variable, capital is also characterised by a longer-lasting adjustment to its steady-state level than investment- even after 60 quarters, capital remains under its steady-state level.

Again, in comparison to the relatively strong response of capital and the output gap the magnitude of the deviation of the marginal product of capital (-0.03 times the shock at its minimum) is relatively weak. Both the sluggish adjustment of marginal product of capital over almost 60 quarters and the overshooting path registered after the forth quarter following the shock can be traced back to the different adjustment dynamics of capital and output gap discussed above. The sluggish adjustment of the real wage is determined by the partial history-dependence of the variable as seen from (3.37) and by the assumption of sticky wages.

---

128 For the values originally proposed by Casares and McCallum (2006), the effective response coefficient assigned to the output gap in (3.39) is so small that no significant difference to the case with a sole inflation target can be observed. The reason for choosing $\lambda_y = \lambda_y^* = 0.5$ is the fact that, as shown in Chapter III, Subsection 4.2.3, the coefficient values $\lambda_\pi^* = \lambda_y^* = 0.5$ yield a determinate rational-expectations equilibrium.

The responses of capital, the output gap and real wage determine the dynamics of real marginal cost, as evident from equation (3.33). Compared to the output gap dynamics, the path of real marginal cost reaches a more moderate peak negative value (0.4 times the shock), but does not adjust monotonically to its steady-state value. Instead, 4 quarters after the shock real marginal cost slightly overshoots the steady-state value; thereafter, it converges monotonically to the steady—state level. While the initial negative impulse to the real marginal cost is mainly a result of the sharp immediate decline of the output gap after the shock, the overshooting part is essentially explained by the slow and lasting response of capital and the real wage.

A monetary policy unit shock has a quantitatively small and non-persistent impact on inflation, transmitted by the real marginal cost. The initial negative blip in inflation is less than 0.01 times the shock. In addition, until the effect subsides completely after 16 quarters, the path of inflation reveals overshooting dynamics before steady-state value is reached 16 quarters after the initial impulse.

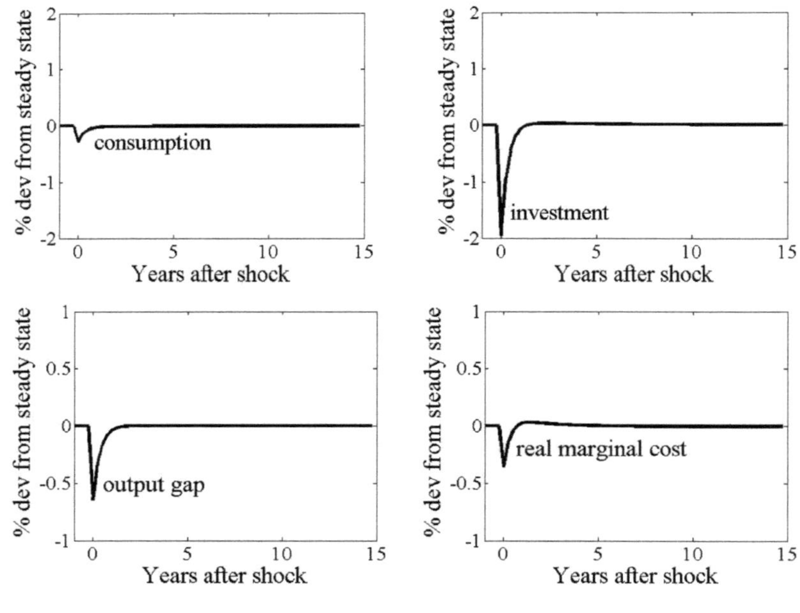

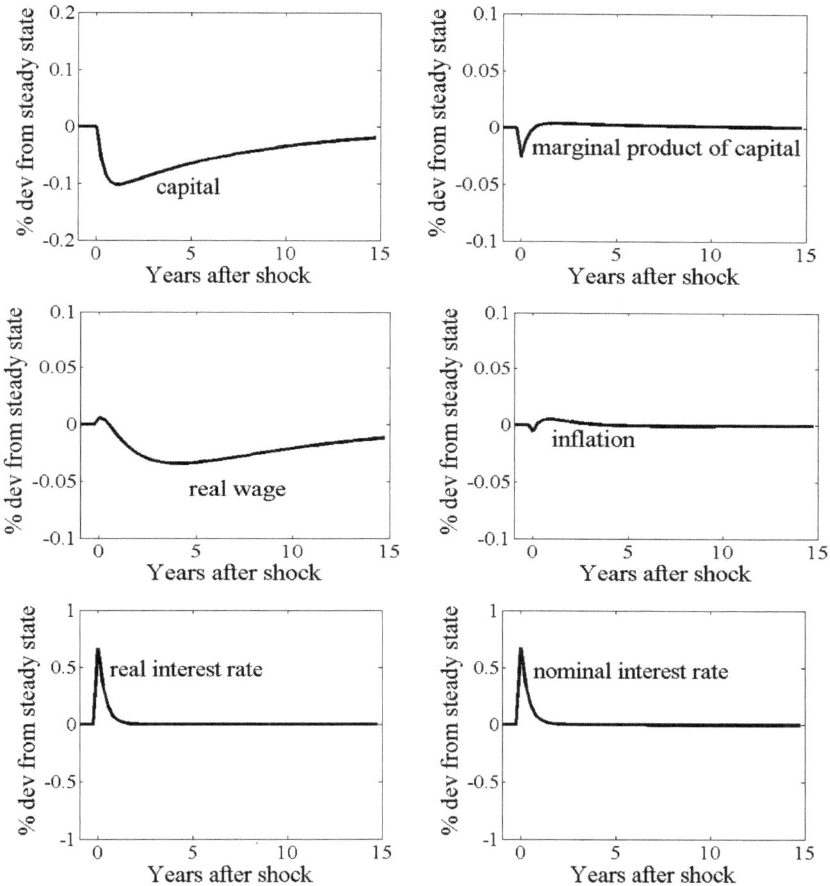

Figure 4.10: Responses to a monetary policy unit shock under a passive rule with inflation- and output-targeting

The nominal interest rate adjustment is triggered the unit shock itself, as well as the responses of the target variables (inflation differential and output gap). The monetary authority's reaction to the unit shock involves an increase in the nominal interest rate of 0.7 times the shock in the first quarter, followed by a gradual convergence to the steady-state level within the next 7 quarters. The Fisher equation $r_t = i_t - E_t\pi_{t+1}$ postulates that the dynamics of the real interest rate is approximated by the difference between the paths of inflation and the nominal interest rate. The real interest rate response (a positive blip with a maximum value of 0.7 times the shock, followed by a monotonic decrease) matches the nominal interest rate dynamics.

In conclusion, the analysis of the impact of a monetary policy unit shock in a model with sticky prices and wages, endogenous capital and adjustment costs shows that the only long-lasting deviations from steady-state values concern the capital stock and the real wage, which take more than 60 quarters to converge. Consumption, the output gap, inflation, the real and the nominal interest rate, on the other hand, all return to their steady-state values within approximately 20 quarters. These results are consistent with the ones under a baseline active Taylor rule.

3.2.2. Technology unit shock

Figure 4.11 reports impulse responses to a technology unit shock (an upward blip of 1 percent in the shock term ε_{A_t} in the AR(1) process $A_t = \rho_A A_{t-1} + \varepsilon_{A_t}$ that enters the real marginal cost condition (3.33) for the model specification with sticky prices and wages, endogenous capital and adjustment costs.

Variable deviations, caused by a technology unit shock, are, with the exception of the real marginal cost, real wage and inflation responses, of a much smaller magnitude that those occurring as a result of a monetary policy unit shock and in each case of a lower value than the shock itself. Moreover, adjustment to the steady-state values of nearly all variables (except capital and the real wage) is more sluggish in the case of a technology shock than under a monetary policy shock.. The strongest deviations are reported for real marginal cost, real wage, investment and inflation.

The initial transmission of the shock occurs through the immediate effect on real marginal cost. A large negative spike of almost 0.9 times the shock is registered immediately after the shock, followed by a gradual return to the steady-state level within the next 60 quarters. This negative initial impulse is then transmitted to inflation as evident from (3.36). The assumption of sticky prices determines the negative, but relatively modest (0.1 times the shock) deviation of inflation from steady state. As a result of the increased inflation differential, the nominal interest rate is reduced in accordance with the policy rule (3.38), initially by slightly over 0.06 times the shock. The initial positive blip in the real interest rate is explained by the initial decrease in expected inflation in (3.36) that in the first 4 quarters quantitatively exceeds the negative effect on the nominal interest rate. Thus, in accordance with the Fisher equation $r_t = i_t - E_t\pi_{t+1}$, the real interest rate reports initially a positive deviation from steady state of almost 0.02.

Investment, consumption, the output gap, capital and the marginal product of capital all reveal an initial negative response to the technology shock, followed by a countervailing positive deviation of a comparatively smaller magnitude before their steady-state values are reached. The strongest deviations in consumption, the output gap and the marginal product of capital all occur within the first eight quarters. The technology shock is channelled to consumption and investment through its impact on the real interest rate; the maximum responses of investment (0.1 times the shock) is much larger than that of consumption (0.01 times the shock). The immediate response of the output gap reaches a fall of about -0.03 times the size of the technology shock at its negative peak. As far as capital is concerned, an initial decline of 0.01 times the shock is followed by a longer-lasting positive deviation of a comparable maximum value.

As a result of the labour-augmenting technology shock, the real wage reaches a quantitatively significant[129] maximum positive deviation from steady state of 0.45 times the shock after 12 quarters and converges monotonically to its steady-state value thereafter. The response is initially triggered by the inflation differential and then sustained by the dynamics of inflation expectations and the history-dependence on own past realisations of the real wage.

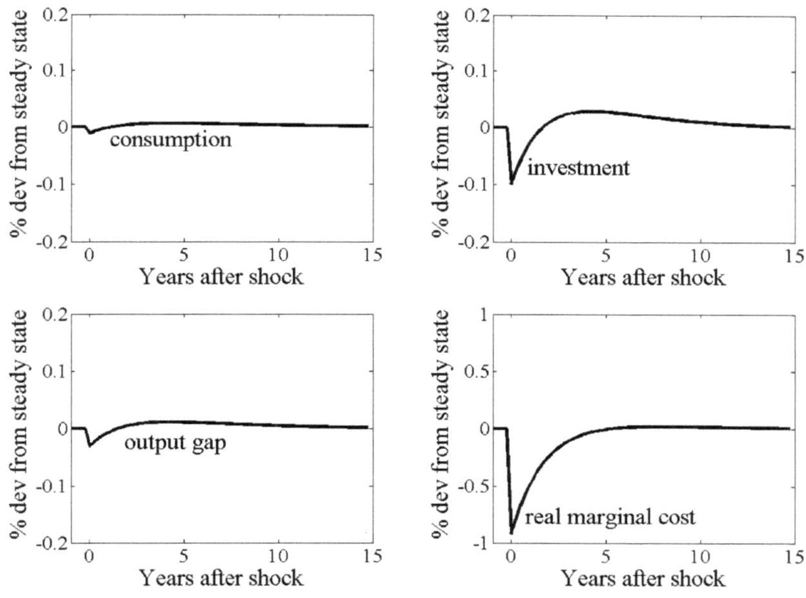

129 The magnitude of the impulse response of real wage is significant especially compared to the magnitude of the responses of the other model variables.

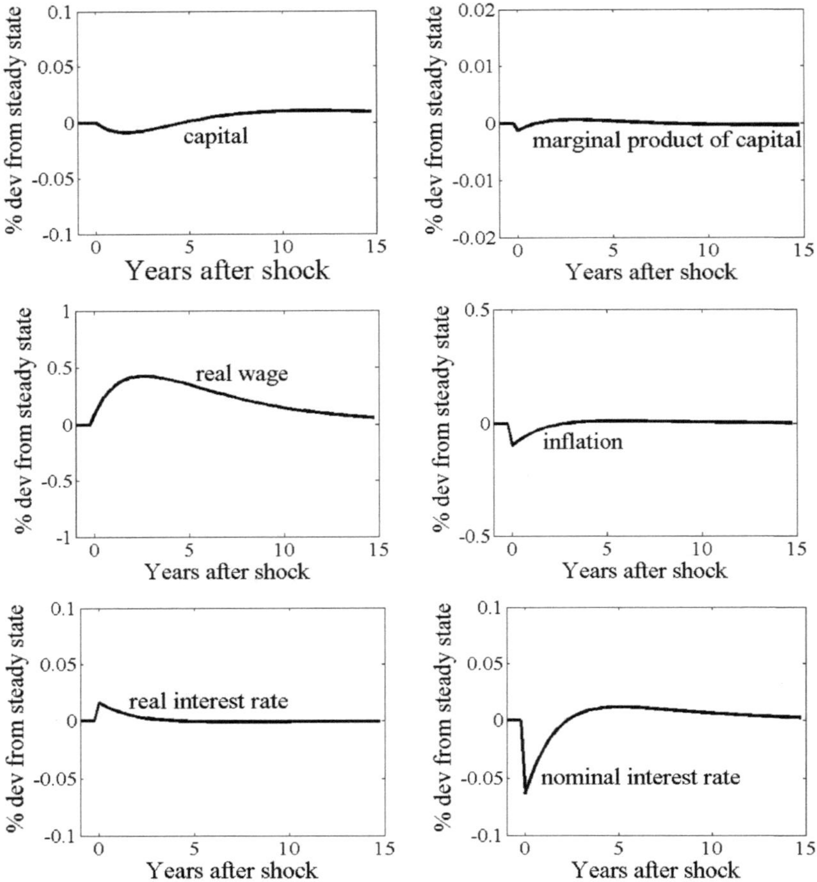

Figure 4.11: Responses to a technology unit shock under a passive rule with inflation- and output-targeting

In conclusion, the analysis of the impact of a technology unit shock in a model with sticky prices and wages, endogenous capital and adjustment costs shows that the only long-lasting deviations from steady-state values concern the capital stock and the real wage that take more than 60 quarters to converge. Compared to the impact of a monetary policy shock convergence to the steady-state values generally appears to be a longer-lasting process. For most variables the magnitude of the observed deviations is relatively smaller than in the case of a monetary policy unit shock. In comparison to the active specification with an inflation and an output gap target, here the technology unit shock has a milder impact as it induces more moderate nominal interest rate cuts as a reaction to the decrease in inflation that cannot offset the latter and thus generate a rise in the real interest rate. Through the real-interest-rate channel investment, consumption and the output gap report negative deviations significantly smaller than the size of the shock.

3.2.3. Consumption preference unit shock

Figure 4.12 reports impulse responses to a consumption preference unit shock (an upward blip of 1 percent in the shock term ε_{υ_t} in the AR(1) process $\upsilon_t = \rho_\upsilon \upsilon_{t-1} + \varepsilon_{\upsilon_t}$ that enters the consumption equation (3.25) for the model specification with sticky prices and wages, endogenous capital and adjustment costs.

The results for a consumption preference unit shock under a passive specification with inflation- and output-targeting do not differ significantly from the findings under a baseline active Taylor rule. Variable deviations are of a very small magnitude and in each case of a much lower value than the shock itself. The adjustment to the steady-state values for all variables occurs much faster than in the case of a technology or a monetary policy shock. Within approximately four quarters after the initial impulse most variables apart from capital and the real wage have returned to their steady-state values. The strongest deviations as a result of the shock are reported for consumption, investment and the output gap.

The initial transmission of the shock occurs through the immediate effect on consumption as in (3.25). A positive blip of almost 0.2 times the shock is observed immediately after the shock, followed by a fast return to the steady-state level within the first 4 quarters. Through its effect on consumption, the preference shock is channelled to the output gap (see equation (3.26) which also reports a sharp rise by 0.12 percent, followed by a rapid convergence to steady state.

As a result of the positive output gap, the nominal interest rate is increased in accordance with the policy rule (3.38) and the response is 0.06 the shock at its peak. After the first quarter, the nominal interest rate is gradually decreased and reaches its steady-state value in the forth quarter

The path of the real interest rate mimics that of the nominal interest rate. The rise in the real interest rate releases an initial fall in investment of 0.12 times the shock, followed by a monotonic adjustment within 4 quarters. Capital initially responds to the negative blip in investment by a gradual decrease, reaching a maximum quantitatively small negative deviation from its steady-state level 4 quarters after the shock. After that, the negative dynamics is reversed and capital converges to steady state after more than 60 quarters. The deviations of capital and the output gap from steady state, entering the term $(\widehat{y}_t - \widehat{k}_t)$ in equations (3.34) and (3.33) determine the responses of marginal product of capital and real marginal cost respectively. Due to the combined impact of the output gap and the capital fluctuations, the maximum response of marginal product of capital (0.005 times the shock) is equal in absolute value to that of capital. The response in real marginal cost shows a similar path – an initial positive spike of 0.06 times the shock, followed by a gradual convergence to steady state within the first 4 quarters.

The positive initial effect on real marginal cost is transmitted to inflation as evident from (3.36), whereby the maximum impact on inflation occurs immediately after the shock and is quantitatively small (an increase of 0.002 times the shock). The impulse disappears in less than 4 quarters. Finally, as in (3.37) the real wage response is driven by the positive inflation differential and then sustained by the dynamics of inflation expectations and the history-dependence on own past realisations of the real wage. Unlike inflation, the real wage takes about 2 quarters to reach its highest negative deviation of 0.002 times the shock. This negative deviation persists until about 60 quarters after the initial impulse.

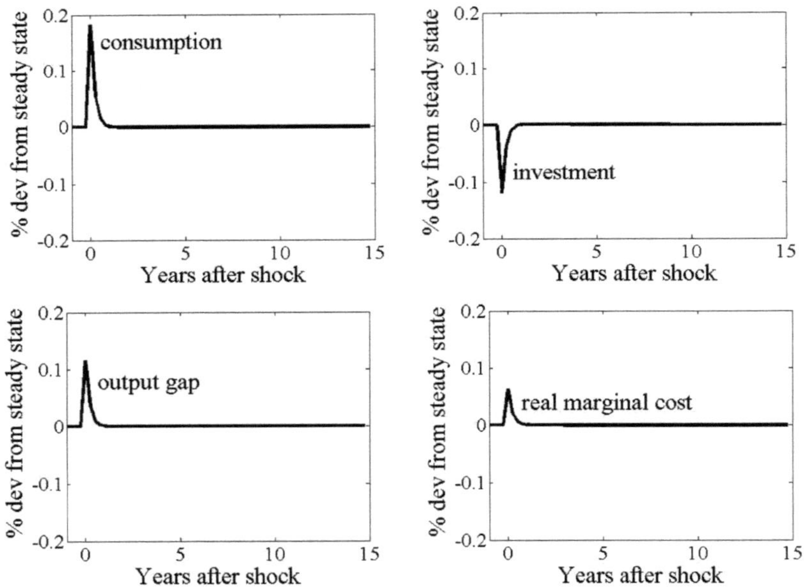

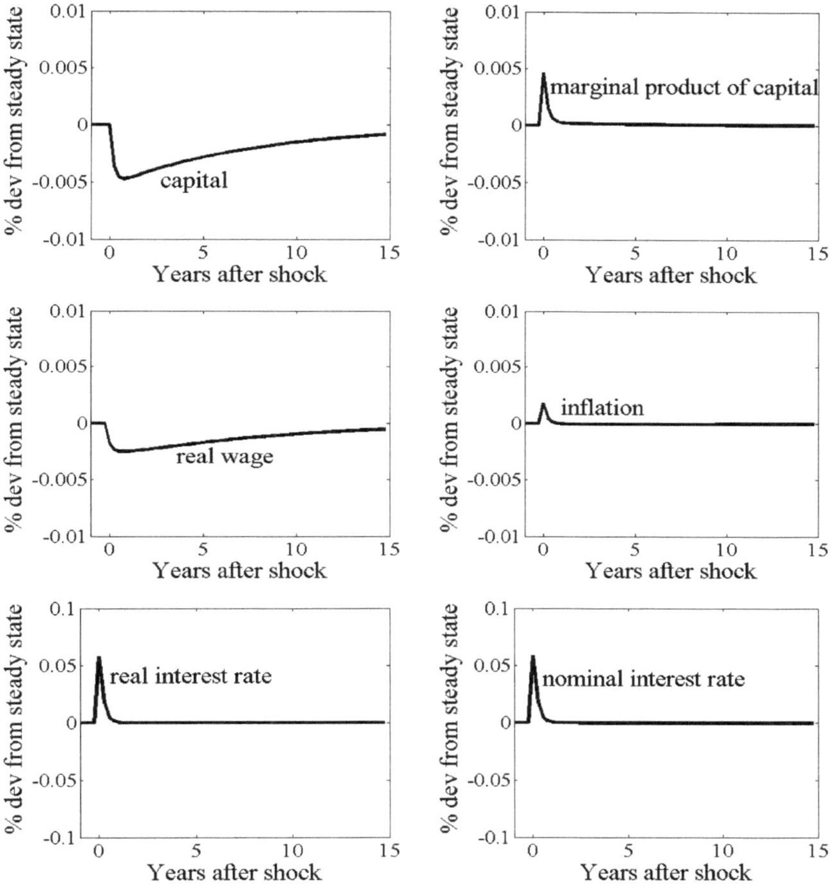

Figure 4.12: Responses to a consumption preference unit shock
under a passive rule with inflation- and output-targeting

In conclusion, a consumption preference unit shock has quantitatively a relatively modest effect on the model variables. Its initial impact on consumption, the output gap and investment is alleviated by the increase in the real interest rate (caused by the nominal interest rate hike). The moderate responses of all other variables are determined by the magnitude of the deviations in the two latter variables in particular.

3.3. The case of inflation- and output-targeting with interest-rate smoothing

The impulse responses in this subsection are calculated based on a passive Taylor rule with inflation and output coefficients both equal to 0.5[130] and interest-rate smoothing, whereby the lagged interest rate coefficient is equal to 0.8 as proposed by Casares and McCallum (2006).

3.3.1. Monetary policy unit shock

Figure 4.13 reports impulse responses to a monetary policy unit shock (an upward blip of 1 percent in the shock term ε_{i_t} in the policy rule (3.38) for the model specification with sticky prices and wages, endogenous capital and adjustment costs.

The results under a monetary policy shock do not differ from these with a passive rule and inflation-targeting only. Negative spikes in investment, consumption and the output gap are observed immediately after the shock, followed by a gradual return to the steady-state level. Investment response is characterised by the sharpest fall (3 times as large as the shock) and gradual adjustment within 32 quarters. Compared to investment, consumption shows a more moderate response (0.5 times the shock) and a faster adjustment to its steady-state value. Since according to equation (3.26) the output gap is a weighted average of consumption and investment, its immediate response has an intermediate value approximately as large as the monetary policy shock. It takes both consumption and the output gap approximately 8 quarters until the effect of the monetary policy unit shock subsides completely. The paths of consumption, investment and output gap plotted on Figure 4.13 reveal the significance of the endogenous capital assumption for the model's quantitative results. Under constant capital, the output gap response to a monetary policy unit shock would still be negative, but of a considerably smaller magnitude, as it would only incorporate the fall in consumption.

The maximum negative response of capital (approximately 0.15 times the size of the shock) is significantly smaller than the initial fall in investment. Contrary to the immediate impact of the shock on investment, it takes 5 quarters until capital reaches its maximum negative response. Moreover, capital is also characterised by a longer-lasting adjustment to its steady-state level than investment- even after 60 quarters, capital remains under its steady-state level.

In comparison to the relatively strong response of capital and the output gap the magnitude of the deviation of the marginal product of capital (-0.04 times the shock at its minimum) might at first seem worth further consideration. Algebraically this is determined by the relatively small value of the steady-state mar-

130 At the end of this subsection, the results under the values originally proposed by McCallum and Casares (2006) for (3.39) are shown.

ginal product of capital (0.04) that enters equation (3.34) as a coefficient, implying a relatively weaker response of marginal product of capital to deviations in output and capital. The sluggish adjustment of the real wage is determined by the partial history-dependence of the variable as seen from (3.37) and by the assumption of sticky wages. The latter is modelled by the inclusion of a fixed probability η_W ($\eta_W = 0.75$) that nominal wages cannot be adjusted in the current quarter, which implies that on average wages are re-set once a year.

The responses of capital, the output gap and real wage determine the dynamics of real marginal cost, as evident from equation (3.33). Compared to the output gap dynamics, the path of real marginal cost reaches a more moderate maximum negative value (0.5 times the shock), but does not adjust monotonically to its steady-state value. Instead, 4 quarters after the shock real marginal cost overshoots the steady-state value; thereafter, real marginal cost converges monotonically to the steady—state level. While the initial negative impulse to real marginal cost is mainly a result of the sharp immediate decline of the output gap after the shock, the overshooting part is essentially explained by the slow and lasting response of capital and the real wage.

A monetary policy unit shock has a quantitatively small and non-persistent impact on inflation. As evident from equation (3.36), the monetary impulse is transmitted by real marginal cost. Under sticky prices, despite the strong response of real marginal cost to the shock, inflation remains hardly affected, as the value of the fixed probability that households cannot adjust their price $\eta_P = 0.75$ (i.e. prices adjusted once a year on average) implies that the real marginal cost coefficient $(1-\beta\eta_P)(1-\eta_P)(1-\alpha_{PF})/\eta_P(1-\alpha_{PF}+\alpha_{PF}\theta)$ equals 0.02. Thus, the initial negative blip in inflation is less than 0.01 the shock. Until the effect subsides completely after 16 quarters, the path of inflation involves overshooting dynamics before steady-state value is reached.

As far as the nominal interest rate is concerned, according to the policy rule (3.38) its deviation depends on the unit shock itself, the responses of the target variables (inflation differential and output gap) and the past deviation of the variable from its steady-state value. The monetary authority's reaction to the unit shock involves an increase in the nominal interest rate half as large as the shock in the first quarter, followed by a gradual convergence to the steady-state level. The effect of the monetary impulse disappears completely after 8 quarters. The Fisher equation $r_t = i_t - E_t\pi_{t+1}$ postulates that the dynamics of the real interest rate is approximated by the difference between the paths of inflation and the nominal interest rate. Due to the quantitatively weak response of inflation, the real interest rate response (a positive blip with a maximum value half as large as the shock, followed by a monotonic decrease) matches to a great extent the nominal interest rate dynamics.

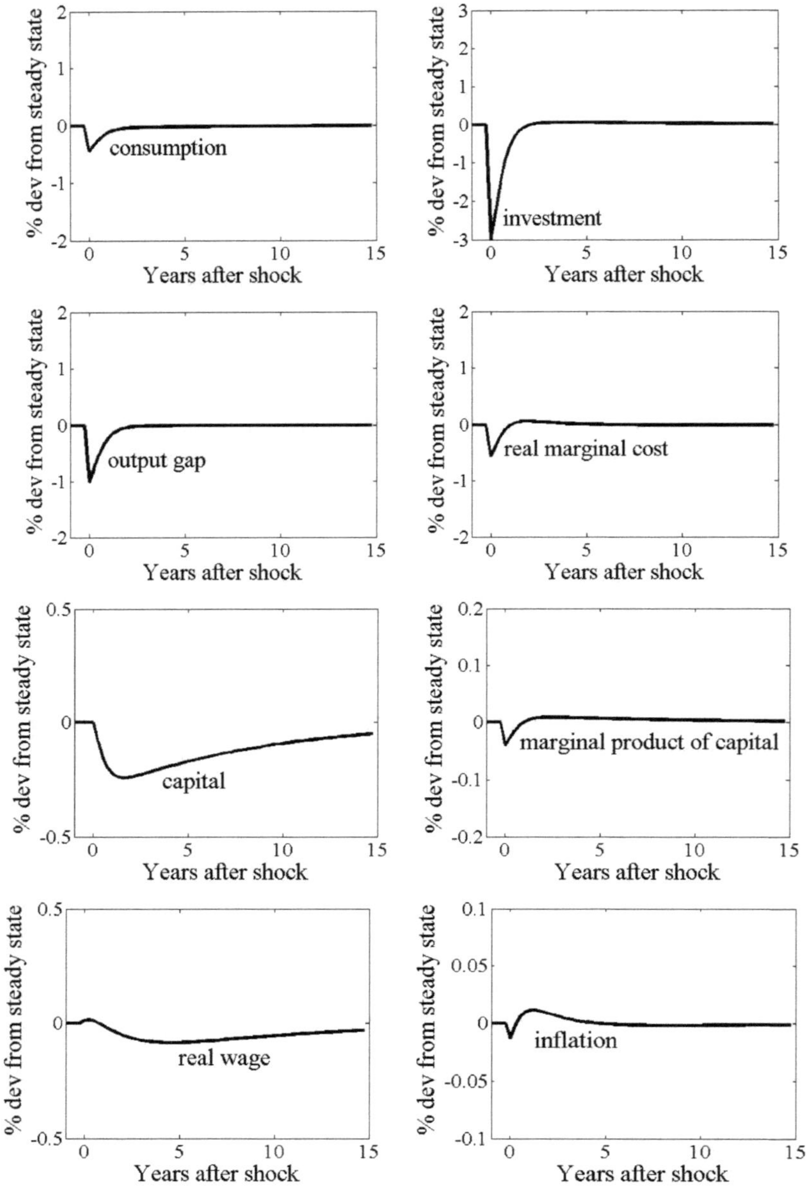
% dev from steady state
consumption
Years after shock
investment
output gap
real marginal cost
capital
marginal product of capital
real wage
inflation
0
5
10
15

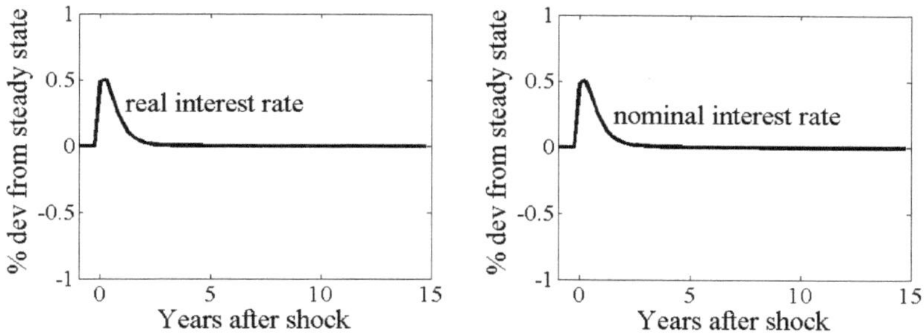

Figure 4.13: Responses to a monetary policy unit shock under a passive rule with inflation- and output-targeting and interest-rate smoothing

In conclusion, the analysis of the impact of a monetary policy unit shock in a model with sticky prices and wages, endogenous capital and adjustment costs shows that the only long-lasting deviation from the steady-state value concern the capital stock, which takes more than 60 quarters to converge. Consumption, the output gap, the real and the nominal interest rate, on the other hand, all return to their steady-state values within 8 quarters. These results basically confirm the long-run monetary neutrality of the model.

3.3.2. Technology unit shock

Figure 4.14 reports impulse responses to a technology unit shock (an upward blip of 1 percent in the shock term ε_{A_t} in the AR(1) process $A_t = \rho_A A_{t-1} + \varepsilon_{A_t}$ that enters the real marginal cost condition (3.33) for the model specification with sticky prices and wages, endogenous capital and adjustment costs.

Variable deviations, caused by a technology unit shock, are generally of a much smaller magnitude that those occurring as a result of a monetary policy unit shock and in each case of a lower value than the shock itself. Another distinction in the case of a technology shock is the slower adjustment to the steady-state values of nearly all variables (except real marginal cost and the nominal and real interest rate). The strongest deviations are reported for real marginal cost, real wage and investment. The adjustment paths of near all variables resemble the ones under a passive interest-rate rule and a sole inflation target. Compared to the active specification with interest-rate smoothing, the impulse responses of consumption, investment and the output gap are of a smaller magnitude. Through the moderate nominal interest rate cuts, passive policy generates a rise in the real interest rate that acts in a stabilising manner.

The initial transmission of the shock occurs through the immediate effect on real marginal cost. A large negative spike of almost 0.9 times the shock is registered immediately after the shock, followed by a gradual return to the steady-state level. This negative initial impulse is then transmitted to inflation as evident from (3.36). The assumption of sticky prices determines the negative deviation of 0.09 times the shock of inflation from steady state. As a result of the increased inflation differential, the nominal interest rate is reduced in accordance with the policy rule (3.38), but the response is quantitatively smaller. The initial positive blip in the real interest rate is explained by the initial decrease in expected inflation in (3.36) that in the first 10 quarters quantitatively exceeds the negative effect on the nominal interest rate. Thus, in accordance with the Fisher equation $r_t = i_t - E_t\pi_{t+1}$, the real interest rate reports a positive deviation from steady state.

Investment, consumption, the output gap, capital and the marginal product of capital all reveal an initial positive response to the technology shock. The strongest deviations in consumption, the output gap and the marginal product of capital all occur within the first 8 quarters, while it takes longer until the maximum impact of the shock on capital unfolds. The technology shock is channelled to consumption and investment through its impact on the real interest rate; the considerably differing magnitudes of the maximum responses of investment (0.18 times the shock) and consumption (0.05 times the shock) are again observed. The immediate response of the output gap reaches a maximum value of about 0.08 times the size of the technology shock.

The maximum positive response of capital is significantly smaller than the strongest increase in investment. In addition, the deviations in investment are channelled with a time lag to the dynamics of capital. Once again, capital is also characterised by a longer-lasting adjustment to its steady-state level.

In comparison to the response of capital and the output gap the magnitude of the deviation of the marginal product of capital (about 0.002 times the shock in both directions) is again quite modest, due to the inclusion of steady-state unit and marginal adjustment costs. Both the sluggish adjustment of marginal product of capital over 60 quarters and the undershooting path registered after the twentieth quarter following the shock can be traced back to the different adjustment dynamics of capital and output gap discussed above.

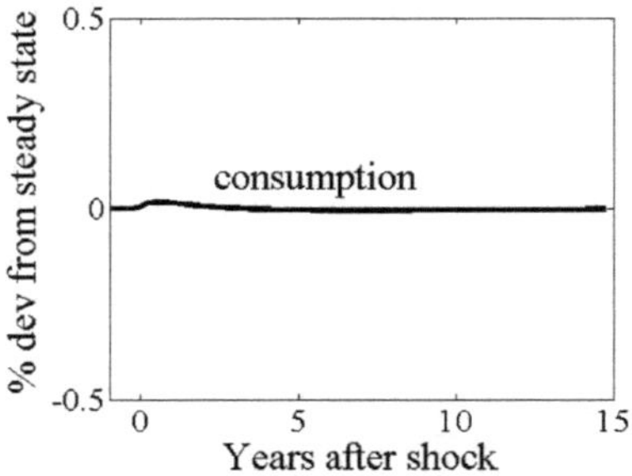

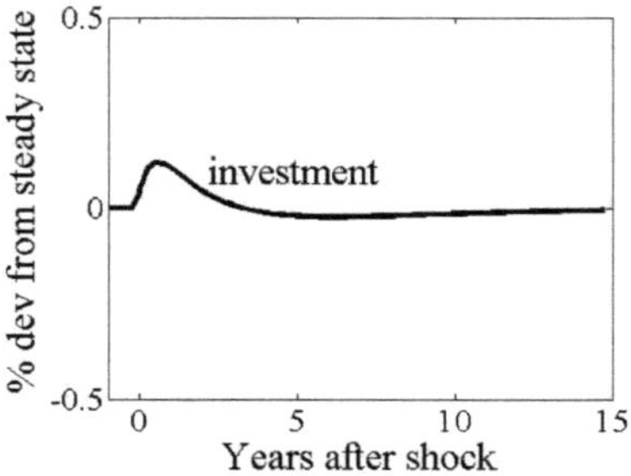

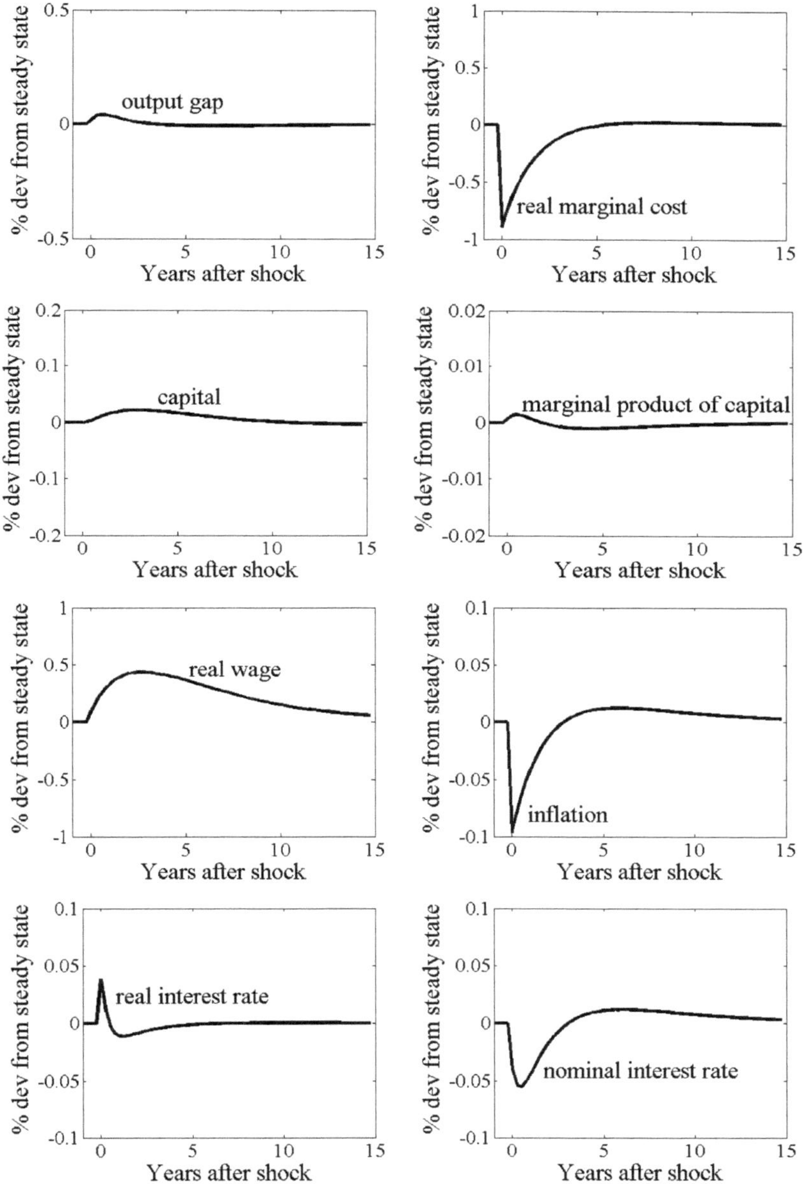

Figure 4.14: Responses to a technology unit shock under a passive rule with inflation- and output-targeting and interest-rate smoothing

Finally, the impulse response of the real wage is worth some consideration. As a result of the labour-augmenting technology shock, the variable reaches a quantitatively significant[131] maximum positive deviation from steady state of 0.4 times the shock after 10 quarters and converges monotonically to its steady-state value thereafter. The response is initially triggered by the inflation differential and then sustained by the dynamics of inflation expectations and the history-dependence on own past realisations of the real wage.

In conclusion, the analysis of the impact of a technology unit shock in a model with sticky prices and wages, endogenous capital and adjustment costs shows that the long-lasting deviations from steady-state values concern the marginal product of capital, inflation and the real wage that take more than 60 quarters to converge. Compared to the impact of a monetary policy shock convergence to the steady-state values generally appears to be a longer-lasting process. For most variables except the real marginal cost, inflation and the real wage the magnitude of the observed deviations is relatively smaller than in the case of a monetary policy unit shock. The reason for the milder impact of a technology unit shock is it induces nominal interest rate cuts as a reaction to the increased inflation differential that quantitatively exceed the latter and thus generate a rise in the real interest rate as well. Through the real-interest-rate channel the positive impulse to investment, consumption and the output gap remains moderate and the variables report positive deviations significantly smaller than the size of the shock.

3.3.3. Consumption preference unit shock

Figure 4.15 reports impulse responses to a consumption preference unit shock (an upward blip of 1 percent in the shock term ε_{υ_t} in the AR(1) process $\upsilon_t = \rho_\upsilon \upsilon_{t-1} + \varepsilon_{\upsilon_t}$ that enters the consumption equation (3.25) for the model specification with sticky prices and wages, endogenous capital and adjustment costs.

Variable deviations, caused by a consumption preference shock, are of a very small magnitude and in each case of a much lower value than the shock itself. Another distinction in the case of a preference shock is that the adjustment to the steady-state values for all variables occurs much faster than in the case of a technology or a monetary policy shock. Within approximately 16 quarters after the initial impulse all variables apart from capital and the real wage have returned to their steady-state values. The strongest deviations as a result of the shock are reported for consumption, the output gap and real marginal cost.

The initial transmission of the shock occurs through the immediate effect on consumption as in (3.25). A positive blip of 0.2 the shock is observed immediately after the shock, followed by a fast return to the steady-state level within the first 4 quarters. Through its effect on consumption, the preference shock is

131 The magnitude of the impulse response of real wage is significant especially compared to the magnitude of the responses of the other model variables.

channelled to the output gap (see equation (3.26) which also reports a sharp rise by 0.1 percent, followed by a rapid convergence to steady state.

As a result of the positive output gap, the nominal interest rate is increased in accordance with the policy rule (3.38), but the response is of a smaller magnitude (0.005 times the shock at its peak). After the first quarter, the nominal interest rate is gradually decreased; the path of the real interest rate mimics that of the nominal interest rate with an initial positive blip of slightly under 0.005.

The rise in the real interest rate releases a positive response of investment, followed by an adjustment within 12 quarters. The impulse to capital is also extremely modest. The deviations of capital and the output gap from steady state determine the responses of marginal product of capital and real marginal cost respectively. Due to the combined impact of the output gap and the capital fluctuations, the maximum response of marginal product of capital (0.004 times the shock) is stronger than that of capital. After the initial positive blip, the marginal product of capital converges to steady state within 6 quarters. The response in real marginal cost shows a similar path – an initial positive spike of 0.06 times the shock, followed by a gradual convergence to steady state within the first 6 quarters.

The positive initial effect on real marginal cost is transmitted to inflation as evident from (3.36), whereby the maximum impact on inflation occurs immediately after the shock and is quantitatively small (an increase of 0.002 times the shock). The impulse disappears in less than 4 quarters. Finally, as in (3.37) the real wage response is driven by the positive inflation differential and then sustained by the dynamics of inflation expectations and the history-dependence on own past realisations of the real wage. Unlike inflation, the real wage takes about 20 quarters to reach its highest negative deviation of 0.005 times the shock. This negative deviation persists for more than 60 quarters after the initial impulse.

In conclusion, a consumption preference unit shock has quantitatively a relatively modest effect on the model variables. Its initial impact on consumption, the output gap and investment is alleviated by the increase in the real interest rate. The moderate responses of all other variables are determined by the magnitude of the deviations in the two latter variables in particular.

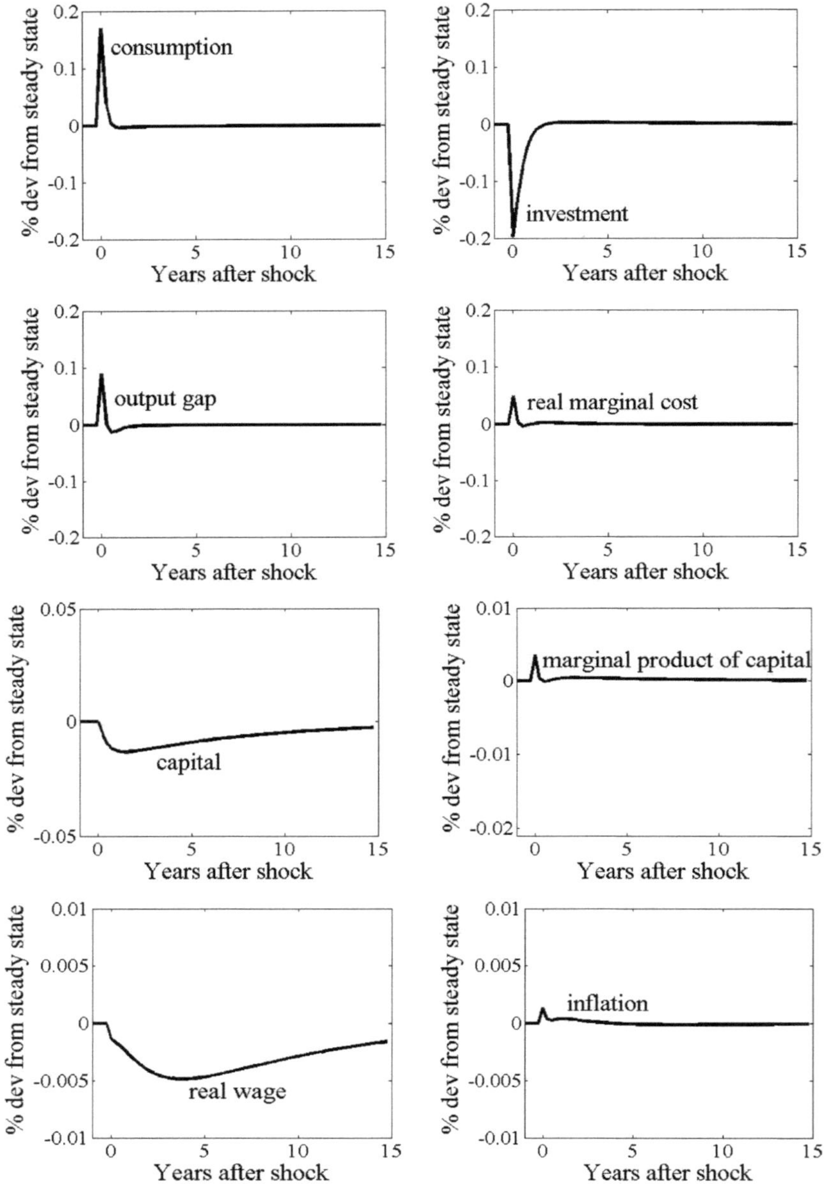
consumption
investment
output gap
real marginal cost
capital
marginal product of capital
real wage
inflation
% dev from steady state
Years after shock

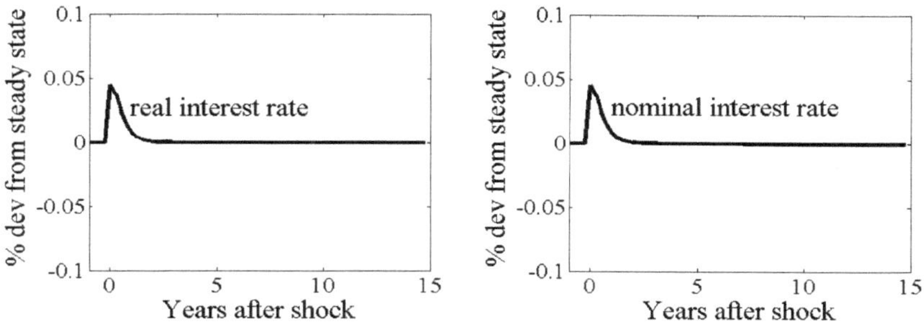

Figure 4.15: Responses to a consumption preference unit shock
under a passive rule with inflation- and output-targeting and interest-rate smoothing

In addition, the impulse responses to a monetary policy unit shock, a technology unit shock and a consumption preference unit shock under the policy rule specification (3.39) with $\lambda_\pi^* = 0.3$, $\lambda_y^* = 0.02$ and $\lambda_i = 0.8$ (as calibrated by Casares and McCallum (2006)) reveal large variable oscillations for all three shocks. This reveals the importance of sufficiently strong responses to inflation and the output gap in the policy rule. These impulse responses are not plotted here, as a "bumpy" convergence path is associated with uncertainty and additional costs in terms of output and thus represents a monetary policy option that should rather be avoided

4. Preliminary summary of results

Using the results from the determinacy analysis in Chapter III, active and passive rules in three possible specifications for each class were tested in this part: (i) rules with a sole inflation target; (ii) rules with an inflation and output target and (iii) rules with inflation and output gap target and interest-rate smoothing. The types of shocks entering the impulse responses are threefold: (i) a monetary policy unit shock; (ii) a technology unit shock and (iii) a consumption preference shock.

There are several important findings resulting from the impulse responses in Sections 2 and 3. Firstly, the distinction between active and passive rules has implications for the sign of the variable deviations, but not for their magnitude or persistence. For instance, a technology unit shock induces a real interest rate decrease under all active rule specifications and the opposite effect under all passive rule specifications[132]. However, the speed and path of the convergence and the maximum deviations from steady state reported differ significantly depending on the choice of target variables, the best performance under all shocks

132 In the case of oscillatory paths the deviations in the direction mentioned above are quantitatively larger than the deviations in the opposite direction.

being reported for the active and passive rule with both an inflation and an output target. As evident from Chapter III, passive policy induces multiple rational-expectations equilibria, so that only the active inflation-targeting rule specification is relevant for monetary policy-making. However, the latter is associated with lengthier and more oscillatory convergence path to steady state, as compared with rules with both an inflation and output gap target.

Secondly, both for active and passive policy, longer-lasting convergence, relatively greater variable deviations and more frequent oscillatory adjustment paths for each shock are reported for the specification with a significant degree of interest-rate smoothing. Thirdly, the sign and exact magnitude of the model variables' responses to a monetary policy unit shock do not differ between the active and the passive specification, as long as identical target variables enter the rule. The responses to a consumption preference unit shock do not differ significantly across the six interest rate rule specifications and therefore offer very limited insights to the analysis.

Lastly, the more significant differences between the active and passive specifications including identical variables are registered in the case of a technology unit shock. This can be traced back to the differing magnitudes of the nominal interest rate responses that induce negative real-interest rate deviations under active policy and positive real-interest rate deviations from steady state under passive policy. Thus, passive policy stance acts stabilising as the technology shock impact is countervailed by the real interest rate increase. By analogy, active policy boosts the shock impulse and contributes to larger deviations of investment, consumption and the output gap. This tendency can be at least partially offset by the introduction of an output target to the policy rule.

V. Discussion and conclusion

Using a model that replicates the structure of the economy as realistically as possible is a crucial prerequisite for delivering practice-relevant policy recommendations. Assuming that the capital stock is constant or inexistent undoubtedly poses significant restrictions on the plausibility of the results obtained. On the other hand, the benefits from the inclusion of endogenous capital and investment depend on the type of the specification chosen. In particular, some degree of inertia in the capital adjustment over time is needed to provide a satisfactory match to empirical business-cycle observations. This study opts for introducing capital adjustment costs as a means to limit the excessive volatility in capital that would have been the case otherwise. However, as seen in Chapter III, Section 2, other solutions to this modelling issue (such as firm-specific capital, for instance) would also be worth some consideration in terms of their policy design implications.

In the foregoing chapters I have based my study on a dynamic optimising IS-LM-type model that incorporates sticky prices and wages, endogenous capital and investment with capital adjustment costs. The framework includes an IS "sector", which allows a more differentiated analysis of the individual aggregate demand components, as well as the impact of their determinants. The main purpose of this work has been to explore different simple interest-rate rule specifications in terms of the target variables included, by applying two criteria: the existence of a determinate rational-expectations equilibrium and the induced variable responses to shocks. Parallel to this analysis, I have presented the Taylor principle (the benchmark criterion for assessing monetary policy rules) and tested whether in the model under standard parameter calibration a more than one-on-one response to inflation (i.e. active policy) is still the only condition needed to ensure determinacy of rational-expectations equilibrium under endogenous capital. The second issue explored has been whether, determinacy notwithstanding, active policy with a sole inflation target actually yields the fastest and least distressful convergence of the economy to the steady-state level under shocks.

The results obtained in Chapters III and IV reveal a very interesting picture. In the first place, in the New Keynesian model with endogenous capital and investment and adjustment costs I use, an inflation response coefficient above unity does not necessarily imply determinacy of rational-expectations equilibrium. For an active rule with inflation-targeting only, adherence to the Taylor principle is a sufficient condition for determinacy of rational-expectations equilibrium only within a small interval of inflation coefficient values, associated with moderately active policy. For all other values, an output gap target is the solution needed to eliminate the indeterminacy problem. Under a passive rule, the equilibrium indeterminacy as implied by the Taylor principle is the case only if inflation is the sole target; the inclusion of an output gap objective alleviates the occurrence of multiple equilibria. Thus, taking into consideration the output gap developments in the economy appears to be crucial for monetary policy design in order to guarantee stable, predictable adjustment path of the economy.

Building upon the insights gained by the determinacy analysis, I then concentrated on assessing the responses to shocks under different specifications of active and passive policy rules (with inflation-targeting only; with inflation and output-targeting; with inflation- and output-gap targeting and interest-rate smoothing). Within both groups of rules, the specification with inflation- and output-targeting was characterised by the best performance in terms of variable deviations and speed and path of the convergence. Thus the results from the determinacy analysis have been complemented by the finding that an output gap target is crucial not only for determinacy of rational-expectations equilibrium, but also for ensuring a less distressful adjustment of the economy after the occurrence of shocks. Both for active and passive policy, introducing a significant degree of interest-rate smoothing appears to be counterproductive, inducing longer-lasting convergence, relatively greater variable deviations and more frequent oscillatory adjustment paths for each shock.

The more significant differences between the active and passive specifications including identical variables are registered in the case of a supply (technological unit) shock. This results from the differing magnitudes of the nominal interest rate responses that induce negative real-interest rate deviations under active policy and positive real-interest rate deviations from steady state under passive policy. Thus, passive policy stance acts stabilising as the technology shock impact is countervailed by the real interest rate increase. By analogy, active policy boosts the shock impulse and contributes to larger deviations of investment, consumption and the output gap. The latter tendency can be at least partially offset by the introduction of an output target to the policy rule.

Appendix: Optimising IS-LM model with endogenous investment and capital adjustment costs

A. Money demand (LM equation)

With respect to money demand, the period utility function (3.22) and equation (3.21) yield

$$m_t = \exp\left[\gamma^{-1}(\varsigma_t - \upsilon_t)\right] c_t^{\frac{\sigma}{\gamma}} \left[\frac{\Upsilon i_t}{(1-\Upsilon)(1+i_t)}\right]^{-\frac{1}{\gamma}}. \tag{A3.1}$$

After approximating $i_t/(1+i_t)$ by i_t, (A3.1) takes the semi-log-linearised form

$$\hat{m}_t = \frac{\sigma}{\gamma}\hat{c}_t - \frac{1}{\gamma \bar{i}}(i_t - \bar{i}_t) + \frac{1}{\gamma}(\varsigma_t - \upsilon_t). \tag{A3.2}$$

In (A3.2), an expression for the composite disturbance $\chi_t = (\varsigma_t - \upsilon_t)/\gamma$ can be substituted to yield the LM equation of the system:

$$\hat{m}_t = \frac{\sigma}{\gamma}\hat{c}_t - \frac{1}{\gamma \bar{i}}(i_t - \bar{i}_t) + \chi_t, \tag{A3.3}$$

where $\chi_t = (\varsigma_t - \upsilon_t)/\gamma$ is the composite disturbance and ς_t and υ_t are real money balances and consumption preference shocks. In (A3.3) real money balances depend positively on a transaction variable (consumption) and negatively on an opportunity-cost variable.

B. Steady-state capital

The first-order condition with capital (3.30) reads

$$1 + r_t = \frac{1 - \delta - E_t C_{t+1} + E_t\left(rmc_{t+1} mpk_{t+1}\right)}{1 + C_t}.$$

After substituting adjustment costs as in (3.29),

$$1 + \rho = \frac{1 - \delta + (1-\delta)\Theta_1(\Theta_2 + 1)\delta^{\Theta_2} + \Theta_1\Theta_2\delta^{\Theta_2+1} + \overline{rmc} * \overline{mpk}}{1 + \Theta_1(\Theta_2 + 1)\delta^{\Theta_2}}, \tag{A3.4}$$

where $\bar{r} = \rho$. After substitution, equation (A3.4) can be transformed into

$$1 + \rho = \frac{1 - \delta + (1 - \delta + \Theta_2)\overline{C} + \overline{rmc} * \overline{mpk}}{1 + \overline{C}_1}, \tag{A3.5}$$

where $\overline{C} = \Theta_1\delta^{\Theta_2}$ is the unit adjustment cost in steady state and $\overline{C}_1 = \Theta_1(\Theta_2 + 1)\delta^{\Theta_2}$ is the marginal adjustment cost in steady state. From (A3.5), the following relation for the marginal product of capital in steady state can be derived:

$$\overline{mpk} = \frac{\rho(1 + \overline{C}_1) + \delta(1 + \overline{C}\,)}{\overline{rmc}}. \tag{A3.6}$$

Capital stock in steady state is then determined by substituting with a Cobb-Douglas technology with steady-state labour of 1 in (A3.6):

$$\alpha_{PF}\overline{k}^{\alpha_{PF}-1} = \frac{\rho(1+\overline{C}_1)+\delta(1+\overline{C}\ )}{\overline{\overline{rmc}}}. \quad \text{(A3.7)}$$

Equation (A3.7) yields the steady-state capital

$$\overline{k} = \left[\frac{\alpha_{PF}\overline{rmc}}{\rho(1+\overline{C}_1)+\delta(1+\overline{C}\ )}\right]^{\frac{1}{1-\alpha_{PF}}}. \quad \text{(A3.8)}$$

C. Inflation and real wage equations under flexible prices and wages

When nominal rigidities are absent, the symmetry conditions $P_t = P_t^A$ and $W_t = W_t^A$ hold in equilibrium. Then, the price symmetry condition equations (3.11) and (3.14) imply a constant real marginal cost rmc_t given by:

$$rmc_t = \frac{\omega_t}{A_t f_1(A_t n_t^d, k_t)} = \frac{\theta-1}{\theta}. \quad \text{(A3.9)}$$

Similarly, the wage symmetry condition and (3.15) imply a constant ratio of the leisure-consumption marginal rate of substitution over the real wage

$$\frac{U_3(c_t, m_t, l_t, \upsilon_t, \varsigma_t)}{\omega_t U_1(c_t, m_t, l_t, \upsilon_t, \varsigma_t)} = \frac{\theta_W - 1}{\theta_W}. \quad \text{(A3.10)}$$

To recall, production technology is given by the Cobb-Douglas function

$$f(A_t n_t^d, k_t) = (A_t n_t^d)^{1-\alpha_{PF}} k_t^{\alpha_{PF}}, \; 0 < \alpha_{PF} < 1. \quad \text{(3.2)}$$

Then, for $W_t = W_t^A$, from (A3.10), the period utility function (3.22), the time constraint (3.7), the overall resources constraint (3.26)[133], and the production function (3.2) yield[134]:

$$\widehat{\omega}_t = \left[\frac{\tau\overline{n}}{\overline{l}(1-\alpha_{PF})} + \frac{\sigma}{\omega_c}\right]\widehat{y}_t - \frac{\sigma\omega_g}{\omega_c}\widehat{g}_t - \frac{\tau\overline{n}}{\overline{l}}A_t - \upsilon_t, \quad \text{(A3.11)}$$

where τ is a leisure risk aversion coefficient from the utility function.

D. Deriving the system's reduced forms

The structural equations (3.25), (3.26), (3.32') and (3.33)-(3.35), together with (3.36), (3.41), (3.39) or (3.38) and (3.41) can be reduced to a system of four equations, expressed in terms of inflation, consumption, capital and the real wage. Equation (3.35) can be written as

---

133 For simplicity, $\omega_g = 0$ is assumed. Later in Chapter III, Subsection 4.1 the calibration is consistent with this assumption.

134 See Casares and McCallum (2006).

$$\widehat{inv}_t = \frac{1}{\delta}\widehat{k_{t+1}} - \frac{1-\delta}{\delta}\hat{k}_t . \qquad (3.35')$$

Equations (3.33) and (3.34) provide the algebraic terms to be substituted for $\widehat{rmc}_t$ and mpk_t in (3.32') and (3.36):

$$\widehat{rmc}_t = \hat{\omega}_t - \frac{\alpha_{PF}}{1-\alpha_{PF}}\left(\hat{k}_t - \hat{y}_t\right) \qquad (3.33)$$

$$mpk_t = \overline{mpk}(\widehat{y}_t - \widehat{k}_t) . \qquad (3.34)$$

Next, $\widehat{y}_t$ can be substituted out according to equations (3.26) and (3.35')[135]:

$$\widehat{y}_t = \omega_c \hat{c}_t + \frac{\omega_{inv}}{\delta}\widehat{k_{t+1}} - \omega_{inv}\left(\frac{1-\delta}{\delta}\right)\widehat{k}_t . \qquad (3.26')$$

From (3.41)

$$r_t = i_t - E_t\pi_{t+1}$$

and after rewriting (3.25) as

$$r_t = \sigma\left(E_t\hat{c}_{t+1} - \hat{c}_t\right), \qquad (3.25')$$

the nominal interest rate can be substituted in the policy rule equation (3.38) or (3.39). After substituting $\widehat{y}_t$ out according (3.26'), the interest-rate rule relation becomes[136]:

$$E_t\widehat{c_{t+1}} = \left(1 + \frac{\lambda_y^*\omega_c}{\sigma}\right)\hat{c}_t + \frac{\lambda_y^*\omega_{inv}}{\sigma\delta}\widehat{k_{t+1}} - \frac{\lambda_y^*\omega_{inv}(1-\delta)}{\sigma\delta}\widehat{k}_t - \frac{1}{\sigma}E_t\pi_{t+1} + \frac{\lambda_\pi^*}{\sigma}\pi_t . \qquad (A3.12)$$

Finally, equations (3.25'), (3.33), (3.34), (3.35'), (3.26') and (3.41) can be combined with (3.32'), (3.36), (3.37) and (A3.12) to yield the system's reduced forms:

$$\begin{aligned}\widehat{k_{t+2}} ={}& \frac{1}{N}\left[2b_4 + \Xi b_1\left(b_6+\delta\right) - \Xi\omega_{inv}\lambda_y^*\left(b_1b_7-1\right) - \Xi\omega_{inv}b_3\left(b_1b_7+b_5-1\right)\right]\widehat{k_{t+1}} + \\ &+ \frac{1}{N}\left[-b_4 + \Xi b_3\left(b_1b_7+b_5-1\right)\left(b_6+\delta\right) + \Xi\lambda_y^*b_6\left(b_1b_7-1\right)\right]\hat{k}_t - \frac{\Xi\omega_c\delta}{N}\left[b_1\left(\lambda_y^*b_7+1\right) + b_3\left(b_1b_7+b_5-1\right) - \lambda_y^*\right]\hat{c}_t + \\ &- \frac{\Xi\delta}{N}\left(\lambda_\pi^* - \frac{1}{\beta}\right)\left(b_1b_7-1\right)\pi_t - \frac{\Xi\delta}{N\beta}\left[b_2\left(b_1b_7+b_5-1\right) + b_5b_9\right]\widehat{\omega}_t + \frac{\Xi\delta b_5}{N\beta}\widehat{\omega_{t-1}}\end{aligned} \qquad (3.32'')$$

$$E_t\pi_{t+1} = \frac{1}{\beta}\pi_t - \frac{\omega_{inv}b_3}{\delta}\widehat{k_{t+1}} + b_3\left(\frac{b_6}{\delta}+1\right)\hat{k}_t - \omega_c b_3\hat{c}_t - \frac{b_2}{\beta}\hat{\omega}_t \qquad (3.36')$$

$$E_t\hat{\omega}_{t+1} = \left(\frac{b_9+b_2}{\beta}\right)\hat{\omega}_t - \frac{1}{\beta}\hat{\omega}_{t-1} + \frac{\omega_{inv}b_3}{\delta}\widehat{k_{t+1}} - \frac{b_3\left(b_6+\delta\right)}{\delta}\hat{k}_t + \omega_c b_3\hat{c}_t \qquad (3.37')$$

---

135 Equation (3.26') dies not include the term $\omega_g\widehat{g}_t$ as in the calibration $\omega_g = 0$.

136 Here λ_π^* and λ_y^* denote the effective values assigned to inflation and the output gap in the monetary rule. For the Taylor rule (3.38) $\lambda_\pi^* = 1 + \lambda_\pi$ and $\lambda_y^* = \lambda_y$. For the policy specification (3.39) $\lambda_\pi^* = (1-\lambda_i)(1+\lambda_\pi)$ and $\lambda_y^* = (1-\lambda_i)\lambda_y$. For the purpose of the subsequent determinacy analysis no interest-rate smoothing is assumed, i.e. $\lambda_i = 0$. The possibility of pursuing interest-rate smoothing will be further considered when the implications of shocks are examined.

$$E_t\hat{c}_{t+1} = \left[1+b_7\left(\lambda_y^*+b_3\right)\right]\hat{c}_t + \frac{1}{\delta}\left(\frac{1}{\sigma}-b_7\right)\left(\lambda_y^*+b_3\right)\widehat{k_{t+1}} - \frac{1}{\sigma\delta}\left[b_3\left(b_6+\delta\right)+\lambda_y^* b_6\right]\hat{k}_t + \frac{1}{\sigma}\left(\lambda_\pi^*-\frac{1}{\beta}\right)\pi_t + \frac{b_2}{\sigma\beta}\hat{\omega}_t \quad \text{(A3.12')}$$

where

$$b_1 = \overline{mpk}\left(\frac{\overline{rmc}*\alpha_{PF}}{1-\alpha_{PF}}+1\right)>0$$

$$b_2 = \frac{(1-\beta\eta_P)(1-\eta_P)(1-\alpha_{PF})}{\eta_P(1-\alpha_{PF}+\alpha_{PF}\theta)},\ 0<b_2<1$$

$$b_3 = \frac{\alpha_{PF}(1-\beta\eta_P)(1-\eta_P)}{\beta\eta_P(1-\alpha_{PF}+\alpha_{PF}\theta)},\ 0<b_3<b_2<1 \text{ for } 0<\alpha_{PF}<\beta<1$$

$$b_4 = \frac{1}{1+\delta},\ 0<b_4<1 \text{ for } \delta>0$$

$$b_5 = \overline{mpk}*\overline{rmc}>0$$

$$b_6 = \omega_{inv}\left(1-\delta\right),\ 0<b_6<1$$

$$b_7 = \frac{\omega_c}{\sigma}>0$$

$$b_8 = \frac{\alpha_{PF}}{1-\alpha_{PF}},\ 0<b_8<1$$

$$b_9 = 1+\beta>1$$

$$N = \frac{1}{1+\delta}+\Xi*\overline{mpk}*\omega_{inv}\left(\frac{\overline{rmc}*\alpha_{PF}}{1-\alpha_{PF}}+1\right)>0.$$

For convenience, the system (3.32''), (3.36'), (3.37') and (A3.12') can be rewritten as:

$$\widehat{k_{t+2}} = a_1\widehat{k_{t+1}}+a_2\hat{k}_t-a_3\pi_t-a_4\hat{c}_t-a_5\hat{\omega}_t+a_6\hat{\omega}_{t-1} \quad \text{(A3.13)}$$

$$E_t\pi_{t+1} = -a_7\widehat{k_{t+1}}+a_8\hat{k}_t+a_9\pi_t-a_{10}\hat{c}_t-a_{11}\hat{\omega}_t \quad \text{(A3.14)}$$

$$E_t\hat{\omega}_{t+1} = a_{12}\widehat{k_{t+1}}-a_{13}\hat{k}_t+a_{14}\hat{c}_t+a_{15}\hat{\omega}_t-a_{16}\hat{\omega}_{t-1} \quad \text{(A3.15)}$$

$$E_t\hat{c}_{t+1} = a_{17}\widehat{k_{t+1}}-a_{18}\hat{k}_t+a_{19}\pi_t+a_{20}\hat{c}_t+a_{21}\hat{\omega}_t \quad \text{(A3.16)}$$

where

$$a_1 = \frac{1}{N}\left[2b_4+\Xi b_1\left(b_6+\delta\right)-\Xi\omega_{inv}\lambda_y^*\left(b_1b_7-1\right)-\Xi\omega_{inv}b_3\left(b_1b_7+b_5-1\right)\right]$$

$$a_2 = \frac{1}{N}\left[-b_4+\Xi b_3\left(b_1b_7+b_5-1\right)\left(b_6+\delta\right)+\Xi\lambda_y^* b_6\left(b_1b_7-1\right)\right]$$

$$a_3 = \frac{\Xi\delta}{N}\left(\lambda_\pi^*-\frac{1}{\beta}\right)\left(b_1b_7-1\right)$$

$$a_4 = \frac{\Xi\omega_c\delta}{N}\left[b_1\left(\lambda_y^* b_7+1\right)+b_3\left(b_1b_7+b_5-1\right)-\lambda_y^*\right]$$

$$a_5 = \frac{\Xi\delta}{N\beta}\left[b_2\left(b_1b_7+b_5-1\right)+b_5b_9\right]$$

$$a_6 = \frac{\Xi \delta b_5}{N\beta}$$

$$a_7 = \frac{\omega_{inv} b_3}{\delta}$$

$$a_8 = b_3\left(\frac{b_6}{\delta} + 1\right)$$

$$a_9 = \frac{1}{\beta}$$

$$a_{10} = \omega_c b_3$$

$$a_{11} = \frac{b_2}{\beta}$$

$$a_{12} = \frac{\omega_{inv} b_3}{\delta}$$

$$a_{13} = \frac{b_3\left(b_6 + \delta\right)}{\delta}$$

$$a_{14} = \omega_c b_3$$

$$a_{15} = \frac{b_9 + b_2}{\beta}$$

$$a_{16} = \frac{1}{\beta}$$

$$a_{17} = \frac{1}{\delta}\left(\frac{1}{\sigma} - b_7\right)\left(\lambda_y^* + b_3\right)$$

$$a_{18} = \frac{1}{\sigma\delta}\left[b_3\left(b_6 + \delta\right) + \lambda_y^* b_6\right]$$

$$a_{19} = \frac{1}{\sigma}\left(\lambda_\pi^* - \frac{1}{\beta}\right)$$

$$a_{20} = \left[1 + b_7\left(\lambda_y^* + b_3\right)\right]$$

$$a_{21} = \frac{b_2}{\sigma\beta}.$$

References

Abel, A. B. (1983). Optimal Investment under Uncertainty. American Economic Review, 73, 228-233.

Abel, A. B. (1985). A Stochastic Model of Investment, Marginal q and the Market Value of the Firm", International Economic Review, 26, 305-322.

Abel, A. B. (1988). Consumption and Investment. NBER Working Paper 2580, National Bureau of Economic Research, Cambridge (Mass).

Abel, A. B. and O. J. Blanchard (1983). An Intertemporal Equilibrium Model of Saving and Investment. *Econometrica* 51, 575-692.

Abel, A. B. and J. Eberly (1994). A Unified Model of Investment under Uncertainty. *American Economic Review* 84, 1369–1384.

Abel, A. B. and J. Eberly (1996). Optimal Investment with Costly Reversibility. *Review of Economic Studies* 63, 581–593.

Alesina, A. and L. H. Summers (1993). Central Bank Independence and Macroeconomic Performance: Some Comparative Evidence. *Journal of Money, Credit and Banking* 25, 151-162.

Allen, R. G. D. (1967). Macro-Economic Theory: A Mathematical Treatment. Macmillan, London.

Altig, D., L. J. Christiano, M. Eichenbaum, and J. Linde (2005). Firm-Specific Capital, Nominal Rigidities and the Business Cycle. NBER Working Paper 11034, National Bureau of Economic Research, Cambridge (Mass).

Arestis, P. and M. Sawyer (2002). Can Monetary Policy Affect the Real Economy? The Levi Economics Institute Working Paper 355.

Arestis, P. and M. Sawyer (2003). Inflation Targeting: A Critical Appraisal. The Levi Economics Institute Working Paper 388.

Barro, J. (1976). Rational Expectations and the Role of Monetary Policy. *Journal of Monetary Economics* 2, 1-32.

Barro, J. and D. Gordon (1983). A Positive Theory of Monetary Policy in a Natural Rate Model. *Journal of Political Economy* 91, 589-610.

Basu, S. and M. Kimball (2005). Investment Planning Costs and the Effects of Fiscal and Monetary Policy. manuscript.

Baumol. W. J. (1959). Economic Dynamics: An Introduction. Macmillan, NY, second edition.

Benhabib, J., and S. Eusepi (2005). The Design of Monetary and Fiscal Policy: A Global Perspective. *Journal of Economic Theory* 123, 40-73.

Benhabib, J., S. Schmitt-Grohe and M. Uribe (1999). Monetary Policy and Multiple Equilibria. CEPR Discussion Paper 2316.

Benhabib, J., S. Schmitt-Grohe and M. Uribe (2001). The Perils of Taylor Rules. *Journal of Economic Theory* 96, 40-69.

Benigno, P. and M. Woodford (2006). Linear-Quadratic Approximation of Optimal Policy Problems. NBER Working Paper 12672, National Bureau of Economic Research, Cambridge (Mass).

Bernanke, B. S. and A. S. Blinder (1988). Credit, Money, and Aggregate Demand. *American Economic Review* 78, 435-439.

Bernanke, B. S. and F. S. Mishkin (1992). Central Bank Behavior and the Strategy of Monetary Policy: Observations from Six Industrialized Countries. *NBER Macroeconomics Annual*, O. J. Blanchard and S. Fischer (eds.), 138-228.

Bernanke, B. S. and F. S. Mishkin (1997). Inflation Targeting: A New Framework for Monetary Policy. *The Journal of Economic Perspectives* 11, 97-116.

Bernanke, B., M. Gertler and S. Gilchrist (1998). The Financial Accelerator in a Quantitative Business Cycle Network. NBER Working Paper 6455, National Bureau of Economic Research, Cambridge (Mass).

Bernanke, B. S., T. Laubach, F. S. Mishkin and A. S. Posen (1999). Inflation Targeting: Lessons from the International Experience. Princeton University Press, Princeton, NJ.

Bernanke, B. and M. Woodford (1997). Inflation Forecasts and Monetary Policy. *Journal of Money, Credit, and Banking* 29, 653-685.

Bernanke, B. and M. Woodford (2006). The Inflation-Targeting Debate. National Bureau of Economic Research Studies in Income and Wealth, University Of Chicago Press.

Bischoff, C. W. (1971). Business Investment in the 1970s: A Comparison of Models. Brookings Papers on Economic Activity 1, 13-63.

Blanchard, O. J. and S. Fischer (1993). Lectures on Macroeconomics. MIT Press, Cambridge (Mass.).

Blanchard, O. and C. Kahn (1980). The Solution of Linear Difference Models under Rational Expectations. *Econometrica* 48, 1305-1311.

Blinder, A. S. and J. Stiglitz (1983). Money, Credit Constraints, and Economic Activity. *American Economic Review* 73, 297-302.

Borio, C. E. V. (1997). The Implementation of Monetary Policy in Industrial Countries: A Survey. Bank of International Settlements Economic Paper 47.

Bray, M. (1982). Learning, Estimation, and the Stability of Rational Expectations. *Journal of Economic Theory* 26, 318-339.

Bullard, J. (2006). The Learnability Criterion and Monetary Policy. Federal Reserve Bank of St. Louis Review 88, 203-217.

Bullard, J. and K. Mitra (2000). Determinacy, Learnability, and Monetary Policy Inertia. Federal Reserve Bank of St. Louis Working Paper 2000-030C.

Bullard, J. and K. Mitra (2002). Learning about Monetary Policy Rules. *Journal of Monetary Economics* 49, 1105-1129.

Burmeister, E., R. Flood and P. Graber (1983). On the Equivalence of Solutions in Rational Expectations Models. *Journal of Economic Dynamics and Control* 5, 311-321.

Caballero, R. (1999). Aggregate Investment. *Handbook of Macroeconomics*, J. Taylor and M. Woodford (eds.), Elsevier, Amsterdam, 813–862.

Caballero, R. and E. Engel (1999). Explaining Investment Dynamics in U.S. Manufacturing: A Generalized (S,s) Approach. *Econometrica* 67, 783–826.

Caballero, R., E. Engel and J. Haltiwanger (1995). Plant-Level Adjustment and Aggregate Investment Dynamics. *Brookings Papers on Economic Activity* 2, 1–39.

Calvo, G. (1978) On the Time Consistency of Optimal Policy in the Monetary Economy. *Econometrica* 46, 1411-1428.

Calvo, G. (1983). Staggered Prices in a Utility Maximization Framework. *Journal of Monetary Economics* 12, 383-98.

Carlstrom, C. and T. Fuerst (1999). Timing and Real Indeterminacy in Monetary Models. Federal Reserve Bank of Cleveland Working Paper 99-10R, revised version.

Carlstrom, C. and T. Fuerst (2000). Forward-Looking versus Backward-Looking Taylor Rules. Federal Reserve Bank of Cleveland Working Paper 00-09.

Carlstrom, C. and T. Fuerst (2001). Taylor Rules in a Model that Satisfies the Natural Rate Hypothesis. Federal Reserve Bank of Cleveland Working Paper 01-16.

Carlstrom, C. and T. Fuerst (2005). Investment and Interest Rate Policy: A Discrete-Time Analysis. Journal of Economic Theory 123, 4-20.

Casares, M. (2002). Time-to-Build Approach in a Sticky Price, Sticky Wage Optimizing Monetary Model. ECB Working Paper 147.

Casares, M. (2006). Time-to-Build, Monetary Shocks, and Aggregate Fluctuations. *Journal of Monetary Economics* 53, 1161–1176.

Casares, M. (2007). Macroeconomic Modelling: Recent Developments. script.

Casares, M. and B. McCallum (2006). An Optimizing IS-LM Framework with Endogenous Investment. *Journal of Macroeconomics* 28, 621-644.

Chari, V. V., P. J. Kehoe and E. R. McGrattan (2000). Sticky Price Models of the Business Cycle: Can the Contract Multiplier Solve the Persistence Problem? *Econometrica* 68, 1151-1179.

Christiano, L., M. Eichenbaum and C. Evans (2001). Nominal Rigidities and the Dynamic Effects of a Shock to Monetary Policy. NBER Working Paper 8403, National Bureau of Economic Research, Cambridge (Mass).

Christano, L. and R. Todd (1996). Time to Plan and Aggregate Fluctuations. Federal Reserve Bank of Minneapolis Quarterly Review 20, 14-27.

Clarida, R., J. Galí and M. Gertler (1999). The Science of Monetary Policy: A New Keynesian Perspective. *Journal of Economic Literature* 37, 1661-1707.
Clarida, R., J. Galí and M. Gertler (2000). Monetary Policy Rules and Macroeconomic Stability: Evidence and Some Theory. *Quarterly Journal of Economics* 115, 147-180.
Clark, P. K. (1979). Investment in the 1970s: Theory, Performance, and Prediction. *Brookings Papers on Economic Activity* 1, 73-113.
Cooper, R. W. and J. C. Haltiwanger (2006). On the Nature of Capital Adjustment Costs. *Review of Economic Studies* 73, 611–633.
Cooper, R. W., J. C. Haltiwanger and L. Power (1999). Machine Replacement and the Business Cycle: Lumps and Bumps. *American Economic Review* 89, 921–946.
Dixit, A. K. and J. E. Stiglitz (1977). Monopolistic competition and optimum product diversity. *American Economic Review* 67, 297-308.
Dupor, B. (2001). Investment and Interest Rate Policy. *Journal of Economic Theory* 98, 81-113.
Edge, R. M. (2007). Time-to-Build, Time-to-Plan, Habit-Persistence, and the Liquidity Effect. *Journal of Monetary Economics* 54, 1644–1669.
Eichenbaum, M., and J. Fisher (2004). Evaluating the Calvo Model of Sticky Prices, NBER Working Paper 10617, National Bureau of Economic Research, Cambridge (Mass).
Eisner, R. and R. H. Strotz (1963). Determinants of business investment. *Impacts of Monetary Policy, Commission on Money and Credit*, Prentice-Hall,.
Erceg, C. J., D. W. Henderson and A. T. Levin (1999). Optimal Monetary Policy with Staggered Wage and Price Contracts. Board of Governors of the Federal Reserve System International Finance Discussion Paper 640.
Evans, G. (1985). Expectational Stability and the Multiple Equilibria Problem in Linear Rational Expectations Models. *Quarterly Journal of Economics* 100, 1217-1233.
Evans, G. and S. Honkapohja (2001). Learning and Expectations in Macroeconomics", Princeton University Press, Princeton, NJ.
Evans, G. and S. Honkapohja (2003a). Expectations and the Stability Problem for Optimal Monetary Policies. *Review of Economic Studies* 70, 807-824.
Evans, G. and S. Honkapohja (2003b). Adaptive Learning and Monetary Policy Design. *Journal of Money, Credit and Banking* 35, 1045-1072.
Federal Reserve Board (1995). Federal Open Market Committee Transcripts. FOMC Meeting January 31-February 1, 43-44.
Fischer, S. (1995a). Central Bank Independence Revisited. *American Economic Review* 85, 201-206.

Fischer, S. (1995b). The Unending Search for Monetary Salvation. *NBER Macroeconomics Annual* 10, 275-286.
Fischer, S. (1996). Why are Central Banks Pursuing Long-Run Price Stability? Federal Reserve Bank of Kansas Proceedings, 7-34.
Friedman, M. (1947). Lerner on the Economics of Control. *The Journal of Political Economy* 55, 405-416.
Friedman, M. (1953). The Effects of Full-Employment Policy on Economic Stabilization: A Formal Analysis. *Essays in Positive Economics*, Friedman, M. (ed.), Chicago University Press, Chicago, 117-132.
Friedman, M. (1960). A Program for Monetary Stability. Fordham University Press, New York.
Friedman, M. (1962a). The Role of Monetary Policy. *American Economic Review* 58, 1-17.
Friedman, M. (1962b). Should There Be an Independent Monetary Authority. *In Search of Monetary Constitution*. LB. Yeager (ed.), Harvard University Press, Cambridge, MA.
Friedman, M. and A. J. Schwartz (1963). A Monetary History of the United States, 1867-1960. Princeton University Press, Princeton.
Fuhrer, J. C. (2000). Habit Formation in Consumption and Its Implications for Monetary-Policy Models. *American Economic Review* 90, 367-390.
Galí, J. (2002). New Perspectives on Monetary Policy, Inflation, and the Business Cycle. NBER Working Paper 8767, National Bureau of Economic Research, Cambridge (Mass).
Galí, J. and M. Gertler (1999). Inflation Dynamics: A Structural Economic Analysis. CEPR Discussion Paper 2246.
Galí, J., M. Gertler, and D. López-Salido (2001). European Inflation Dynamics. *European Economic Review* 45, 1237-1270.
Galor, O. (2007). Discrete Dynamical Systems. Springer-Verlag, Berlin-Heidelberg.
Giannoni, M. (2006). Robust Optimal Policy in a Forward-Looking Model with Parameter and Shock Uncertainty. NBER Working Paper 11942, National Bureau of Economic Research, Cambridge (Mass).
Giannoni, M. and M. Woodford (2002a). Optimal Interest-Rate Rules: I. General Theory. NBER Working Paper 9419, National Bureau of Economic Research, Cambridge (Mass).
Giannoni, M. and M. Woodford (2002b). Optimal Interest-Rate Rules: II. Applications. NBER Working Paper 9420, National Bureau of Economic Research, Cambridge (Mass).
Giannoni, M. and M. Woodford (2003). Optimal Inflation Targeting Rules. NBER Working Paper 9939, National Bureau of Economic Research, Cambridge (Mass).

Goodfriend, M. (1990). Interest Rates and the Conduct of Monetary Policy. Federal Reserve Bank of Richmond Working Paper 90-6.

Goodfriend, M. and R. G. King (1997). The New Neoclassical Synthesis and the Role of Monetary Policy. *NBER Macroeconomics Annual* 12, 231-283.

Gould, J. P. (1968). Adjustment Costs in the Theory of Investment of the Firm. *The Review of Economic Studies* 35, 47-55.

Groth, C. and H. Khan (2007). Investment Adjustment Costs: Evidence from UK and US Industries. Bank of England Working Paper 332.

Hairault, J.-O. and F. Portier (1993). Money, New Keynesian Macroeconomics, and the Business Cycle. *European Economic Review* 37, 1533-1568.

Hall, R. E. (1988). Intertemporal Substitution in Consumption. Journal of Political Economy 96, 339-57.

Hall, S. (2001). Credit Channel Effects in the Monetary Transmission Mechanism. Bank of England Quarterly Bulletin (Winter), 442-448.

Hamermesh, D. S. and G. A. Pfann (1996). Adjustment Costs in Factor Demand. *Journal of Economic Literature* 34, 1264-1292.

Hayashi, F. (1982). Tobin's Marginal and Average q: A Neoclassical Interpretation. *Econometrica* 50, 213-224.

Heijdra, B. J. and F. van der Ploeg (2000). Foundations of Modern Macroeconomics. Oxford University Press, Oxford.

Henderson, D. W. and W. J. McKibbin (1993). A Comparison of Some Basic Monetary Policy Regimes for Open Economies: Implications of Different Degrees of Instrument Adjustment and Wage Persistence, Carnegie-Rochester Conference Series on Public Policy 39, 221—317.

Hetzel, R. L. (2000). The Taylor Rule: Is It a Useful Guide to Understanding Monetary Policy? Federal Reserve Bank Richmond Economic Quarterly 86, 1—33.

Hicks, J. R. (1939). Value and Capital; an Inquiry into Some Fundamental Principles of Economic Theory. Clarendon Press, Oxford.

Ho, C. (2008). Implementing Monetary Policy in the 2000s: Operating Procedures in Asia and Beyond. Bank of International Settlements Working Paper 253.

Holt, C., F. Modigliani, J. Muth, and H. Simon (1960). Planning Production, Inventories, and Work Force. Prentice-Hall, Englewood Cliffs, NJ.

Huang, K. and Q. Meng (2007). Capital and Macroeconomic Instability in a Discrete-Time Model with Forward-Looking Interest Rate Rules. Federal Reserve Bank of Philadelphia Working Paper 07-4.

Jaffee, D. and F. Modigliani (1969). A Theory and Test of Credit Rationing. *American Economic Review* 59, 850-872.

Jorgenson, D. W. (1963). Capital Theory and Investment Behaviour. *American Economic Review* 53, 247-256.

Jorgenson, D. W. and C. D. Siebert (1968). A Comparison of Alternative Theories of Corporate Investment Behavior. *American Economic Review* 58, 681-712.

Jorgenson, D. W. and J. A. Stephenson (1969) Issues in the Development of the Neoclassical Theory of Investment Behavior.*The Review of Economics and Statistics* 51, 346-353.

Judd, J. and G. Rudebusch (1998). Taylor's Rule and the Fed: 1970-1997", Federal Reserve Bank of San Francisco Economic Review 3, 3-16.

Kerr, W. and R. King (1996) Limits on Interest Rate Rules in the IS-LM Model. Federal Reserve Bank of Richmond Economic Quarterly 82.

Keynes, J. M. (1936). The General Theory of Employment, Interest and Money. Macmillan, New York.

Kimball, M. S. (1995). The Quantitative Analytics of the Basic Neomonetarist Model. *Journal of Money, Credit and Banking* 27, 1241-1277.

King, M. (1997). Changes in UK Monetary Policy: Rules and Discretion in Practice. *Journal of Monetary Economics* 39, 81-97.

King, R. and M. Watson (1996). Money, Prices, Interest Rates and the Business Cycle. *Review of Economics and Statistics* 78, 35-53.

King, R. and A. Wolman (1996). Inflation Targeting in a St. Louis Model of the 21st Century. NBER Working Paper 5507, National Bureau of Economic Research, Cambridge (Mass).

Kozicki, S. (1999). How Useful Are Taylor Rules for Monetary Policy? Federal Reserve Bank Kansas City Economic Review 2, 5—33.

Kurozumi, T., Van Zandweghe, W. (2008). Investment, Interest Rate Policy, and Equilibrium Stability. *Journal of Economic Dynamics and Control* 32, 1489-1516.

Kuttner, K. N. (1994). Estimating potential output as a latent variable", *Journal of Business and Economic Statistics* 12, 361–368.

Kydland, F. E. and E. C. Prescott (1982). Time to Build and Aggregate Fluctuations. *Econometrica* 50, 1345-1370.

Leeper, E. M. (1991). Equilibria under "Active" and "Passive" Monetary and Fiscal Policies. Journal of Monetary Economics 27, 129-147.

Leeson, R. (1994). A. W. H. Phillips, Inflationary Expectations and the Operating Characteristics of the Macroeconomy. *Economic Journal* 104, 1420-1421.

Leeson, R. (1997a). The Trade-off Interpretation of Phillips's Dynamic Stabilization Exercise. *Economica* 64, 155-171.

Leeson, R. (1997b). The Political Economy of the Inflation-Unemployment Trade-off. *History of Political Economy* 29, 117-156.

Levin, A. and J. Williams (2003). Robust Monetary Policy with Competing Reference Models. Federal Reserve Bank of San Francisco Working Paper 2003-10.

Levin, A., Wieland, V. and J. Williams (1999). Robustness of Simple Monetary Policy Rules under Model Uncertainty. *Monetary Policy Rules,* Taylor (ed.).

Li, Hong (2002). Inflation Determination under a Taylor Rule: Consequences of Endogenous Capital Accumulation. Princeton University Working Paper, (May).

Lowe, P. and L. Ellis (1997). The Smoothing of Official Interest Rates. *Monetary Policy and Inflation Targeting*, Reserve Bank of Australia Annual Conference Volume, Lowe, P. (ed.).

Lucas, R. E. (1967). Adjustment Costs and the Theory of Supply. *Journal of Political Economy* 75, 321-343.

Lucas, R. E. (1972). Expectations and the Neutrality of Money. *Journal of Economic Theory* 4, 103-124.

Lucas, R. E. (1973). Some International Evidence on the Output-Inflation Tradeoffs. *American Economic Review* 63, 326-334.

Lucas, R. E. (1976). Econometric Policy Evaluation: A Critique. Carnegie-Rochester Conference Series on Public Policy 1, 19-46.

Lucas, R. E. (1987). Adaptive Behavior and Economic Theory. *Rational Choice: The Contrast Between Economics and Psychology*. Hogarth, R. M. and M. W. Reder (eds.), University of Chicago Press, Chicago, 217-42.

Lucas, R. E., and E. C. Prescott (1971). Investment under Uncertainty. *Econometrica* 39, 659–681.

Marcet, A. and T. Sargent (1989). Convergence to Least Squares Learning Mechanisms in Self-Referential Linear Stochastic Methods. *Journal of Economic Theory* 48, 337-368.

McCallum, B. (1981). Price Level Determinacy with an Interest Rate Policy Rule and Rational Expectations. *Journal of Monetary Economics* 8, 319-329.

McCallum, B. (1988). Robustness Properties of a Rule for Monetary Policy. Carnegie-Rochester Conference Series on Public Policy 29, 173-204.

McCallum, B. (1989). Targets, Indicators, and Instruments of Monetary Policy. NBER Working Paper 3047, National Bureau of Economic Research, Cambridge (Mass).

McCallum, B. (1993). Specification and Analysis a of Monetary Policy Rule for Japan. Bank of Japan Monetary and Economic Studies 11, 1-45.

McCallum, B. (1994). Monetary Policy Rules and Financial Stability. NBER Working Paper No. 4692, National Bureau of Economic Research, Cambridge (Mass).

McCallum, B. (1997). Issues in the Design of Monetary Policy Rules. NBER Working Paper 6016, National Bureau of Economic Research, Cambridge (Mass).

McCallum, B. (1999). Roles of the Minimal State Variable Criterion in Rational Expectations Models. NBER Working Paper 7087, National Bureau of Economic Research, Cambridge (Mass).

McCallum, B. (2000a). The Present and Future of Monetary Policy Rules. NBER Working Paper 7916, National Bureau of Economic Research, Cambridge (Mass).

McCallum, B. (2000b). Alternative Monetary Policy Rules: A Comparison with Historical Settings for the United States, the United Kingdom, and Japan. NBER, Working Paper 7725, National Bureau of Economic Research, Cambridge (Mass).

McCallum, B. (2001a). Should Monetary Policy Respond Strongly to Output Gaps? NBER Working Paper 8226, National Bureau of Economic Research, Cambridge (Mass).

McCallum, B. (2001b). A course in Macro and Monetary Economics. script.

McCallum, B. (2002a). The Non-Optimality of Proposed Monetary Policy Rules Under Timeless-Perspective Commitment. NBER Working Paper 8882, National Bureau of Economic Research, Cambridge (Mass).

McCallum, B. (2002b). Consistent Expectations, Rational Expectations, Multiple-Solution Indeterminacies, and Least-Square Learnability. NBER Working Paper 9218, National Bureau of Economic Research, Cambridge (Mass).

McCallum, B. (2003a). The Unique Minimum State Variable RE Solution is E-Stable in All Well Formulated Linear Models. NBER Working Paper 9960, National Bureau of Economic Research, Cambridge (Mass).

McCallum, B. (2003b). Multiple-Solution Indeterminacies in Monetary Policy Analysis. NBER Working Paper 9837, National Bureau of Economic Research, Cambridge (Mass).

McCallum, B. (2004). On the Relationship between Determinate and MSV Solutions in Linear RE Models. NBER Technical Working Paper 297, Na-tional Bureau of Economic Research, Cambridge (Mass).

McCallum, B. and E. Nelson (1999a). An Optimizing IS-LM Specification for Monetary Policy and Business Cycle Analysis. *Journal of Money, Credit and Banking* 31, 296-316.

McCallum, B. and E. Nelson (1999b). Performance of Operational Policy Rules in an Estimated Semiclassical Structural Model. *Monetary Policy Rules*, J.B. Taylor (ed.), University of Chicago Press, Chicago IL.

McCallum, B. and E. Nelson (2000). Timeless Perspective vs. Discretionary Monetary Policy in Forward-Looking Models. NBER Working Paper 7915, National Bureau of Economic Research, Cambridge (Mass).

McCallum, B. and E. Nelson (2004). Targeting vs. Instrument Rules for Monetary Policy. NBER Working Paper 10612, National Bureau of Economic Research, Cambridge (Mass).

Meltzer, A. H. (1987). Limits of Short-Run Stabilization Policy. *Economic. Inquiry* 25, 1—14.
Mishkin, F. S. (1999). International Experiences with Different Monetary Regimes. *Journal of Monetary Economics* 43, 579-606.
Mishkin, F. S. (2000). What Should Central Banks Do? Federal Reserve Bank of St. Louis Review (November/December), 1-13.
Mishkin, F. S. (2006). Monetary Policy Strategy: How Did We Get There? NBER Working Paper 12515, National Bureau of Economic Research, Cambridge (Mass).
Muth, J. F. (1961). Rational Expectations and the Theory of Price Movements. *Econometrica* 29, 315-335.
Nelson, E. (2008). Friedman and Taylor on Monetary Policy Rules: A Comparison. Federal Reserve Bank of St. Louis Review (March/April), 95-116.
Onatski, A. and N. Williams (2003). Modeling Model Uncertainty. NBER Working Paper 9566, National Bureau of Economic Research, Cambridge (Mass).
Orphanides, A. (1998). Monetary Policy Evaluation with Noisy Information. Board of Governors of the Federal Reserve System Finance and Economics Discussion Series Working Paper 1998–50.
Orphanides, A. (2001). Monetary Policy Rules Based on Real-time Data. *American Economic Review* 91, 964-985.
Orphanides, A. and S. van Norden (2004). The Reliability of Inflation Forecasts Based on Output Gap Estimates in Real Time. Federal Reserve Board Washington Finance and Economics Discussion Paper 68.
Orphanides, A., R. D. Porter, D. Reifschneider, R. Tetlow and F. Finan (2000). Errors in the Measurement of the Output Gap and the Design of Monetary Policy. *Journal of Economics and Business* 52, 117-141.
Paez-Farrell, J. (2003). Endogenous Capital in New Keynesian Models. Centre for Economic Policy Research Memorandum 39.
Peck, S. C. (1974). Alternative Investment Models for Firms in the Electric Utilities Industry. *The Bell Journal of Economics and Management Science* 5, 420-458.
Phelps, E. S. (1967). Money-Wage Dynamics and Labor-Market Equilibrium. *Journal of Political Economy* 76, 678-711.
Phillips, A. W. (1958). The Relation Between Unemployment and the Rate of Change of Money Wage Rates in the United Kingdom, 1861-1957. *Economica* 25, 283-299.
Poole, W. (1970). Optimal Choice of Monetary Policy Instruments in a Simple Stochastic Macro Model. *The Quarterly Journal of Economics* 84, 197-216.
Prescott, E. C. (1986). Theory Ahead of Business Cycle Measurement", Federal Reserve Bank of Minneapolis Staff Report 102.

Reither, F. E. (2003). Grundzüge der Neuen Keynesianischen Makroökonomik. Diskussionspapier 19, Fächergruppe Volkswirtschaftslehre, Universität der Bundeswehr Hamburg.

Reither, F. E. (2008). Sinn und Grenzen des "Taylor-Prinzips". Forthcoming.

Roberts, J. M. (1995). New Keynesian Economics and the Phillips Curve. *Journal of Money, Credit and Banking* 27, 975-984.

Roberts, J. M. (1998). Inflation Expectations and the Transmission of Monetary Policy. Federal Reserve Board Paper 43.

Rotemberg, J. (1982). Sticky Prices in the United States. *Journal of Political Economy* 90, 1187-1211.

Rotemberg, J. and M. Woodford (1998a). Interest-Rate Rules in an Estimated Sticky-Price Model. NBER Working Paper 6618, National Bureau of Economic Research, Cambridge (Mass).

Rotemberg, J. and M. Woodford (1998b). An Optimization-Based Econometric Framework for the Evaluation of Monetary Policy. NBER Technical Working Paper 233, National Bureau of Economic Research, Cambridge (Mass).

Rouwenhorst, K. G. (1991). Time to Build and Aggregate Fluctuations. A Reconsideration. *Journal of Monetary Economics* 27, 241–254.

Rudebusch, G. (1995). Federal Reserve Interest Rate Targeting, Rational Expectations, and the Term Structure. *Journal of Monetary Economics* 35, 245-274.

Rudebusch, G. and L. Svensson (1998). Policy Rules for Inflation Targeting. NBER Working Paper 6512, National Bureau of Economic Research, Cambridge (Mass).

Sack, B. (1998). Does the Fed Act Gradually? A VAR Analysis. Board of Governors of the Federal Reserve System Finance and Economics Discussion Paper 17.

Samuelson, P. A. (1947). Foundations of Economic Analysis. Harvard University Press, Cambridge, MA.

Samuelson, P. A. and R. Solow (1960). Analytical Aspects of Anti-Inflation Policy. *American Economic Review* 50, 177-194.

Sargent, T. J. (1973). Rational Expectations, the Real Rate of Interest, and the Natural Rate of Unemployment. *Brookings Papers on Economic Activity* 2, 169-183.

Sargent, T. J. and N. Wallace (1975). Rational Expectations, the Optimal Monetary Instrument, and the Optimal Money Supply Rule. *The Journal of Political Economy* 83, 241-254.

Sargent, T. J. and N. Wallace (1976). Rational Expectations and the Theory of Economic Policy . *Journal of Monetary Economics* 2, 169-183.

Sbordone, A. (2001). An Optimizing Model of U.S. Wage and Price Dynamics. Department of Economics Working Paper 200110, Rutgers University.

Sbordone, A. (2002). Prices and Unit Labor Costs: A New Test of Price Stickiness. *Journal of Monetary Economics* 49, 265-292.
Schmitt-Grohé, S. and M. Uribe (2004). Optimal Simple and Implementable Monetary and Fiscal Rules. NBER Working Paper 10253, National Bureau of Economic Research, Cambridge (Mass).
Sellon, G. H. and V. V. Roley (1995). Monetary Policy Actions and Long-term Interest Rates. Federal Reserve Bank of Kansas City Economic Review (Fourth Quarter).
Smets, F. (1998). Output Gap Uncertainty: Does it Matter for the Taylor Rule? Bank of International Settlements Working Paper 60.
Snowdon, B. and H. R. Vane (2005). Modern Macroeconomics: Its Origins, Development and Current State. Edward Edgar Publishing Ltd.
Stiglitz, J. E and A. Weiss (1981). Credit Rationing in Markets with Imperfect Information. *American Economic Review* 71, 393-410.
Sveen, T. and L. Weinke (2004). Pitfalls in the Modelling of Forward-Looking Price Setting and Investment Behaviour. Norges Bank Working Paper 1.
Sveen, T. and L. Weinke (2005). New Perspectives on Capital, Sticky Prices and the Taylor Principle. *Journal of Economic Theory* 123, 21-39.
Svensson, L. (1997a). Inflation Forecast Targeting: Implementing and Monitoring Inflation Targets. *European Economic Review* 41, 1111-1146.
Svensson, L. (1997b). Inflation Targeting: Some Extensions. NBER Working Paper 5962, National Bureau of Economic Research, Cambridge (Mass).
Svensson, L. (1999a). How Should Monetary Policy Be Conducted in an Era of Price Stability? *New Challenges for Monetary Policy,* Federal Reserve Bank of Kansas City, 195-259.
Svensson, L. (1999b). Inflation Targeting as a Monetary Policy Rule. *Journal of Monetary Economics* 43, 607-654.
Svensson, L. (1999c). Price Stability as a Target for Monetary Policy: Defining and Maintaining Price Stability. NBER Working Paper 7276, National Bureau of Economic Research, Cambridge (Mass).
Svensson, L. (2000). The First Year of the Eurosystem: Inflation Targeting or Not. *American Economic Review: Papers and Proceedings* 90, 95-99.
Svensson, L. (2002). What is Wrong with Taylor Rules? Using Judgment in Monetary Policy through Targeting Rules. NBER Working Paper 9421, National Bureau of Economic Research, Cambridge (Mass).
Svensson, L. (2004). Targeting Rules vs. Instrument Rules for Monetary Policy: What is Wrong with McCallum and Nelson? NBER Working Paper 10747, National Bureau of Economic Research, Cambridge (Mass).
Svensson, L. and M. Woodford (1999). Implementing Optimal Policy Through Inflation-Forecast Targeting. NBER Working Paper 9747, National Bureau of Economic Research, Cambridge (Mass).

Svensson, L. and M. Woodford (2000). Indicator Variables for Optimal Policy. ECB Working Paper 12.

Taylor, J. B. (1980). Aggregate Dynamics and staggered contracts, *Journal of Political Economy* 88, 1-23.

Taylor, J. B. (1983). Optimal Stabilization Rules in a Stochastic Model of Investment with Gestation Lags. NBER Working Paper 1225, National Bureau of Economic Research, Cambridge (Mass).

Taylor, J. B. (1986). An Appeal for Rationality in the Policy Activism Debate, in: The Monetary versus Fiscal Policy Debate: Lessons from Two Decades. *Proceedings of the Ninth Annual Economic Policy Conference of the Federal Reserve Bank of St. Louis,* The Federal Reserve Bank of St. Louis Review, 151-63.

Taylor, J. B. (1993). Discretion versus Policy Rules in Practice. Carnegie-Rochester Conference Series on Public Policy 39, 195-214.

Taylor, J. B. (1995). Monetary Policy Implications of Greater Fiscal Discipline. *Budget Deficits and Debt: Issues and Options*, A Symposium Sponsored by the Federal Reserve Bank of Kansas City, Jackson Hole.

Taylor, J. B. (1998). A Historical Analysis of Monetary Policy Rules. NBER Working Paper 6768, National Bureau of Economic Research, Cambridge (Mass).

Taylor, J. B. (1999). The Robustness and Efficiency of Monetary Policy Rules as Guidelines for Interest Rate Setting by the European Central Bank. *Journal of Monetary Economics* 43, 655-679

Taylor, J. B. (2000). The Monetary Transmission Mechanism and the Evaluation of Monetary Policy Rules. Central Bank of Chile Working Paper 87.

Thomas, J. (2002). Is Lumpy Investment Relevant for the Business Cycle? *Journal of Political Economy* 110, 508–534.

Tobin, J. (1969). A General Equilibrium Approach to Monetary Theory. *Journal of Money, Credit and Banking* 1, 15-29.

Treadway, A. B. (1969). On Rational Entrepreneurial Behavior and the Demand for Investment. *Review of Economic Studies* 36, 227-240.

Uhlig, H. (1997). A Toolkit for Analyzing Nonlinear Dynamic Stochastic Models Easily. Federal Reserve Bank of Minneapolis, Institute for Empirical Economics, Discussion Paper 101, updated version.

Walsh, Carl E. (2003). Speed Limit Policies: The Output Gap and Optimal Monetary Policy. *American Economic Review* 93, 265-278.

Wicksell, K. (1898). Geldzins und Güterprise. Jena: Gustav Fischer. English translation 1936: Interest and Prices. Reprinted 1965. Augustus M. Kelley, Bookseller, New York.

Woodford, M. (1995). Price-level Determinacy without Control of a Monetary Aggregate. Carnegie-Rochester Conference Series on Public Policy 43, 1-46.

Woodford, M. (1996). Control of the Public Debt: A Requirement for Price Stability. NBER Working Paper 5684, National Bureau of Economic Research, Cambridge (Mass).

Woodford, M. (1999). Optimal Monetary Policy Inertia. NBER Working Paper 7261, National Bureau of Economic Research, Cambridge (Mass).

Woodford, M. (2001a). Inflation Stabilization and Welfare. NBER Working Paper 8071, National Bureau of Economic Research, Cambridge (Mass).

Woodford, M. (2001b). The Taylor Rule and Optimal Monetary Policy. *American Economic Review: Papers and Proceedings* 91, 232-237.

Woodford, M. (2003). Interest and Prices. Princeton University Press, Princeton, NJ.

Woodford, M. (2004). Inflation and Output Dynamics with Firm-Specific Investment. manuscript, Princeton University.

Woodford, M. (2005). Firm-Specific Capital and the New Keynesian Phillips Curve. NBER Working Paper 11149, National Bureau of Economic Research, Cambridge (Mass).

Wright, S. (1998). Monetary Policy, Nominal Interest Rates, and Long-horizon Inflation Uncertainty. University of Cambridge DAE Working Paper 9820.

Yun, T. (1996). Nominal Price Rigidity, Money Supply Endogeneity, and Business Cycles. *Journal of Monetary Economics* 37, 345-370.

SCHRIFTEN ZUR WIRTSCHAFTSTHEORIE UND WIRTSCHAFTSPOLITIK

Herausgegeben von Klaus Beckmann, Michael Berlemann, Rolf Hasse, Jörn Kruse, Franco Reither, Wolf Schäfer, Thomas Straubhaar, Klaus W. Zimmermann

Band 1 Lars Bünning: Die Konvergenzkriterien des Maastricht-Vertrages unter besonderer Berücksichtigung ihrer Konsistenz. 1997.

Band 2 Andreas Henning: Beveridge-Kurve, Lohnsetzung und Langzeitarbeitslosigkeit. Eine theoretische Untersuchung unter Berücksichtigung des Insider-Outsider-Ansatzes und der Entwertung des Humankapitals. 1997.

Band 3 Iris Henning: Die Reputation einer Zentralbank. Eine theoretische Untersuchung unter besonderer Berücksichtigung der Europäischen Zentralbank. 1997.

Band 4 Rüdiger Hermann: Ein gemeinsamer Markt für Elektrizität in Europa. Optionen einer Wettbewerbsordnung zwischen Anspruch und Wirklichkeit. 1997.

Band 5 Alexander Tiedtke: Japan und der Vorwurf des Trittbrettfahrerverhaltens in der US-amerikanisch-japanischen Allianz. 1997.

Band 6 Wolfgang Grimme: Ordnungspolitisches Konzept der Regionalpolitik. Darstellung der Defizite und des Reformbedarfs der Regionalpolitik am Beispiel Mecklenburg-Vorpommerns. 1997.

Band 7 Christian Ricken: Determinanten der Effektivität der Umweltpolitik. Der nationale Politikstil im Spannungsfeld von Ökonomie, Politik und Kultur. 1997.

Band 8 Christian Schmidt: Real Convergence in the European Union. An Empirical Analysis. 1997.

Band 9 Silvia Marengo: Exchange Rate Policy for MERCOSUR: Lessons from the European Union. 1998.

Band 10 Jens Kleinemeyer: Standardisierung zwischen Kooperation und Wettbewerb. Eine spieltheoretische Betrachtung. 1998.

Band 11 Stefan M. Golder: Migration und Arbeitsmarkt. Eine empirische Analyse der Performance von Ausländern in der Schweiz. 1999.

Band 12 Stefan Kramer: Die Wirkung einer Internationalisierung des Yen auf die japanischen Finanzmärkte, die japanische Geldpolitik und die Usancen der Fakturierung. 1999.

Band 13 Antje Marielle Gerhold: Wirtschaftliche Integration und Kooperation im asiatisch-pazifischen Raum. Die APEC. 1999.

Band 14 Tamim Achim Dawar: Deutsche Direktinvestitionen in Australien. Eine Evaluation der theoretischen Erklärungsansätze und der Standortattraktivität des Produktions- und Investitionsstandortes Australien. 1999.

Band 15 Hans-Markus Johannsen: Die ordnungspolitische Haltung Frankreichs im Prozeß der europäischen Einigung. 1999.

Band 16 Annette Schönherr: Vereinigungsbedingte Dimensionen regionaler Arbeitsmobilität. Wirkungen unter analytisch einfachen Bedingungen und potentielle individuelle Migrationsgewinne in Deutschland nach der Vereinigung. 1999.

Band 17 Henrik Müller: Wechselkurspolitik des Eurolandes. Konfliktstoff für die neue währungspolitische Ära. 1999.

Band 18 Lars H. Wengorz: Die Bedeutung von Unternehmertum und Eigentum für die Existenz von Unternehmen. Eine methodenkritische Analyse der Transformation des Wirtschaftssystems in Russland. 2000.

Band 19 Eckart Bauer: Konzeptionelle Grundfragen eines Kinderleistungsausgleichs im Rahmen einer umlagefinanzierten zwangsweisen Rentenversicherung. 2000.

Band 20 Hubertus Hille: Enlarging the European Union. A Computable General Equilibrium Assessment of Different Integration Scenarios of Central and Eastern Europe. 2001.

Band 21 Tobias Just: Globalisierung und Ideologie. Eine Analyse der Existenz und Persistenz von Partisaneffekten bei zunehmender Internationalisierung der Märkte. 2001.

Band 22 Simone Claber: Großbritannien und die Europäische Integration unter besonderer Berücksichtigung ordnungspolitischer Aspekte. 2002.

Band 23 Silvia Rottenbiller: Essential Facilities als ordnungspolitisches Problem. 2002.

Band 24 Peggy Dreyhaupt von Speicher: Die Regionen Polens, Ungarns und der Tschechischen Republik vor dem EU-Beitritt. Interregionale Disparitäten, Bestimmungsfaktoren und Lösungsansätze. 2002.

Band 25 Gerhard Rösl: Seigniorage in der EWU. Eine Analyse der Notenbankgewinnentstehung und -verwendung des Eurosystems. 2002.

Band 26 Jörn Quitzau: Die Vergabe der Fernsehrechte an der Fußball-Bundesliga. Wohlfahrtsökonomische, wettbewerbspolitische und sportökonomische Aspekte der Zentralvermarktung. 2003.

Band 27 Małgorzata Stankiewicz: Die polnische Telekommunikation vor dem EU-Beitritt. 2003.

Band 28 Sarah Schniewindt: Einführung von Wettbewerb auf der Letzten Meile. Eine ökonomische Analyse von Netzinfrastruktur und Wettbewerbspotential im Teilnehmeranschlussbereich. 2003.

Band 29 Jens Bruderhausen: Zahlungsbilanzkrisen bei begrenzter Devisenmarkteffizienz. Ein kapitalmarkttheoretischer Ansatz. 2004.

Band 30 Philip Jensch: Einkommensteuerreform oder Einkommensteuerersatz? Alternative Ansätze einer Reform der direkten Besteuerung unter besonderer Berücksichtigung steuerpraktischer Gesichtspunkte. 2004.

Band 31 Karsten J. Adamski: Mikroanalyse eines Grundrentenkonzeptes der Alterssicherung. Eine empirische Studie zur Wirkung einer Grundrente auf Basis des Sozioökonomischen Panels. 2004.

Band 32 Sven Schulze: Anreizwirkungen und Arbeitsmarkteffekte der Ausgestaltung einer Arbeitslosenversicherung. 2004.

Band 33 Alkis Henri Otto: Makroökonomische Effekte der Direktinvestitionen. 2005.

Band 34 Stefan Hardege: Informationstechnologische Entwicklung und der Schutz von Verfügungsrechten für Informationsgüter. Eine ökonomische Analyse zur Ausgestaltung des Urheberrechts. 2006.

Band 35 Christoph Kimmel: Vermögenspreisinflation als wirtschaftspolitische Herausforderung. 2008.

Band 36 Axel Czaya: Das Europäische Normungssystem aus der Perspektive der Neuen Institutionenökonomik. 2008.

Band 37 Jana Brandstätter: International divergierende demographische Entwicklungen und internationale Kapitalbewegungen. 2008.

Band 38 Annette Olbrisch: Die Zinsmarge und ihre Determinanten. Eine theoretische und empirische Analyse unter besonderer Berücksichtigung von Protektion im Bankensektor. 2009.

Band 39 Hien Phuc Nguyen: National Competitiveness of Vietnam: Determinants, Emerging Key Issues and Recommendations. 2009.

Band 40 Heiko Geruschkat: Zur Ökonomie politischer Systeme. 2010.

Band 41 Reto Schemm-Gregory: Europa als ein Club voller Clubs. Eine clubtheoretische Betrachtung des politischen Systems der Europäischen Union. 2010.

Band 42 Cordula Wandel: Industry Agglomerations and Regional Development in Hungary. Economic Processes during European Integration. 2010.

Band 43 Klaus Beckmann / Christian Müller / Katrin Röpke (Hrsg./eds.): Politikberatung für Marktwirtschaft in Transformationsstaaten: Grundlagen, Visionen und Anwendungen. Policy Advice on the Social Market Economy for Transformation Economies: Principles Vision, and Applications. 2010.

Band 44 Elena Pavlova: Interest-Rate Rules in a New Keynesian Framework with Investment. 2011.

www.peterlang.de

Peter Lang · Internationaler Verlag der Wissenschaften

Ralf Fendel

Monetary Policy, Interest Rate Rules, and the Term Structure of Interest Rates

Theoretical Considerations and Empirical Implications

Frankfurt am Main, Berlin, Bern, Bruxelles, New York, Oxford, Wien, 2007.
XIII, 187 pp., num. tab. and graphs
Studien zu internationalen Wirtschaftsbeziehungen. Edited by Michael Frenkel.
Vol. 8
ISBN 978-3-631-55894-2 · pb. € 43,20*

Interest rate rules play an important role in the empirical analysis of monetary policy as well as in modern monetary theory. Besides giving a comprehensive insight into this line of research the study incorporates the term structure of interest rates into interest rate rules. This is performed analytically as well as empirically. In doing so, state of the art techniques of modern finance for the analysis of the term structure of interest rates are introduced into the macroeconomic concept of interest rate rules. The study implies that from the theoretical perspective term structure effects are an important extension of interest rate rules. From an empirical perspective it shows that including term structure effects in interest rate reaction functions improves our understanding of the interest rate setting of the Deutsche Bundesbank and the European Central Bank.

Contents: Analysis of the monetary policy of the ECB and the Bundesbank · Derivation and estimation of interest rate rules · Special focus on the term structure of interest rates · Combination of the concept of interest rate rules with affine no-arbitrage term structure models

Frankfurt am Main · Berlin · Bern · Bruxelles · New York · Oxford · Wien
Distribution: Verlag Peter Lang AG
Moosstr. 1, CH-2542 Pieterlen
Telefax 0041(0)32/3761727

*The €-price includes German tax rate
Prices are subject to change without notice

Homepage http://www.peterlang.de